Comparative Study on the Promotion of Common Prosperity

Zhou Hong et al.

Paths Publishing Group

中国社会科学出版社
CHINA SOCIAL SCIENCES PRESS

About the Author

ZHOU Hong, member of Chinese Academy of Social Sciences, director of the Academic Division of International Studies of Chinese Academy of Social Sciences, honorary professor at University of Chinese Academy of Social Sciences. ZHOU has for long worked in the fields of welfare state, European integration, China-Europe relations, international development assistance, diplomacy of German unification, etc.

About the Contributors

Other prominent authors of this book are introduced as follows:

LI Kaixuan, author of The United States, PhD in Political Science, associate researcher at Academy of Marxism, Chinese Academy of Social Sciences. Her main research areas include Italian politics and social policy, left-wing politics in Europe, and new trends in the development of contemporary capitalist political and economic systems.

CHAI Yu, the first author of South American, researcher, director of the Institute of Latin American Studies, Chinese Academy of Social Sciences, mainly engaging in research on international trade and foreign direct investment, regional economic integration, and emerging economies.

YUE Yunxia, the second author of South American, director of the Economic Research Department of the Institute of Latin American Studies, Chinese Academy of Social Sciences. She mainly involves in international trade and investment as well as Latin American economic research.

HE Bingzi, the third author of South America, PhD in Sociology, currently works in the Social Culture Research Office of the Institute of Latin American Studies, Chinese Academy of Social Sciences, mainly engaging in the research of Latin American social issues.

LIU Tao, author of German, professor and doctoral supervisor of School of Public Affairs, Zhejiang University, Leading Personnel of the Humanities of Zhejiang University.

PENG Shuyi, author of French, PhD, researcher at Institute of European Studies, Chinese Academy of Social Sciences.

LIN Ka, author of Northern Europe, professor of Zhejiang University, chair lecturer at University of Tampere and University of Turku, guest lecturer at Lingnan University, mainly engaging in the research on social security, social policy, social work, and social management.

ZHANG Min, author of Spain, researcher and doctoral supervisor at Institute of European Studies of Chinese Academy of Social Sciences, director of Spanish Research Center of Chinese Academy of Social Sciences.

DING Chun, author of European Union, professor of Fudan University, director of the European Studies Center of Fudan University, vice president of Fudan Institute of Belt and Road & Global Governance.

ZHENG Chunrong, author of Britain, professor and doctoral supervisor at Shanghai University of Finance and Economics, vice president of the Institute of Public Policy and Governance.

XU Yanli, author of Russia, PhD in Sociology, professor at China University of Labor Relations, and executive dean of the School of Hotel Management, China University of Labor Relations.

HUANG Guan, author of Japan, PhD in Political Science, professor at Xiamen University Tan Kah Kee College, specializing in research related to social security and the evolution of political and economic systems.

GAO Chunlan, author of the Republic of Korea, PhD in Social Welfare, professor at School of Public Administration, Changchun University of Technology. Her main research areas include social policy and international comparison of social welfare systems.

ZHANG Jun, researcher at Institute of European Studies, Chinese Academy of Social Sciences, participates in the drafting and editing of the report.

Abstract

Abstract: Promoting common prosperity is closely linked to all-round economic and social progress. For the purpose of measuring common prosperity, a variety of indicators are invented, covering economic income, social distribution, public services and so on. In western countries with full - fledged market economy, various state intervention measures are taken to correct "market failure", thus affect the distribution of wealth. The paths and methods of these interventions are different, forming various modes of national governance in the world today. This study analyzes the important factors affecting wealth creation and distribution by combing the main relevant systems, mechanisms, policies, principles and ideas of each case country in the process of national wealth creation and distribution, summarizing the experience and lessons of the case countries in achieving common prosperity. The study demonstrates that establishing market norms and rule of law is essential for constructing a fair, reasonable and common prosperous society, meanwhile, systematic social policies are indispensable. The social elements should be embedded in regulating the market to ensure market fairness, therefore, it is important to improve the institutions and tools of intervention in the fields of social employment, social distribution, public service and so on.

Key Words: Common prosperity; social distribution; comparative study

Contents

Introduction*

1. How to Understand and Measure Common Prosperity?

Internationally, there are multiple ways to measure common prosperity, among which the Gini Coefficient (with zero indicating perfect equality) and the S80/S20 ratio (the ratio of the average income of the 20 percent richest to the 20 percent poorest) are the most widely used. International institutions such as the World Bank and the Organization for Economic Co-operation and Development (OECD) regularly publish the ranking of the estimated Gini Coefficient by country and the S80/S20 ratio. In addition, there are many other indicators. Take the Human Development Index (HDI) introduced by the United Nations Development Programme for example. It combines economic indicators with social ones, putting even more emphasis on human development rather than just income status. The *Human Development Report 2020* introduced three new measurement indices, namely, the Income Inequality Index (III), the Gender Inequality Index (GII) and the Multidimensional Poverty Index (MPI), and adopted life expectancy at birth, education, life quality and even satisfaction as indicators to comprehensively reflect the common prosperity of society. Moreover, the report also contained calculation methods of poverty risk, among others.

---

* Author: ZHOU Hong, Chinese Academy of Social Sciences.

The social average wealth and the social prosperity (GDP per capita) often overlap but are not positively correlated. The Gini Coefficient of countries with GDP per capita of over USD 30,000 is mostly below 0.35. However, countries with high GDP per capita do not consequentially have low Gini Coefficients. For example, the Gini Coefficients of the United States (US) and the United Kingdom (UK) are above 0.4, while the Gini Coefficient of Russia, with GDP per capita of USD 10,000, is lower than 0.35[①]. Some think tanks also include personal income, social activities, health and life expectancy, freedom of lifestyle, views on governance, care for vulnerable groups, accessibility to social services, and even the acceptance of idealism and Utopian spirit as indicators of happiness index. Furthermore, some studies focus on the sources of citizens' income in various countries and investigate the share of labor income, property income, transfer income, and other non-labor income. Except for such static indicators as population, economy, society, distribution and effectiveness, the dynamic development indicators of the above elements should also be measured, especially the potential of some long-term projects and cost indicators changing actual conditions.

The focus of this study is not to detail the current situation of poverty and wealth in various countries around the world, but to discuss the main relevant systems, mechanisms, policies, development laws and concepts each case country adopted in the creation and distribution of national wealth. The world experienced a relatively stable period of economic growth after World War II. During this period, some national governance models emerged, which feature relatively stable economic and social development and relatively balanced growth of national income, with

① According to the OECD (2021), Income inequality (indicator) . doi: 10. 1787/459 aa7f1-en (Accessed on 04 September 2021) and data released by the World Bank.

those of the Nordic countries, Germany, and Japan standing out in particular. Although these countries have inherent institutional issues and these models are based on imbalanced global development and are increasingly becoming unstable and unbalanced, there are still many governance models and social policies worth exploration. This study also investigates Anglo-Saxon countries and South American countries. Spain, Russia and the Republic of Korea (ROK) are selected as reference countries. In spite of different reasons for the gap between rich and poor in different countries (some are caused by institutions and policies and some are due to age, race, industry, and regional differences), positive experiences and negative lessons can still be concluded through this study.

2.Regulating the Market Benefits the Society

Contemporary capitalist countries, whether they are free-market capitalism (such as Britain and America), social market economies (such as mainland Europe), or welfare capitalism (such as Nordic Europe), are not absolutely "laissez-faire" economies. Countries intervene in the market in similar but different ways, resulting in different distribution patterns of national income.

2.1 Regulating the Market is Regulating the Society

The fair scale of market rules varies among countries globally, but the original intention of establishing market rules to influence resource and income distribution is the same. After World War II, Germany rebuilt a free market economy, but this "freedom" was a standardized market order rather than completely a "laissez-faire" policy, which was also named as "ordered capitalism". As the social equity is considered as an element in the system design of the market, the German policy is also known as the "social market economy". Ludwig Wilhelm Erhard, a German politician and economist, once said, "if the competitive market order can avoid monopolies, then the market economy itself can be regarded as a social market economy." Due to the injection of social element, German labors receive higher returns from the market.

The United States is the proponent of free market economy, which regulates the market to ensure free competition, encouraging entrepreneurial spirit, maintaining capital investment profits, demonstrating the principle of efficiency and effectiveness, and cracking down on monopolistic industries that affect the free operation of the market. The disintegration of AT&T in history and the fragmentation faced by the four major technology giants in the current are typical cases.

Nordic countries are another market economy model where the private properties are protected in accordance with the law and the interests of the capital are vigorously safeguarded. Private enterprises are the main component of the national economy regardless of industries. Let us take Sweden as an example, whose corporate tax rate is only 20-25 percent, which is relatively low in industrialized capitalist countries and it even dropped to 17-18 percent from 2012 to 2014 to stimulate innovation and vitality of enterprises. Therefore, Sweden and other Nordic countries have created a large number of internationally renowned large enterprises and relatively high average income levels. The main reason for this is not only the high-quality human resources, but also the loose investment environment.

In contrast to the Nordic countries, the finance of southern European countries has long been highly dependent on corporate tax. The corporate tax rate of Spain was as high as 35 percent in the 1980s, but in the process of European integration, there has been a convergence with other member countries. The government has continuously lowered corporate tax rates, which have been reduced to 25 percent by 2018 and newly established companies are provided with tax incentives, which can be as low as 15 percent in the first two years. Enterprises can enjoy tax credits and incentives for investment in R&D, reinvestment, export promotion, employee training, employment creation and social house supply.

The characteristic that distinguishes France from other developed Western countries is the high degree of nationalization, which affects the operation of the market economy. Due to historical factors, almost all industries that are linked to the national economy and people's livelihood or have important strategic significance are nationalized. Although they since been privatized, the number of state-owned enterprises is still large, forming various interest groups that cannot be regulated. Meanwhile, small and medium-sized enterprises in France are severely underdeveloped. The segmented market affects the income of labors, and as a result, the country has to make great efforts to establish a social redistribution mechanism.

Almost all countries use strict legal means to regulate the market, crack down on market violations, and punish rent-seeking behaviors and have established strict legal enforcement and punishment mechanisms for illegal activities. For example, tax evasion in Spain carries up to 50 percent -150 percent of unpaid taxes in fines and deprives other tax exemption rights within 5 years.

2.2 Intervention of the Labor Market

Another common feature of the countries mentioned above is their emphasis on employment policy. The employment rate and quality are directly related to national income and prosperity, but the specific practices of each country in terms of the employment policy are not the same.

American employment policy focuses on the market, and various intervention policies are formulated to stimulate employment and create a more flexible labor market. U.S. Department of Labor regularly publishes employment information and trends. Cross state employment is very common in the United States, which is related to the early use of English as the unified working language of all ethnic groups. The nationwide highway network, unified social security network, and national employment services promote the rational movement of labor. To some extent, the United States took the lead in achieving the free movement of accessible labor on a large scale nationwide. As a result, labor resources can be optimized and allocated according to market demand.

One of the founding principles of the European Union/European Community is the "free movement of labor across borders", which is not easy to achieve due to language barriers and cultural differences. The EU's policy is to promote "good job opportunities", which are so-called "decent employment" and "employment with high income". Through the "open consultation system", EU coordinates social policies of various countries and promotes countries to advance high-quality employment.

During the Schroder's ruling period (1998-2005), Germany firmly implemented a freer and more relaxed labor market policy, with the main focus on breaking barriers and reducing unemployment rates. Starting from 2005, the unemployment rate decreased from 11.7 percent to 5 percent in 2019, and the employment rate increased from 69.4 percent to 80.1 percent in 2020. In 2020, due to the pandemic, the unemployment rate in Germany rebounded slightly to 5.9 percent but the income stability of German core labor force and labors was ensured through a range of protective measures such as "short-time duty system".

Since the 21st century, Nordic countries have adopted proactive labor policies to promote employment. In the past decade, employment rate in Nordic countries has remained above 70 percent , and the registered unemployment rate has maintained from 3 percent to 8 percent, ensuring basic national income. Nordic labor market rules are also very strict, with personal income taxes reaching around 70 percent, which are used for various "social union" projects, aiming to improve the national welfare system and achieve a significant convergence of national income and social services.

Affected by regional differences in industrial structure, weak R&D innovation, less development of modernization construction, Spain faces challenge in achieving full employment. Unemployment rates, especially among young people and women, have remained high for a long time. Since 1982, successive Spanish governments have implemented more than 50 labor market reforms. In 1984, the Socialist Workers' Party introduced a dual structure labor market system, flexibly combining short-term and long-term contract employment and attracting a large number of temporary employment in tourism industry, service industry and and other industries. In 2012, the People's Party carried out the strictest labor market reform, changing the rigid characteristics of the labor market and giving employers greater decision-making power in employment, dismissal, and other aspects.

France Government has intervened in the employment market through social policies. On the one hand, it has tightened the quality for unemployment insurance and expanded the scope of unemployment insurance, forcing unemployed labors to return to the labor market.

On the other hand, it has introduced assistance measures, deeply and comprehensively intervening in the job process from both supply and demand sides. In terms of recruiters, the Government has dispatched consultants to follow up on the recruitment process, helping enterprises solve recruitment difficulties. With regard to job seekers, it has increased employment consultants, provided improvement training and communicated with enterprises. Meanwhile, it has established hundreds of childcare institutions with a mission of career immersion to provide childcare services for impoverished families, especially single mothers so that they are available to find jobs. Furthermore, the Government has offered public beneficial employment positions.

The *Russian Federal Employment Act* (1996) clearly specifies that the government implements policies ensuring residents' employment rights which are full, productive and allow employees to choose their job freely. It encourages reasonable labor mobility and flexible employment through measures such as financial investment and tax incentives. Russia has also established the federal employment agency, and the federal government can allocate funds from the federal budget in accordance with the law to alleviate the pressure on the labor market.

ROK pursues a policy of collaborative employment promotion involving labors, capital, civil society, and government. It formulates adaptive policies targeting different objects and introduces distinctive employment promotion policies for special groups. From central government to local authorities, measures and institutions have been created to provide support for the employment of youth, women, and the elderly.

South American countries have also intervened in employment, mainly by adjusting the employment structure, expanding the service sector, scaling up labor income, increasing labor protection, improving the stability of labor income, amplifying the proportion of wage income in labor income, and promoting equality in primary distribution.

2.3 Investment in Human Resource Development: "Social Investment State"

The main background for the emergence of the concept of "social investment country" is the increasing economic competition between countries in the age of globalization, and the core meaning of competitiveness lies in the quality and ability of labors. Labors with high quality is also a necessary prerequisite for maintaining high income. Based on this understanding, Nordic countries have long focused on human resource policy, providing the complete set of social policy interventions including newborn care, education, vocational training and elderly reemployment. The proportion of investment in education and research to GDF ranks the first globally and the proportion of citizens with college diploma in the five Nordic countries from 25 to 39 years old is higher than the average in EU. Citizens generally possessing a high level of knowledge, educational quality is a prerequisite to become innovative countries. It also creates conditions for young people to be employed in the innovation field, and provides a high-level and highly skilled labor force for enterprise innovation. With these efforts, Nordic countries have cultivated a variety of leading enterprises, such as Ericsson, Nokia, Skype, Spotify, Lego, Ikea, Volvo, etc., and their national income has been maintained at a high level. Based on Nordic experience, EU has begun to advocate for "social investment state" and promoted this policy to EU member states.

Macron has decided to learn the Nordic concept of "social investment" since he took office as president of France, expanding child-care centers and kindergartens with an emphasis on education. The Macron Government has transformed the policy from adjusting social distribution to investing in human resources, from passive relief to improving individuals with knowledge and skills, so as to ensure individuals enjoy the right of access to stable employment and achieve lifelong sustainable development, i.e. from outcome equality to opportunity equality.

South American countries are also focusing on labors skills to narrow the wage gap and promote equalization of primary distribution.

2.4 Standardization of Primary Distribution

The standardization of primary distribution is mainly the governance model of continental European countries. The formulation of national intervention in wage policies guarantees the reasonable income of labors and ensures that labors pay taxes in accordance with the law. Such social intervention in the market makes national income reach a relatively average level after primary distribution.

Germany has created a collective bargaining mechanism called "social partnership", which allows labors to gain a favorable position in the primary distribution. This system is negotiated by German industry unions and employers' associations on wage levels and working conditions within the industry to reach a package of agreements, thus forms fixed principles of high-degree social autonomy and social self-management. The German Government provides directional guidance and basic data on the labor market rather than directly intervening in collective bargaining. Through collective bargaining, wages reach a reasonable and balanced level. After primary distribution, the proportion of disposable income of German employees in national income has increased from 66.8 percent in 2010 to 69 percent in 2018. Labor reward has become the main component of German national wealth, reflecting the value of labor to capital and ensuring effective consumption.

Some studies believe that Northern Europe, which practiced social democracy, had introduced the tripartite negotiation mechanism as early as the 1950s, which has played a critical role in ensuring labor return, working conditions, employment conditions, enterprises development planning and employ welfare. Collective negotiation on income distribution and working environment has indeed helped workers to gain more reasonable and equal benefits in the process of primary distribution.

Like Germany, France also has collective bargaining mechanisms for social partners on issues such as wage, enterprise supplementary insurance. Furthermore, France establishes improved labor supervision system, strict tax system and banking supervision system (cash transaction is prohibited). All employment (including part-time employment, hourly worker, seasonal worker and short-term worker, etc.), regardless of size, must be declared to the government tax department and regarded as registered employment, and employment without signing a labor contract and tax declaration is illegal. Labors paying tax enjoy relevant social security rights and payment qualifications and receive state support in the event of unemployment.

Different from European countries, Japan has a system of lifelong employment and seniority pay, centering on the enterprises-based labor union. Due to the highly stable employment, losses caused by economic crises often undertaken by business owners and top managers. Currently, over 90 percent of graduates (high school and college degree or above) stepping into the career each year sign traditional lifelong employment contracts with enterprises. Stable employment also makes business owners more willing to invest in employ training and career development. As a result, Japan features a high degree of income equalization after primary distribution, ranking second or third in the world, and its Gini Coefficient remains stable below 0.35 for a long period.

The intervention of the United States in primary distribution has been minimized. Although the Department of Labor provides standard wage for various industries, wage negotiations mostly happen between employees and employers. In recent years, due to the widening gap between high-end and low-end service industries and the rapid expansion of capital, although the employment rate in the United States is relatively high, the proportion of capital, land and technology in distribution iis relatively high compared to labors. The gap between the rich and the poor remains significant after primary distribution.

The main approach of South American countries to intervene in primary distribution is to implement income security for low-income groups, that is, to promote policies such as relating the minimum wage to economic growth and inflation.

3.Institutional Social Redistribution Offsets "Market Default"

In addition to ensuring the functioning of the markets mentioned above (primary distribution as a part of market operation), countries reintervene in social distribution through a package of social policies, social legislation and social administration based on their own social identities and political operations. One of the reasons is to prevent the risks brought by the industrial market economy to society, and the other is to control the unfair social distribution under the market economy system to make up for the "market default".

There are various mechanisms for social redistribution, the most common and institutionalized of which is social insurance. Furthermore, there are social assistance specially designed for poverty alleviation and social welfare allowance formulated to achieve social objectives. As the policy objectives of these mechanisms are to protect society, the concept of "social protection" adopted by many countries covers the policies participated by social entities mentioned above. The direct goal of "social protection" is not to equalize the rich and the poor, but kinds of income transfers implemented to protect the society actually play a role in wealth redistribution and narrowing the wealth gap. In 2018, the average Gini Coefficient of employees in OECD member countries was 0.41, which decreased to 0.31 after such policy intervention as taxation and transfer payments system[①].

3.1 Social Insurance (Social Security)

Social insurance is a social redistribution system with a history of over a hundred years. Originated in Germany at the end of the 19th century, it was popularized after the global economic crisis in the 1930s and shaped up in the 1970s. According to the types of income reduction risks brought to human society by industrialization and urbanization, a complete social security system, commonly known as the "five insurances" has been constructed, including medical insurance, work-related injury insurance, endowment insurance, unemployment insurance and family insurance. In recent years, with the intensification of increasing aged population, some countries have begun to establish long-term care insurance. The essence of social insurance is a shared responsibility and risk mechanism. Most countries adopt a system where employees and employers jointly pay the insurance and the national finance supports necessary subsidies. The

① OECD (2021), Income inequality (indicator). doi: 10.1787/459aa7f1-en (Accessed on 04 September 2021).

system varies in different countries but the contents are highly consistent, indicating the rationality of social insurance as a modern social system.

Due to the differences in contribution methods (employers and employees jointly pay the insurance according to a specific proportion) and claim methods (based on necessary conditions such as age, unemployment, illness, etc.), the transfer of personal income among all insured individuals is inevitable, resulting in social redistribution. After establishing a social insurance system and adjusting income through this system, the wealth gap in general countries has been significantly narrowed.

The governments' financial support in social insurance in countries is quite different. France's endowment insurance is jointly paid by employers and employees, and the excess part is supplemented by the government. The national subsidy rate in France is as high as 60-70 percent, similar to the German system. Spain's national strength is far inferior to Germany and France, but its modern social insurance mechanism is similar to Western European countries. The endowment insurance, medical insurance, work-related injury insurance, unemployment insurance and family insurance cover almost all Spanish, although the national subsidy rate is lower than that of France and Germany. Some pension plans vary by industries, but contribute to maintaining the Gini Coefficient below 0.35. Some developed European countries even promote equal social insurance plans, such as France and the United Kingdom, where patients are not required to pay extra for insurance. During the outbreak of COVID-19, the medical security system of European countries has been under great pressure, but it is still stable as a system model.

In 1899, the Japanese government launched "A Ten-year Planning Strategy" to promote the health and well-being of the elderly and introduced a series of expansionary reform measures for social security plans, including the introduction of long-term care insurance, which strengthened the redistribution of income. Through these efforts, the Gini Coefficient of primary income distribution of 0.4 in the mid-1990s fell back to around 0.3, ensuring the income equality in Japan.

ROK's Gini Coefficient based on market income has exceeded 0.4 in most years, but the Gini Coefficient of household disposable income decreased significantly through national annuity, basic pension, child subsidies and other public transfer income, which hit bottom in 2019.

In South America, there are obvious weaknesses in the social security system that most countries have not established the unemployment insurance system. Chile has implemented structural reforms in public pension system and adopted the "Defined Contribution" (DC) plan. However, due to insufficient coverage, vulnerable social redistribution, low mandatory contribution rate and relatively low retirement age, it fails to provide "sufficient" pension. Brazil, Colombia, Guyana, Paraguay, Peru and Venezuela adopt "Defined Benefit" (DB) plan, while Argentina, Bolivia, Ecuador, Guyana and Uruguay implement the mixed plan, but they all confront with financial difficulties. Because of system absence, the wealth gap in South America is large and the Gini Coefficient is above 0.45 for a long time.

3.2 Social Welfare and Social Assistance

"Social assistance" is generally a backing policy to prevent into absolute poverty and is also a component of the overall social security system in most countries. As many countries provide targeted distribution after means test, it has become another root cause of social inequality and discrimination.

There are different interpretations of "social welfare". In some countries, "social welfare" generally refers to social policy payments, including backing projects such as social assistance, which are excluded from the "five insurances". However, in some countries, "social welfare" stands for social policy payments or social allowance that are prior to social insurance. The implementation of such allowance projects can not only targeted increase the income of those in need, but also involve such national policies as population policies and gender policies. Furthermore, it can also be used to narrow the gap between the rich and the poor.

The social welfare policy in France tends to favor vulnerable groups such as the elderly, the disabled, and the poor. The family allowance system is totally contributed by employers and has a wide range of subsidies, demonstrating high social identity in terms of social development.

Nordic countries implemented child allowance as early as the 1930, which could be received by people with legal residency right. Since the 1980s, with the development of feminism, the welfare of mothers in Nordic countries has also been further improved. In addition, there are such kind of universal allowances as housing allowance, housekeeping allowance and student allowance aiming to ensure people live with dignity and strengthen civic awareness and social cohesion.

Spain is not obviously wealthy, but it has established a complete family allowance system. Families with two or more kids can receive various allowances without means test. Therefore, Spanish has remained social stability under the severe impact of the COVID-19 pandemic. The Gini Coefficient of Spain was 0.32 in 2019, and the S80/S20 ratio (the ratio of the average income of the 20 percent richest to the 20 percent poorest) was 5.8 in 2019, decreasing by 0.1 from 2018.

The state governments in the United States practice a wide range of subsidy systems, such as single parent family assistance program for raising juveniles, short-term support for impoverished families, state-level supplemental nutrition assistance program and housing allowance program, etc. These programs are targets and some of them are designed based on means test, which are equivalent to poverty alleviation and are completely different from the Nordic family allowances in terms of goals and operational methods.

The governments of various states in the United States implement a wide range of subsidy systems, such as single parent family assistance programs for raising minors, short-term support for impoverished families, state supplementary nutrition assistance programs, and housing allowance programs. These plans have clear targeting and some are based on household surveys, which are equivalent to poverty alleviation and are completely different from the Nordic family allowance system in terms of goals and operational methods.

3.3 The Third Distribution: Charity Policy and Progressive Income Tax

After primary distribution and social redistribution, capital gains in some countries are still relatively high and the gap between the rich and the poor is serious. Under such conditions, some countries have enhanced their efforts to intervene in society. For example, European countries have adopted high progressive income taxes and increased social service expenditures. In the United States, in order to ensure capital gains, equalizing the rich and the poor is considered a voluntary behavior and governments guide the wealthy to voluntarily transfer money through inheritance tax, real estate tax as well as loose charity laws. The voluntarily transferred wealth usually forms various foundations and non-profit organizations, which are targeted to support the development of certain social groups or special fields. Its direct goal is not to balance the rich and the poor, but the indirect function can promote the development of specific fields. The US government even allocates funds to charitable organizations to purchase social welfare services.

Due to the relatively equal distribution of wealth within Germany, the vast majority of donations from charity have been invested in humanitarian causes abroad. According to data provided by the German and European statistical website "Statista", German citizens donated a total of EUR 5.139 billion in 2019, with 75.3 percent of the endowments being used for humanitarian assistance[①], improving Germany's international image.

There are also many volunteers in Nordic countries, without the goal for poverty alleviation. Due to the small number of private welfare resources and private property, when the main financial resources are transferred to the national treasury through tax payment, the remaining financial resources of the people are very limited. Therefore, in Nordic society, the supply of social welfare is mainly achieved through public finance or redistribution by the country, while the strength of private charity is relatively weak.

Spain focuses on cultivating and developing social welfare organizations and private donations. In 2018, there were 15,865 social welfare organizations receiving a total of EUR 3.643 billion in donations. In 2019, the total number of donors donating to various types of charities reached 21.8 million, mainly used for cancer treatment, development assistance to the third world, child assistance, disaster relief, humanitarian assistance, education, healthcare, etc. The Spanish's participation in voluntary services

---

① Refer to the German and European statistical website "Statista" for statistics on social volunteer services in Germany: https: //de. statista. com/themen/71/ehrenamt/.

and social donations has become an important component of citizens' involvement in social affairs. The income of various public welfare organizations is returned to society and used to help people in urgent need, forming a social morality and public welfare concept of mutual assistance.

4. Government Direct or Indirect Investment in Public Facilities

In most Western industrialized countries, society has reached a basic understanding of "market default" and expectations for government intervention in public facility construction, which is also universally beneficial to different groups. The European Union has launched structural funds in economically underdeveloped southern European countries, with the initial goal of creating employment through the construction of public facilities such as highways and subways, but while creating employment, it has also formed a public investment that equalizes regional wealth. The EU Structural Fund and Solidarity Fund have achieved fiscal transfer payments between different regions within the EU. These two Funds support the development of small and medium-sized enterprises in underdeveloped areas, promote investment, improve infrastructure and provide financial support for the adoption of new agricultural technologies, improvement of agricultural industry structure, and development of non-agricultural industries in rural areas, playing a role in balancing the development of member countries. After the outbreak of the COVID-19, the EU launched an urgent employment support plan of EUR 100 billion, and promoted the "short-term work system" existed in Germany to protect employment stability in the EU region. Meanwhile, EUR 750 billion European Recovery Fund which was collectively borrowed is invested in areas closely related to European development. The benefit of such public investment is not only economic, but also social.

In addition to government direct investment in public facilities, many countries adopt measures such as guidance, promotion, and incentives to encourage the participation of large enterprises in social infrastructure construction and achieve their social responsibility. For example, in 2006, Russia incorporated corporate social responsibility into its national socio-economic development strategy through the "public-private partnership model". The local governments introduced commercial resources through formal cooperation agreements, focusing on the development of areas such as sports, art, healthcare, and education that were left over from the Soviet era as "social infrastructure" with insufficient capital investment, making them the fastest developing areas and the best areas for Russian enterprises to fulfill their social responsibilities.

Although lacks financial tools, EU takes advantage of soft power tools such as laws, regulations and guidelines to advocate for corporate social responsibility, guiding enterprises to invest public goods in social, environmental, and other fields. The "corporate social responsibility" was first proposed in EU's Green Paper - *Promoting a European Framework for Corporate Social Responsibility*. Its concept is companies integrate social and environmental issues into their operations and interactions with stakeholders on a voluntary basis. In October 2011, EP passed the Corporate Social Responsibility Strategy, promoting member states to introduce policies, legislation, and regulatory measures to corporate social responsibility.

Many countries also support public facilities or activities through tax exemptions. For example, people in Sweden can enjoy 25 percent tax exemption by donating SEK 2,000 every year or SEK 200 in a lump sum, with a maximum exemption of SEK 1,500 per year, which is the tax exemption of SEK 6,000. The Spanish government promotes solidarity fund or financial transfer fund between regions to help backward regions improve their socio-economic development and narrow regional regional income gaps. It also adjusts income distribution through Progressive Tax and Regressive Tax①.

5. Public Expenditure on Social Areas

Social expenditure accounts for the first place in the financial expenditure of various countries, far higher than expenditure on fields such as national defense and diplomacy. According to the OECD, public social expenditure in mainland European countries is relatively high. For example, the proportion of public social expenditure to GDP in 2019 in Germany was 25.9 percent, in Sweden was 25.5 percent, in Norway was 25.3 percent, with a maximum of 31 percent in France, 28.2 percent in Italy and 24.7 percent in Spain. The proportion of public social expenditure to GDP in 2019 in some Nordic countries, such as Finland, was 29.1 percent, Denmark, was 28.3 percent, while the proportion in Anglo Saxon countries was relatively low, with the United States at 18.7

① Regressive Tax mainly refers to specific tax reduction and exemption. For example, the basic individual tax exemption for people under 65 years old in Spain is EUR 5,550, for people above 65 is EUR 6,700 and for people above 75 is EUR 8,100. The elderly living with children under the age of 25 can apply for additional allowances: EUR 2,400 for one child, EUR 2,700 for two children, EUR 4,000 for three children and EUR for four children. The additional allowance for each child under 3 years old is EUR 2,800. If a child lives with parents or grandparents with a total income less than EUR 8,000, people over 65 years old can apply for an annual subsidy of EUR 1,150 and people over 75 years old can apply for EUR 2,250. Furthermore, expenses for charitable donations, union dues, renovating or renting houses can also enjoy tax exemption.

percent, UK at 20.6 percent, Canada at 18 percent, and Australia at 16.7 percent. In 2019, the average proportion of OECD countries was 20 percent. In 2018, public social expenditure of France accounted for 30 percent of its GDP, much higher than the average value of 21 percent of OCED. In 2019, Russia's social expenditure accounted for 61.2 percent of the national total expenditure, followed by the expenditure on national defense, national security, and law enforcement activities and the expenditure on national economic development, accounting for 13.9 percent and 12 percent respectively. In other countries, including the United States, public expenditure ranks first in terms of social expenditure. This indicates that the social functions of contemporary countries are well developed, and the social responsibilities they bear are also extremely great. Social stability and unity within the country are the primary responsibilities of national governance.

6. Social Policies' Importance in the Construction of a Modern Socialist China

As the world today is marked by changes unseen in a century, transformations occur in economic structure, technical fields and international policies, with the social changes bearing the brunt. Maintaining social stability is one of the prerequisites for ensuring a smooth transition to a new era, while remaining relative equality of national income, stable growth of the middle class, and the achievement of labor benefits for all classes is a crucial part in achieving harmonious economic and social development.

In the process of summarizing the experiences and lessons learned from other countries, we have found that the importance of formulating systematic social policies is no less than the establishment of a market economy system and the solidity of national defense.

Social policy is a systematic project shared by all, including the embedding of social elements by the state when regulating the market, compensating for market default while ensuring market equality, and conducting institutional interventions in social employment, social distribution, and public services. To formulate social policies that are in line with the goal of developing China into a great modern socialist country, it is necessary to consider various indicators measuring common prosperity and harmonious development in the world, so as to have an objective understanding of China's own development.

After entering the 21st century, the short-term balance of capitalist society seems to falter, and various governance models of capitalist society are in a state of dynamic transformation as their inherent institutions and mechanisms are becoming increasingly apparent. Countries around the world have different social policy systems, mechanisms, and regulations due to their different concepts and endowments, which directly affect national income, social common prosperity, and even the future of national development. We need to attach great importance to this. However, the practice of governance systems and social policies in modern industrialized countries can still provide us with positive experiences or negative lessons learned in terms of common prosperity.

The United States*

Why does poverty still exist in the prosperous America? In 1879, Henry George, an American political economist, put forward such a question in his book *Progress and Poverty*. He analyzed it from the perspective of private ownership of land and distribution of wealth and proposed the concept of Single Tax as the response. Since surpassing the UK as the world's largest economy in 1894, the US GDP has ranked first in the world for 127 consecutive years. However, over the past hundred years, the United States has not only failed to overcome poverty, but the wealth gap has also continued to widen. This social phenomenon is closely related to the values of laissez-faire and Social Darwinism prevailing in the United States as well as the primary distribution and redistribution system under the guidance of the values.

1. Economic and Social Development

The United States is a multi-ethnic country. According to the 2020 national census data released by the U.S. Census Bureau on August 12, 2021, the proportion of white people in the total population has shown a downward trend, dropping from 63.7 percent in 2010 to 57.8 percent, the

* Author: LI Kaixuan, Academy of Marxism, Chinese Academy of Social Sciences.

Hispanic population has surged by 23 percent to 62 million, accounting for 18.7 percent of the total population, the population of African-American is 46.9 million, accounting for 12.4 percent of the total population, which has remained stable over the past 10 years and the fastest-growing population of Asian-American reaches to 24 million, with an increase of more than one-third over the past decade, accounting for 6 percent of the total number.①

According to the World Bank, in the past decade, the GDP per capita of the United States has increased from USD 49,814 in 2011 to USD 63,415 in 2020, with an increase of 27.3 percent. Meanwhile, the per capita GNI growth increased from USD 50,580 in 2011 to USD 65,910 in 2019, with a growth rate of 30.3 percent (from 2011 to 2019), witnessing a relatively rapid growth trend (see Table 1-1).

However, the sustained strong economic growth and achievements of the United States over the years have not equally benefited everyone, and the gap between the rich and the poor has been on the rise in the past decade. The Gini Coefficient of the United States has shown a slow upward trend in the past decade, from 40.9 in 2011 (0 is full equality, 100 is full inequality) to 41.4 in 2018 (see Table 1-1). According to the latest statistics on wealth distribution released by the OECD in July 2021, the average net wealth of households in the United States in 2019 was USD 63,4591, while the median household wealth was only USD 90,298 (both at constant prices in 2015). Due to factors such as high debt, in 2019, 20 percent of the lowest income population in the United States had -1 percent of their total national wealth, while the wealthiest 5 percent and 1 percent of the population had 68 percent and 40 percent of their total

① According to OECD (2021), Income inequality (indicator) . doi: 10. 1787/459 aa7f1-en (Accessed on 04 September 2021) and data released by the World Bank.

wealth, respectively.[①]

Overall, the poverty in the United States also features prominent age, gender, ethnic group, and regional characteristics. As shown in Chart 1-1, according to data released by the U.S. Census Bureau, the poverty rate in the United States as a whole was 10.5 percent in 2019, with 9.4 percent for male and 11.5 percent for female, while the overall poverty rate is 14.4 percent for those under 18 years old, 9.4 percent for those between 18 and 64, and 8.9 percent for those over 65. However, the poverty rate varies among different ethnic groups in the United States, with a poverty rate of 7.3 percent for white people(excluding Latinos), 18.8 percent for black people, 7.3 percent for Asian-Americans, and 15.7 percent for Latinos and other ethnic groups. In terms of age, the poverty rates for black people under 18, adults from 18 to 64 and seniors above 65 were 26.4 percent, 15.9 percent and 18.0 percent respectively, while the corresponding values for white people were 8.3 percent, 7.1 percent and 7.7 percent.[②] The overall poverty rate of black people by age is more than twice that of white people, especially for the juvenile group, which has a poverty rate as high as three times. In terms of gender, the poverty rate among males aged 18 to 64 in the United States is 4 to 6 percent lower than that of females in most cases.[③] Geographically, the poverty rate in the southern region is the highest in the United States, reaching 12 percent, and the poverty rate in the northeast, midwest and west is 9.4 percent, 9.7 percent and 9.5 percent respectively. The overall poverty rate of the employed population aged 18 to 64 is 9.4

① Source: OECD Wealth Distribution Database (WDD).

② Poverty Status of People by Age, Race and Hispanic Origin: 1959 to 2019, https://www2.census. gov/programs-surveys/cps/techdocs/cps-mar20.pdf.

③ Poverty rate in the U. S. by age and gender 2019, https://www.statista.com/statistics/233154/us-poverty-rate-by-gender/

Table 1-1

Item / Year	2011	2012	2013	2014	2015	2016	2017	2018	2019	2020
Per Capita GDP (USD)	49814	51548	53057	55008	56832	58001	60092	63043	65240	63415
Per Capita GNI (USD, Atlas method)	50580	52760	53930	55840	56740	57270	59460	63510	65910	A.
Gini Coefficient (0-1)	0.409	0.409	0.407	0.415	0.412	0.411	0.412	0.414	N.A.	N.A.
Life Expectancy	78.6	78.7	78.7	78.8	78.6	78.5	78.5	78.6	78.8	N.A.
Doctors (per 1000 inhabitants)	2.46	2.50	2.56	2.58	2.58	2.59	2.61	2.61	2.64	N.A.
Hospital Beds (per 1000 inhabitants)	2.97	2.93	2.89	2.83	2.8	2.77	2.87	2.83	N.A.	N.A.

Source: http://data.worldblank.org/indicator/SP.DYN.LE00.IN?end=2019&locations=US&start=2011;http://data.oecd.org/healthres/doctors.htm.

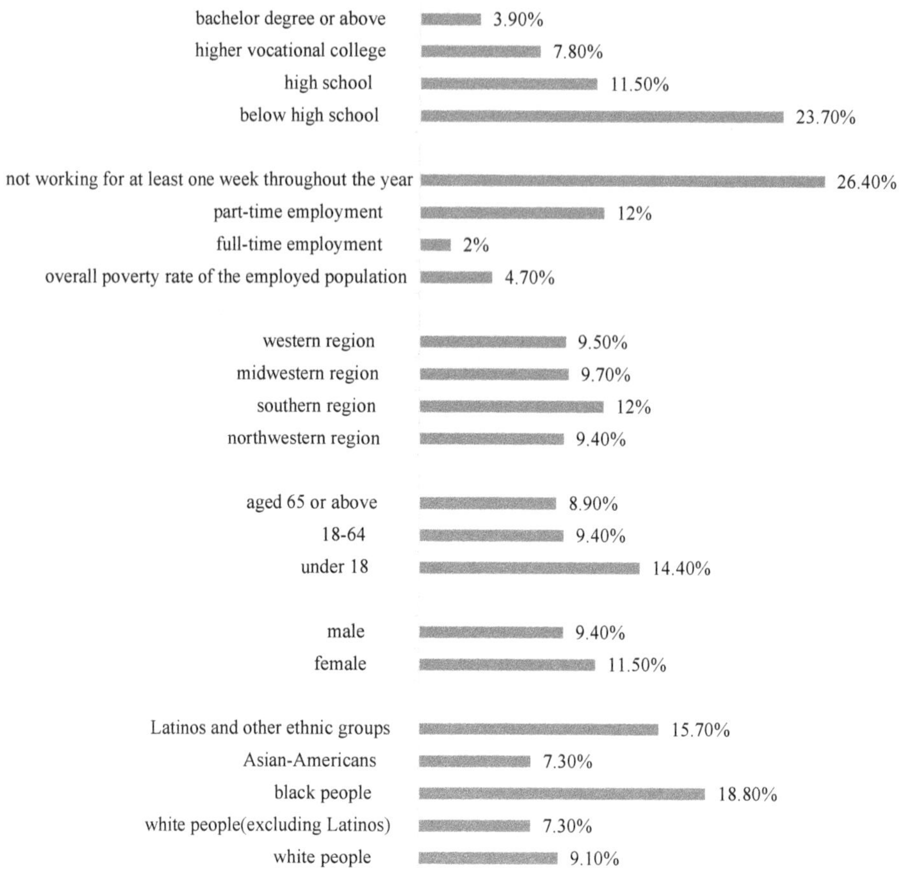

Chart 1-1 Poverty in U.S. (2019)

Source: U.S. Census Bureau, Current Population Survey, 2019 and 2020 Annual Social and Economic Supplements (CPS ASEC).

percent, with a poverty rate of 2 percent for full-time employment, 12 percent for part-time employment and 26.4 percent for the group who does not work for at least one week throughout the year.[1]

In recent years, the middle class of the olive-shaped society in the United States has been constantly shrinking, with the proportion of middle-income groups significantly below the OECD average. As shown

---

① Source: U. S. Census Bureau, Current Population Survey, 2019 and 2020 Annual Social and Economic Supplements (CPS ASEC).

in Chart 1-2, the share of middle-income groups in the United States is 51 percent, which is 10 percent lower than the average of OECD member countries, while the proportion of high-income groups is 14 percent, 5 percent higher than the OECD average.

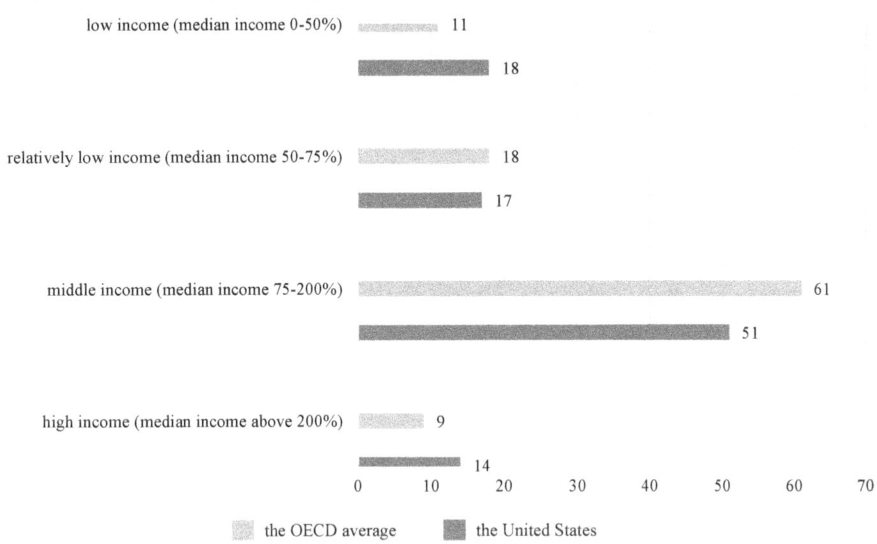

Chart 1-2 The Proportion of Middle-income Groups to the Total Population in U.S. and OECD Member Countries

Source: https://www.oecd.org/unitedstates/Middle-class-2019-United-States.pdf.

2. Primary Distribution

The primary distribution in the United States mainly prioritizes the efficiency, which is to distribute the income based on the efficiency functions of production factors such as labor, capital, land, and technology. Among them, labor-capital relationship is an important influencing factor.

In 1935, during President Franklin Roosevelt's New Deal, the U.S. Congress passed the *National Labor Relations Act*, and on this basis, the National Labor Relations Board (NLRB) was established to arbitrate and adjust labor relations. However, after the World War II, with the rise of anti-communism and "cold war" ideology, the force of anti union prevailed. In 1947, the United States enacted the *National Labor Relations Act*, which restricted union activities and broke the employment monopoly of unions. Furthermore, the *Labor-Management Reporting and Disclosure Act* (LMRDA) was promulgated in 1959 with the main purpose of regulating the leadership power of unions and further restricting union activities. Since then, trade unions in the United States have plunged into a long-term decline, and the trade union density has continued to decrease, which puts them at a disadvantage in labor-capital negotiations. According to the OECD, the trade union density and the collective bargaining coverage in the United States have continued to fall in recent years. Specifically, the trade union density has decreased from 12.9 percent in 2000 to 10.3 percent in 2020, the collective bargaining coverage has declined to 12.1 percent in 2020, which was 14.9 percent in 2000 (see chart 1-3). Especially, the

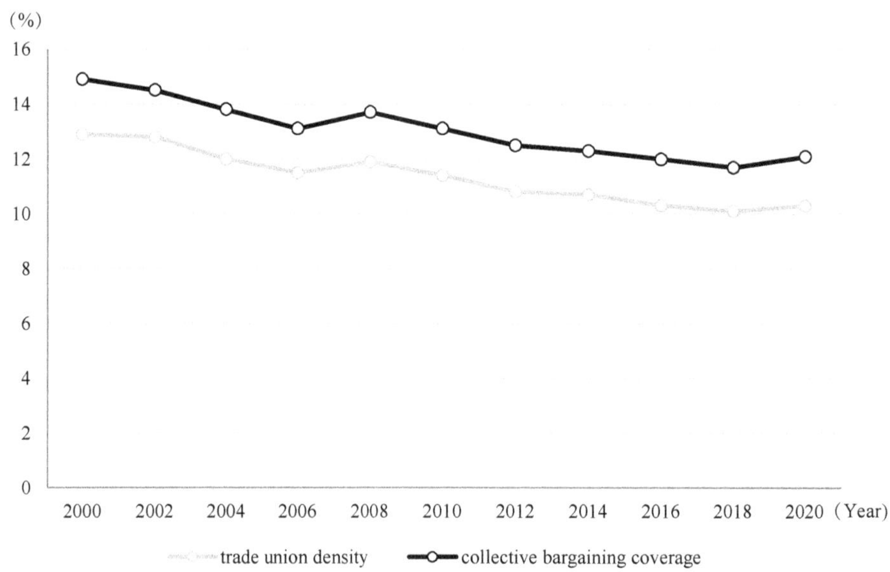

Chart 1-3 Trade Union Density and Collective Bargaining Coverage in U.S.

Source: Trade Union Dataset, https://stats.oecd.org/Index.aspx?DataSetCode=TUD.

collective bargaining coverage is far below that of France (9.8%) and Nordic countries (ranging from 82% to 90%).[1] This has negatively impacted the proportion of wage income in the primary distribution.

Therefore, although employment rate has been relatively stable in the United States, at over 67 percent from 2011 to 2020, reaching 71.36 percent in 2013, the proportion of wage income to total income has rapidly declined since 2000 due to low trade union density and collective bargaining coverage, from 63.3 percent to 56.7 percent in 2016, which was 65.4 percent in 1947.[2]

In addition, the proportion of women in part-time employment to the female workforce is 16. 8 percent and that of men is 8.3 percent. As a result, the median wage gap between men and women is 18.9 percent, much higher than Denmark's 4.9 percent and France's 11.5 percent but lower than Japan's 23.5 percent and ROK's 34.1 percent.[3] Compared horizontally with European countries such as Germany and France, the United States shows the lowest "middle class" share of the total population.

In terms of tax, turn over tax including consumption tax, value-added tax and business tax is a part of primary distribution. Unlike European countries, the United States doesn't have value-added tax but there exists consumption tax, which refers to the general sales tax levied by most states. 45 states and the District of Columbia generally have excise taxes ranging from 2.9 percent to 7.25 percent. General sales tax accounts for 34.7 percent of states revenue and 10 percent of local government revenue. The federal government does not impose general sales tax,

---

① Source: Trade Union Dataset, https://stats.oecd.org/Index.aspx?DataSetCode=TUD.

② Source: BLS; OECD STAN; McKinsey Global Institute analysis.

③ Source: Social Protection and Well-being, https://stats.oecd.org/index.aspx?queryid=54744.

except on motor vehicle fuel, alcoholic beverages, tobacco, and a few other goods, which account for less than 10 percent of federal revenue.①

In conclusion, although the overall employment rate in the United States is relatively stable, due to factors such as low trade union density and collective bargaining coverage, as well as the tax incidence of consumption tax, the proportion of capital and labor income in the primary distribution in the United States is severely unbalanced and the wealth gap is constantly widening.

3. Social Redistribution System

After the primary distribution, social redistribution mainly readjusts income through social security, public services and some subsidy systems. Compared with the primary distribution, it mainly exists in the non-production phase.

Since its founding, the United States has been a country that advocates individualism, while liberalism and limited government are the basic concepts of its political and economic development. Therefore, it was not until the 1930s, under the heavy economic and social background of the Great Depression, that the United States began to build a complementary social security system, establishing the pension insurance system and the unemployment relief system. In the 1960s, it further promoted Medicare for seniors aged 65 and above, and Medicaid for impoverished group.

The public assistance programs in the United States are relatively complete, including the Supplemental Nutrition Assistance Program (SNAP, formerly known as the Food Stamp Program), the Supplemental Security

① [U.S.] Harvey S. Rosen, Ted Gayer: *Public Finance* (Tenth Edition), China Renmin University Press, 2019: 394.

Income (SSI), and the Temporary Assistance for Needy Families (TANF).

3.1 The Structure and Coverage of Five Major Social Security Programs

The current pension system in the United States consists of three pillars. The first pillar is the Social Security Program enforced by the federal government, which mainly includes the Old-Age, Survivors, and Disability Insurance (OASDI), currently covering 96 percent of the employed population nationwide.[①] This is the cornerstone of the U.S. pension system. The proportion of expenditure on OASDI to GDP in 2019 was 4.9 percent.[②] The net replacement rate of public pensions in the United States reached 49.4 percent in 2018.[③]

The second pillar is the government or employer funded pension programs. The government funded pension programs are the Public Sector Plans, which refer to the various pension plans offered by federal, state and local governments to their labors. The employer funded pension programs are the Employer Based Pension plans, which refer to the pension plans provided by enterprises and some non-profit organizations and institutions for their employees, also known as Private Pension Plans. The third pillar is the Individual Retirement Accounts (IRAs), which are supplementary pension plans initiated by the federal government through tax incentives and voluntarily participated by individuals. The voluntary participation in fund-based and private pension plans in the United States

---

① Old-Age, Survivors, and Disability Insurance, https://www.ssa.gov/policy/docs/progdesc/sspus/oasdi.pdf.

② 2019 OASDI Trustees-Report-Social-Security-Administrations, https://www.ssa.gov/OACT/TR/201 9/VI_G2_OASDHI_ GDP.html.

③ Net pension replacement rates, https://data.oecd.org/pension/net-pension-replacement-rates. htm#indicator-chart.

accounts for 40 percent of the employed population.[1] Such kind of tax-deferred individual income adjustment plan is not related to social redistribution.

The United States doesn't establish a universal health insurance plan, but has a special health insurance plan for the elderly and the poor. Among them, Medicare is a program established by the U.S. government in 1965 to increase access to high-quality healthcare services for people aged 65 and above. Medicare, administered by the federal government with unified eligibility standards across states, covers almost all populations aged 65 and older without the needs for means test. The only requirement is that the person or spouse works and pays payroll tax for at least 10 years. Medicare consists of mandatory Hospital Insurance (HI) derived from payroll taxes, voluntary Supplementary Medical Insurance (SMI) and Prescription Drug Insurance (PDI). Among them, the participation rate of Supplementary Medical Insurance among eligible elderly people reaches 92 percent, and the participation rate of Prescription Drug Insurance is over 90 percent.[2] Medicare is the second largest social security expenditure item in the United States after the Old-Age, Survivors, and Disability Insurance. In 2019, expenditure on Medicare accounted for 3.72 percent of GDP and 21 percent of total healthcare expenditure in the United States.[3]

---

① Coverage of funded and private pension plans, https://www.oecd-ilibrary.org/sites/983bdeef-en/index.html?itemId=/content/component/983bdeef-en.

② [U.S.] Harvey S. Rosen, Ted Gayer: *Public Finance* (Tenth Edition), China Renmin University Press, 2019: 172-173.

③ National Health Expend Data, https://www.cms.gov/Research-Statistics-Data-and-Systems/Statistics-Trends-and-Reports/National-HealthExpendData/NHE-Fact-Sheet#:~:text=NHE% 20grew% 204. 6% 25% 20to% 20% 243 . 8 % 20trillion% 20in% 202019% 2C, in% 20201 9%2C%20or%2016%20percent%20of%20total%20NHE .

Medicaid promoted in 1965 aimed to provide health care to beneficiaries of cash welfare programs, which are jointly administered by the federal government and state governments. In the 1980s, eligibility for Medicaid was loosened to include children from low-income, two-parent families and pregnant women. In 1997, the State Children's Health Insurance Program (SCHIP) was enacted. States could expand Medicaid coverage at their discretion or develop new, independent insurance programs for children. The number of beneficiaries of Medicaid (including the Children's Health Insurance Program) has increased significantly as a result of two large-scale relaxation of eligibility. There were only 22.9 million beneficiaries in 1990, which increased to 62.4 million in 2009. According to the latest data, in March 2011, 81.698 million people were covered by the Medicaid, of which 38.716 million were covered by the Children's Health Insurance Program or the independent insurance programs for children, and children accounted for 48.6 percent of the Medicaid.[①]

The Unemployment Insurance (UI) program in the United States is mandatory and is established by each state. The funding for unemployment insurance is payroll tax contributed by employers. The gross replacement rate of unemployment insurance in most states is about 50 percent, and the federal individual income tax is required.

In the field of relief, there are dozens of relief programs based on means test in the United States, featured with the continuous growth of physical assistance and the decline of cash assistance. Currently, cash assistance in the United States accounts for about 18 percent of total assistance. From 1935 to 1996, the main cash welfare program of the U.S. government was Aid to Families with Dependent Children (AFDC). The major

---

① March 2021 Medicaid & CHIP Enrollment, https://www.medicaid.gov/medicaid/program-information/medicaid-and-chip-enrollment-data/report-highlights/index.html.

beneficiaries of this program are generally single parent families with dependent children. In 1996, the United States established Temporary Assistance for Needy Families through new legislation, replacing previous family assistance programs. The new temporary assistance program emphasizes the temporary nature of cash subsidies, clarifies the duration (generally no more than 5 years) and imposes stricter requirements on job. The federal government provides fixed funding to each state, and state governments independently control the specific expenditure structure and assistance targets, as well as reduces the proportion of subsidies as household income increases. Therefore, temporary assistance for needy families varies significantly among different states in the United States.

Actually, the profound cash transfer support program provided by the United States to low-income individuals is not implemented through welfare institutions, but through the tax system, namely "tax expenditure". The Earned Income Tax Credit (EITC) is an income support for the poor labors. It is the same as the temporary assistance system for needy families, combining welfare with work. Empirical literature indicates that the earned income tax credit to some extent encourages low-income single mothers to join the labor market.

Since 1972, the United States has also provided Supplementary Security Income (SSI) for the elderly in poverty, the blind, and the disabled. The federal government has set a minimum coverage amount for supplementary security income. Starting from January 2021, the average monthly subsidy is USD 794 for individuals and USD 1,191 for couples. [①] The Supplemental Security Income has an implicit tax rate of 50 percent on increased income tax and encourages beneficiaries to work

① SSI Benefits-Social Security Administration, https://www.ssa.gov/ssi/text-benefits-ussi.htm.

harder.

The Supplementary Nutrition Assistance Program (SNAP) is also another relief program for the poor in the United States[①], costs of which are borne by the federal government and managed by each state. Since October 1, 2021, the average monthly subsidy for individuals has increased to USD 250, and the subsidy for a family of four has increased to USD 835.[②] Currently, over 42 million people are eligible for this assistance.

United States has been providing housing allowance to the poor since 1937. Public housing is developed, owned, and operated by local governments (cities, counties, or a consortium of several counties), with partial allowance provided by the federal government. But the number of public housing is limited, only 1.2 million units, making it difficult to meet the needs of up to 46 million impoverished people. Therefore, in the 1980s, the United States launched a housing voucher program. For many years, this program has enabled 3 million low-income families to search for housing in the private market and have the potential access to better living spaces.

The Supplementary Nutrition Assistance Program and housing allowance are both social welfare programs aimed at promoting consumption. According to American scholars, the amount of assistance provided by rescuers for supplementary nutrition program is estimated to be 80 percent of the face value. Therefore, poverty relief in the United States is more focused on ensuring the basic income and consumption

---

① Previously known as the Food Stamp Program, mainstream media and scholars in the United States still refer to the Supplementary Nutrition Assistance Program as the Food Stamp Program. To reduce the shame of poor families participating in this program, the United States provides such assistance only applicable to food through Electronic Benefits Transfer (EBT) cards, similar to credit cards.

② SNAP Eligibility| USDA-FNS, https://www.fns.usda.gov/snap/recipient/eligibility.

of the poor, rather than increasing their asset savings, investment, and accumulation. In other words, relief can only maintain expenditure and consumption. However, consumption often promotes asset savings, investment, and accumulation, while asset accumulation is increasingly tilted towards a few asset owners.

Although the social redistribution system in the United States is relatively complete (such as medical insurance programs), it lacks profound impact and reflects the concept of "Small government". In 2019, the proportion of the Old-Age, Survivors, and Disability Insurance (OASDI) to GDP in the United States was 4.9 percent, medical care-hospital indemnity insurance and supplemental medical insurance accounted for 3.72 percent of GDP and Medicaid (including SCHIP, State Children's Health Insurance Program) accounted for only 2.83 percent.

3.2 Federal Tax Structure and Tax expenditure

The tax system in the United States is complex, with two levels of taxation, namely federal-level and state-level. According to the OECD (see Table 1-2), the main characteristic of the U.S. federal tax structure is that it is highly dependent on individual income tax and payroll social security tax, and the proportion of corporate profit tax is meager. At the same time, the scale of tax expenditure mainly flowing to individuals is huge.

In recent years, both per capita GDP and per capita income in the United States have shown a slow growth trend, but the proportion of various taxes to GDP has decreased to different extents. Among them, the proportion of total tax revenue to GDP decreased from 28.3 percent in 2000 to 24.3 percent in 2019. The proportion of individual income tax to GDP slightly reduced from 11.994 percent in 2000 to 10.143 percent in 2019, as well as the social security tax, which fell from 6.6 percent to 6.1 percent, while the proportion of corporate profit tax to GDP correspondingly decreased from 2.24 percent to 0.957 percent. In other words, 66 percent of the U.S. tax revenue comes from the tax categories that tax individuals, which is significantly higher than the average level of OECD member countries.

Table 1-2 The Proportion of Major Taxes to GDP in U.S.

Item \ Year	2000	2013	2015	2016	2017	2018	2019
Social Security Contribution	6.663	6.137	6.171	6.155	6.168	6.066	6.101
Individual Income Tax	11.944	9.914	10.571	10.387	10.422	10.037	10.143
Payroll Tax	—	0.009	0.010	0.010	0.010	0.011	0.011
Corporate Profit Tax	2.24	2.099	2.113	1.949	1.566	0.998	0.957
Property Tax	2.922	2.998	2.958	3.009	4.352	2.997	2.958
General Tax Revenue	28.29	25.57	26.18	25.81	26.74	24.41	24.47

Source: https://data.oecd.org/tax/tax-revenue.htm#indicator-chart.

The tax system in the United States greatly reduces the tax evasion possibility of the working class. The Form W-2 for the working class in the United States covers over 90% of the income of the working class. Related research shows that the undeclared income of the bottom 50 percent of Americans accounts for 7 percent of the actual income, while the corresponding proportion of the richest 1 percent reaches 21 percent, and the corresponding proportion of the wealthiest 0.1 percent group is more than 66 percent.[①]

The tax system in the United States provides legal paths for large enterprises to reduce and evade taxes. Meanwhile, large corporations have managed to push for a revision of tax law to evade taxes. In 2017, the *Tax Cuts and Jobs Act* reduced the corporate income tax rate from 35 percent to 21 percent. However, the actual tax rates of many corporations are much lower than this. Taking Amazon for example, during the COVID-19, its profits soared to USD 20 billion in 2020, only 9.4 percent of which were levied as corporate profit tax. In the fiscal year 2020, at least 55 large corporations did not pay taxes while enjoying tax exemptions of up to USD 12 billion, including USD 8.5 billion in (legal) tax avoidance and USD 3.5 billion in tax refunds.[②]

In addition, according to the Federal Tax Law, the special tax-free, tax exemptions or tax reductions granted by the federal government to certain organizations and individuals with tax obligations, or the provision of special credit, preferential tax rates or deferred tax obligations, belong to tax expenditure. In other words, it is the federal government's fiscal expenditure in the form of reducing tax revenue.[③] Tax expenditure accounts for a large part of the federal budget. The report released by U.S. Joint Committee on Taxation in January 2020 shows that the total amount of tax expenditure in the fiscal year 2020 was close to USD 1.8 trillion.

The beneficiaries of tax expenditure in the United States are mainly the high-income class and the group with the most wealth. Because

---

① John Guyton (ed.), "Tax Evasion at the Top of the Income Distribution: Theory and Evidence", Social Science Electronic Publishing.

② Matthew Gardner and Steve Wamhoff, "55 Corporations Paid MYMO in Federal Taxes on 2020 Profits", https://itep.org/55-profitable-corporations-zero-corporate-tax/.

③ Wei Nanzhi: An Analysis of US Income Distribution System under the COVID-19 Epidemic, *World Socialism Studies*, 2021(6).

the higher an individual's tax rating, the greater the tax benefits that are deducted, exempted, or excluded. Taking the fiscal year 2019 as an example, 58 percent of tax expenditure went to the households in the top 20 percent of income in the United States, and 24 percent of tax expenditure were shared by households in the top 1 percent of income in the United States.①

In conclusion, the redistribution system in the United States has extremely demonstrated the values of individualism, liberalism, and limited government. On the one hand, the financial source of direct welfare transfer payments in the United States mainly comes from the working class itself. Its poverty relief is based on the purpose of filling vacancies, meeting basic needs, and promoting consumption among the poor, with weak function in poverty reduction. On the other hand, the tax system, which should play an important role in social redistribution, has largely shown a distinct tilt towards capital and the wealthy in the United States.

4. The Third Distribution System

In the third distribution system, social resources and wealth are distributed by various social classes voluntarily through charitable activities such as fundraising, donation, and funding, which is beneficial supplement to the primary distribution and redistribution and conducive to narrowing social gap and achieving more reasonable income distribution.

In 1601, the British Parliament passed the *Poor Relief Act* and

① Ward Williams, "Why Do We Spend So Much Federal Tax Money on the Rich in the US?" https://bettertomorrowfinancial.com/2020/04/29/ why-do-we-spend-so-much-federal-tax-money-on-the-rich-in-the-us/.

the *Charitable Uses Act*, which defined the property categories for compulsory taxation and the donation objects in detail. Since then, philanthropy has begun its popularization in Britain. In the mid-17th century, it launched in North America with early colonizers and began to develop from charitable relief to public welfare. By the latter half of the 19th century, American capitalism had developed rapidly and social wealth had grown fast. From 1870 to 1892, the number of millionaires increased from 100 to over 4,000. Influenced by the philanthropic culture of the Old World, new rich Americans chose to donate their huge wealth, or build universities or public service institutions such as libraries, hospitals and museums. As Daniel Coit Gilman, one of the founders of the American Social Science Association (1865) advocated, new philanthropy is not a temporary solution to the issues of poverty, while its ultimate goal is to find the root causes of poverty, continuously enhance the national strength of the United States, and even promote human progress.① This has also been the development direction of American philanthropy since the 20th century.

"Americans with unequal wealth and cultural differences have learned to transform market profits and methods into powerful driving forces for charity, which can influence the course of history".② Americans return their "interests" to society with a motivation to benefit from them, and investment in American philanthropy abroad is no exception, especially represented by the rise of the so-called profitable "new public welfare" model in the 21st century. Therefore, the American philanthropy is a

---

① [U.S.] Oilvier Zunz: *Philanthropy in America: A History*, Yang Min (translator), Shanghai University of Finance & Economics Press, 2016: 2.

② [U.S.] Oilvier Zunz: *Philanthropy in America: A History*, Yang Min (translator), Shanghai University of Finance & Economics Press, 2016: 170.

dialectical combination of altruism and egoism as well as a combination of donation and investment.

Nowadays, the United States has the hugest scale of charitable organization in the world and enjoys high credibility domestically. In 2019, there were 154,000 charitable organizations in the United States, and the main bodies of charitable organizations in the United States are public charities and private foundations that comply with Article 501(c)(3) of the *Internal Revenue Code*, which enjoy more reliability among the American public than the government and business enterprises. Charitable organizations and donors that comply with Article 501(c)(3) of the Internal Revenue Code are exempt from federal income tax, which is a major institutional factor in promoting the United States as world's largest charitable country.

The funding of U.S. charitable organizations mainly comes from cash and physical donations from ordinary people. In 2018, charitable donations in the United States accounted for 2.1 percent of its GDP, which is one-third of its stock market value. In 2019, the largest charitable donations came from individual donations, reaching USD 309,6600 billion, accounting for 69 percent of the total donation amount. Other sources of charitable donations included foundation donations (USD 75.69 billion, 17 percent of total donations in the United States) and bequests (USD 43.21 billion, 10 percent of total donations) and corporate donations (USD 21.09 billion, 5 percent of total donations). About 90 percent of high net worth households involved in donation. In 2017, donors from high net worth households donated an average of USD 29,269 to charitable organizations, while ordinary households donated an average of USD 2,514. Charitable donations accounted for 2.1 percent of the U.S. GDP in 2018 and reached one-third of its stock market value.①

It is worth re-emphasizing that the large-scale public philanthropy in the United States is not a mechanism for equalizing the rich and the poor with a single goal of poverty alleviation and poverty alleviation is only a negligible part of its expenditure. According to Article 501(c)(3), charitable organizations in the United States refer to any legal entity, community welfare fund, foundation (or fund) that is fully committed to religion, charity, science, public safety testing, literature, education, promotion of national and international amateur competitive sports, prevention of abuse of children and animals and other undertakings. They are more established to meet the diverse development needs of the whole society, including religion, education, scientific research, art, health, environmental protection, peace, etc. In 2019, the majority of charitable funds in the United States were invested in religion (29 percent), education (14 percent), human services (12 percent), sponsored foundations (12 percent), and health (9 percent). Among them, compared to 2018, the field with more than 10 percent growth rate in donations is education (12.1 percent), public social welfare (13.1 percent), arts, culture and humanities (12.6 percent), environment and animal organizations (11.3 percent).

The United States has formed a comprehensive regulatory system for public welfare and philanthropy at the federal, state, and local levels. *The Constitution of the United States* is the legal foundation of this system, while the *Internal Revenue Code* is the "basic principle" of this system. The main regulatory direction of the system is the credibility, fundraising, and fund utilization of public welfare charitable organizations. The

---

① Giving USA 2020, https://givingusa.org/giving-usa-2020-charitable-giving-showed-solid-growth-climbing-to-449-64-billion-in-2019 -one-of-the-highest-years-for-giving-on-record/.

main agency at the federal level is the Tax Exempt and Government Entities Division (TE/GE) of the Internal Revenue Service. In addition to traditional audits and reviews, the Internal Revenue Service also conducts comprehensive tracking and comparison through archival data and publicly available information. The regulatory work of the state governments on charitable organizations focus on providing various assistance and information services and educating the board members of various organizations on their legal responsibilities, rather than "management". The state governments are "Board Governs, Attorney General Enforces" of the charitable organizations. The role of local governments focuses on fundraising management and event management. The charitable organizations therefore enjoy great freedom within the U.S. legal framework.[①]

It is worth noting that there are professional institutions for supervision in different public welfare fields. For example, the Department of Health and Human Service (HHS), the Health Resources and Services Administration (HRSA), Centers for Medicare & Medicaid Services (CMS) and the Food and Drug Administration (FDA) all have the responsibility to supervise and regulate charitable organizations engaged in non-profit health care according to law.

In short, the values of individualism, liberalism, and limited government in the United States are also fully reflected in the fundraising, fund utilization, and regulation of public welfare and philanthropy . Therefore, public welfare philanthropy in the United States is regarded as a "third-party department" that is independent of the government and surpasses the market, featuring outstanding "independence" and "citizenship". Relying

---

① Refer to Xu Tongwu's *US Government's Management on Public Welfare Philanthropy and Experiences, Report on US Issues in 2011*, Social Science Academic Press, 2012.

on abundant material resources and social capital, in terms of their role of independence from the government and surpassing the market, it has repaired the damage caused by "market default" to a certain extent, and made up for the deficiency of public services due to the "limited government".

The vigorous development of U.S. charitable organizations is an important aspect of the self-adjustment and self-improvement of the capitalist system over the centuries, and it is also a necessary means for the power elite in the United States, such as the Ford Foundation, Rockefeller Foundation and Carnegie Foundation, which boast non-ideology and political neutrality, to achieve social control and safeguard the global strategic interests of the United States.

5. Conclusion

In recent years, the United States has been at the forefront of the OECD in terms of economic growth and employment rate as well as the gap between the rich and the poor, which is closely related to the serious imbalance in the proportion of capital income and labor income in primary distribution.

The highlighted concepts of individualism, laissez-faire and limited government lay the foundation for the U.S. redistribution system. The financial source of direct welfare transfer payments such as social security mainly comes from the working class itself. The poverty relief mechanism is based on the purpose of filling vacancies, meeting basic needs, and promoting consumption by the poor, and its poverty reduction role is very weak. At the same time, the tax system balance, which should play an important role in social redistribution, is significantly tilted towards capital and the wealthy. On the one hand, the financial source of direct welfare transfer payments such as social security in the United States mainly comes from the working class itself. Its poverty relief is based on the purpose of filling vacancies, meeting basic needs, and promoting consumption among the poor, with a weak function in poverty reduction. On the other hand, the tax system, which should play an important role in social redistribution, has essentially shown a distinct tilt towards capital and the wealthy.

Due to the fact that the redistribution mechanisms such as social security in the United States have not fundamentally improved income inequality and have not effectively slowed down the shrinking trend of the "middle class", the function of third distribution of massive public welfare philanthropy is often paid high expectations. However, facts have shown that the public welfare philanthropy that enjoys high independence and almost universal participation in the United States is not a mechanism for equalizing wealth, but focuses more on guiding and shaping economic and political norm, promoting all-round social development and progress, and maintaining the sustained compctitiveness and leading position of the United States in the world as its ultimate goal.

In other words, the system of primary distribution, redistribution and third distribution constructed centering on individualism, liberalism, and limited government, is one of the important reasons accounting for maintaining its attraction and capitalist economic vitality for decades. Of course, this is also the main reason why polarization between the rich and the poor is much more severe than European countries.

South America*

1. Basic Information

Since the 1970s, South American countries have successively advanced industrialization, paving the way for continuous improvement of income and access to the middle-income stage. However, affected by the debt crisis in the 1980s, South American countries launched neoliberal reforms, and gradually formed a commodity centered industrial layout model driven by resource endowments and comparative advantages. The increased external vulnerability and volatility and the decreased independence of economic policies made the economic growth and poverty reduction performance unstable and the polarization of wealth distribution countries in South America has not fundamentally changed. On the whole, in term of the development level, wealth creation ability, reality gap and sharing degree, South American countries show a pronounced "wealth imbalance", and there is still a long way to achieve common prosperity.

According to UNDP's estimation, South American countries are in the upper middle of the global human development (see Table 2-1). The mean values of HDI, life expectancy, and average years of education in the South American region are higher than the world average and the

---

* Author: CHAI Yu, YUE Yunxia, HE Bingzi, Institute of Latin American Studies, Chinese Academy of Social Sciences.

average level in developing countries, while per capita GNP in the South America is higher than the average of developing countries, but lower than the world average. There are considerable gaps between HDI and its sub-indexes in South American and that in developed OECD economies. Therefore, in terms of overall development, South American countries are generally at medium-high global level, with higher life expectancy demonstrating advancement in medical services, environment, education and life quality. However, the economic development in South America is slightly behind the regional well-being.

Table 2-1 Human Development Index of South American Countries (2019)

Ranking	Country	Index Value	Life Expectancy	Average Schooling Year	Per Capita GNP (USD, 2017 PPP)
Very High Human Development					
43	Chile	0.851	80.2	10.6	23, 261
46	Argentina	0.845	76.7	10.9	21, 190
55	Uruguay	0.817	77.9	8.9	20, 064
High Human Development					
79	Peru	0.777	76.7	9.7	12, 252
83	Columbia	0.767	77.3	8.5	14, 257
84	Brazil	0.765	75.9	8.0	14, 263
86	Ecuador	0.759	77.0	8.9	11, 044
97	Suriname	0.738	71.7	9.3	14, 324
103	Paraguay	0.728	74.3	8.5	12, 224
107	Bolivia	0.718	71.5	9.0	8, 554
113	Venezuela	0.711	72.1	10.3	7, 045
Medium Human Development					
122	Guyana	0.682	69.9	8.5	9, 455
	Average of South American Countries	0.763	75.1	9.3	13, 994
	Average of Developing Countries	0.689	71.3	7.5	10, 583
	Average of OECD	0.900	80.4	12.0	44, 967

continued

Ranking	Country	Index Value	Life Expectancy	Average Schooling Year	Per Capita GNP (USD, 2017 PPP)
	World Average	0.737	72.8	8.5	16, 734

Source: UNDP, 2020 Human Development Report (HDR).

In terms of absolute per capita wealth, South American countries are above the middle-income level. The per capita GDP of South America is nearly USD 7,700, which is relatively leading among emerging markets and developing countries. According to the World Bank's classification of income, among the 12 countries in South America, Uruguay and Chile are high-income countries, Bolivia and Venezuela are in the lower middle-income economies, and the other 8 countries belong to the upper middle-income countries (see Chart 2-1). In comparison, except for the latter two countries with relatively lower per capita GDP, other South

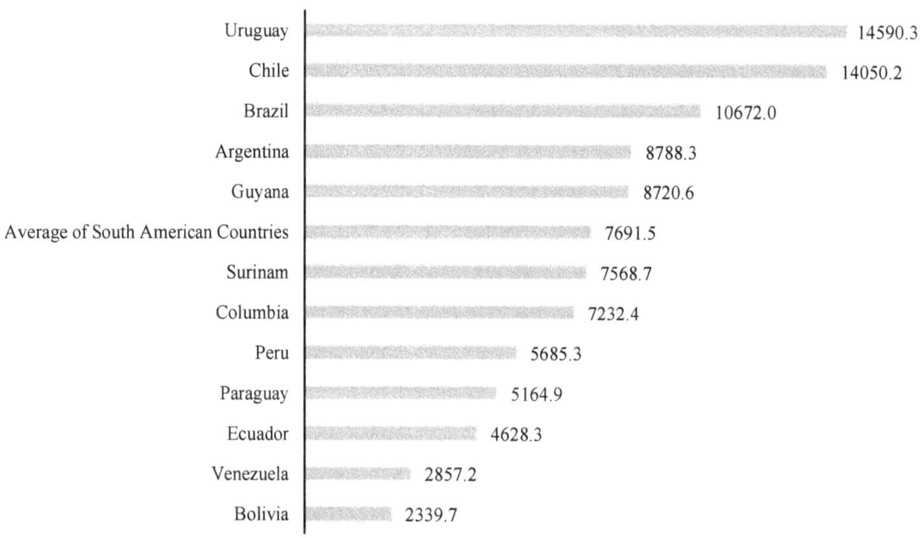

Chart 2-1　Per capita GDP of South American countries (2020, USD)

Source: CEPALSTAT

American countries have exceeded the world median level, and the strong ability to create per capita wealth contributes to the achievement of “prosperity”.

In terms of the distribution of income groups, the proportion of lower-middle income groups in South American countries is relatively high. As populism prevails in South America, especially in the early 21st century combined with the governance of left-wing parties and the “commodity supercycle”, and higher social expenditures bring changes in the population and social structure, according to data from EURO International, in terms of relative income, the proportion of middle class households in South America in absolute numbers and in the total number of households is constantly increasing. At the national-level, data from the World Bank and Socio-Economic Database for Latin America and the Caribbean (SEDLAC) show, by absolute income measurement, as of 2017, the proportion of the middle class in South American countries such as Argentina, Chile, and Uruguay had exceeded half, while the proportion of the middle class in other South American countries had also exceeded 30 percent (see Chart 2-2). However, there is still a certain gap in most South American countries compared to the stable “olive-shaped society” requiring the proportion of middle income class over 60 percent. At the same time, poverty and absolute poverty in South American countries have not been eliminated. High income countries such as Uruguay and Chile still exist extreme poverty, the proportion of destitute population in Uruguay and Chile exceed 10 percent, while Ecuador, Argentina, Bolivia, and Colombia have more than a quarter of the population living in poverty (see Chart 2-3). Therefore, South American countries are far from common prosperity.

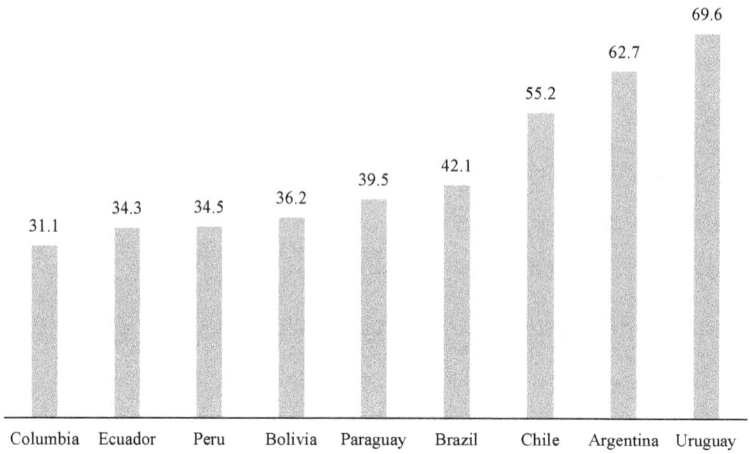

Chart 2-2 Proportion of Middle Class in South America (%)

Note: The standard for the middle class is based on the World Bank and CEDLAS standards, where the per capita daily income is between USD 13 and USD 70 (calculated at purchasing power parity in 2011)

Source: CEPALSTAT

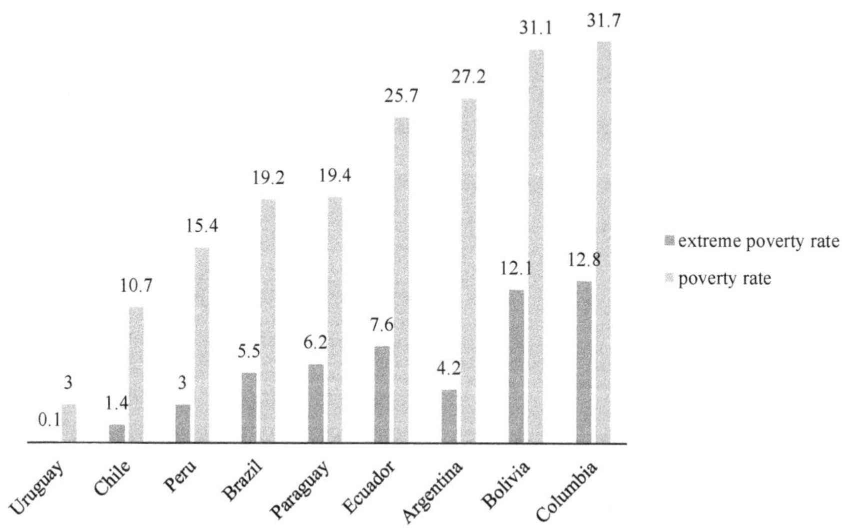

Chart 2-3 Poverty Rate in South America

Source: ECLAC, Social Panorama of Latin America, 2020

In terms of the wealth distribution, South American countries show obvious polarization. Since the early 21st century, the South American economy has experienced relatively stable and sustained growth, and the income gap has narrowed. However, South America remains one of the most unequal regions in global income. In terms of Gini Coefficient, except Uruguay, where the coefficient is slightly below 0.4, Gini Coefficient in most Latin American countries is between 0.4 and 0.5, indicating a large income gap and Colombia and Brazil have wide income gap with the coefficient even greater than 0.5. In terms of the ratio of per capita income between the highest 10 percent group and lowest 10 percent group, the index value in Brazil is as high as 40 times, while Ecuador, Colombia, Paraguay, and Bolivia have a value exceeding 20 times. The value in Argentina, Peru, Venezuela, and Chile also is also beyond 15 times, with a value slightly higher than 12 times in Uruguay (see Chart 2-4).

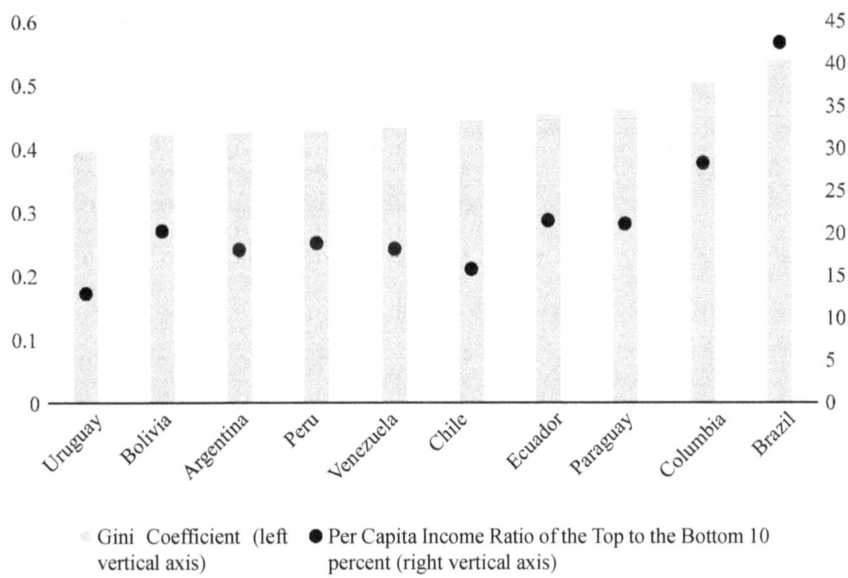

Chart 2-4 Income Gap in South American Countries

Note: the most recent year available for data from various countries

Source: CEPALSTAT

It's obvious that South American countries have a relatively high level of social development, but they have not yet achieved common prosperity which is shared by all, and there are differences in countries' development. Uruguay is close to common prosperity, while Chile still encounters the problem of "prosperous but unequal". Argentina has made relatively remarkable achievements in social development, but is still left behind in terms of the total amount and distribution of wealth. Meanwhile, other countries are facing challenges of wealth growth and sharing in varying degrees, and need continuous efforts in poverty alleviation and income expansion.

2. South American Policies to Promote Common Prosperity and Effectiveness

Common prosperity is the comprehensive development of people and the society. The social development of South American countries is ahead of economic development, and the prominent problem in economic development is reflected in the wealth realization and distribution gap. Therefore, in promoting common prosperity, the relevant policies of South American countries focus on the efforts of income expansion and distribution equality that match their income structure.

The main income sources of South American countries include labor income, transfer income, pension income, property income, and other non-labor income (see Table 2-2). The composition of income shows structural characteristics. According to data from the World Bank's "LAC Equity Lab", labor income is the main source of income for all income groups, accounting for an average of about two-thirds of income in major countries in South America. Especially in middle-income groups in the second, third, and fourth quintile of income, the average proportion of labor income is close to 70 percent, while countries such as Bolivia, Colombia, Paraguay, and Peru account for almost 80 percent. Other non-labor income, mainly from overseas remittances, is the second largest income source with South American characteristics, accounting for an average of 16 percent of the income of major South American countries, especially among the lowest income group, accounting for an average of 20 percent. In Chile, Paraguay, and Peru, the proportion even exceeds 20 percent. Pension income accounts for an average of 9 percent of the income of South American countries, and the proportion of pension income in high and middle-income countries such as Chile, Uruguay, Brazil, and Argentina significantly surpasses the average level. The distribution of pension income is also obviously positively correlated with income levels, with an average proportion of 10 percent and 12 percent among middle and upper-income groups and high income groups. Transfer income accounts for an average of 7 percent of income in South American countries, and its distribution is significantly negatively correlated with income levels. It is the third largest source of income among the first and second quintile of income. Property income accounts for an average of 1 percent of South American income, mainly occupied by the group with medium to high income or above.

Based on the structure of income distribution, Latin American policies to promote common prosperity are reflected in primary distribution, redistribution, and third distribution of income, as well as the adjustment of social public policies, and have shown different policy effectiveness.

2.1 Primary Distribution

In the early 21st century, due to the improvement of commodity prices in the international market, income in South American countries increased. Most countries began to implement more active labor policies,

Table 2-2 **Income Sources of South American Countries**

	Argentina	Bolivia	Brazil	Chile	Columbia	Ecuador	Paraguay	Peru	Uruguay
The First Quintile of Income (low income)									
Labor Income	54%	74%	56%	58%	68%	62%	58%	65%	57%
Transfer Income	16%	8%	18%	11%	16%	21%	14%	7%	16%
Pension Income	10%	7%	8%	9%	1%	2%	4%	3%	9%
Property Income	0%	0%	0%	0%	1%	0%	0%	0%	0%
Other Non-labor Income	20%	11%	17%	22%	16%	15%	25%	24%	18%
The Second Quintile of Income (low and middle income)									
Labor Income	64%	80%	63%	61%	77%	68%	71%	73%	63%
Transfer Income	6%	6%	8%	6%	8%	12%	8%	5%	6%
Pension Income	11%	4%	14%	11%	2%	2%	3%	2%	14%
Property Income	0%	1%	0%	0%	1%	0%	0%	1%	0%
Other Non-labor Income	18%	10%	14%	21%	12%	17%	18%	19%	16%
The Third Quintile of Income (middle income)									
Labor Income	61%	79%	63%	63%	78%	69%	75%	74%	61%
Transfer Income	4%	6%	5%	4%	6%	9%	6%	4%	4%
Pension Income	15%	5%	18%	12%	4%	3%	3%	3%	18%
Property Income	1%	1%	1%	1%	1%	1%	0%	1%	1%
Other Non-labor Income	20%	10%	14%	20%	11%	18%	15%	18%	16%

continued

	Argentina	Bolivia	Brazil	Chile	Columbia	Ecuador	Paraguay	Peru	Uruguay
The Fourth Quintile of Income (middle and upper-income)									
Labor Income	59%	79%	61%	66%	76%	67%	78%	74%	62%
Transfer Income	3%	4%	3%	3%	4%	7%	4%	4%	3%
Pension Income	17%	5%	19%	11%	7%	4%	3%	3%	18%
Property Income	1%	2%	1%	1%	2%	1%	1%	1%	1%
Other Non-labor Income	21%	10%	16%	19%	11%	21%	13%	17%	16%
The Fifth Quintile of Income (high income)									
Labor Income	58%	72%	62%	75%	71%	60%	76%	70%	59%
Transfer Income	1%	4%	1%	2%	2%	4%	3%	3%	2%
Pension Income	18%	8%	18%	7%	12%	12%	6%	5%	20%
Property Income	4%	4%	3%	4%	6%	4%	3%	4%	4%
Other Non-labor Income	19%	12%	16%	13%	9%	21%	13%	17%	15%

Note: The data of Chile is for 2017, while the rest are for 2019. The data of Argentina is based on urban data, while the rest are based on national data.

Source: World Bank, LAC Equity Lab: Inccme Inequality-Composition by Quintile.

which had an impact on labor income from aspects such as employment structure, tax structure, minimum wage system, and wage collective bargaining mechanism.

2.1.1Employment Policies

The employment policies of South American countries can be divided into three categories. The first is to adjust the employment structure, expand the proportion of service industry, stabilize and increase new employment and expand the scale of labor income. The second is to intensify the protection of labors, promote the normalization of the labor market, expand the proportion of wage income in labor income and improve the stability of labor income. The third is to improve labors' skill, narrow the wage gap between high and low skilled workers and promote the equality of primary distribution.

Because of above policies, South American countries have made significant progress in the labor market. From 2000 to 2015, unemployment rates in all South American countries steadily decreased, with unemployment rates even halving in countries such as Argentina, Brazil, Colombia, and Uruguay, and employment rates saw an increase. ① This has reduced the size of the working poor population the South America by more than half, and income inequality in most countries has sharply decreased. However, after 2015, most countries in South America experienced a long-term economic slowdown, with regional labor market indicators, unemployment rates and poverty rates rising(see Chart 2-5). The outbreak of COVID-19 has led to a sharp exacerbation of employment and rapid expansion of poverty rate.

① Escudero, V., López Mourelo, E. and Pignatti, C., "What Works Active Labour Market Policies in Latin America and the Caribbean", *Studies on Growth with Equity*, 2016.

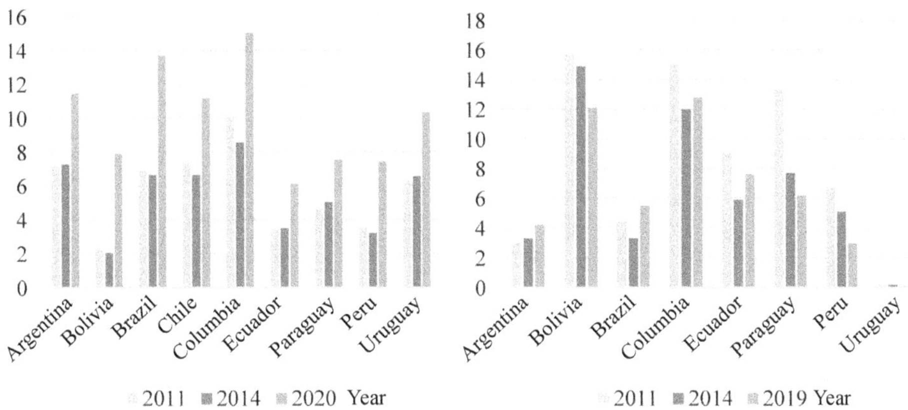

Chart 2-5 Changes in Unemployment Rates (left) and Poverty Rates (right) in Major South American Countries

Source: Unemployment Rates: ILOSTAT; Poverty Rates: CEPALSTAT.

2.1.2 Tax Policies

The primary distribution of South American countries mainly relies on value-added tax and consumption tax. In 2019, these two major tax categories accounted for 47. 9 percent of the total annual tax revenue, higher than the average of 32.4 percent for the OECD countries (See Table 2-3). Among them, value-added tax is the largest tax category in South American countries, with an average contribution of 29.58 percent, and even more than 35 percent in Chile, Peru, and Paraguay, which is higher than the average for the Latin American countries and the OECD. The average consumption tax is 18.34 percent, much higher than the average level of OECD. Compared with these two major taxes, the average proportion of individual tax and corporate tax used for redistribution is 7.37 percent and 16.06 percent respectively, and the social security tax is 18.91 percent. In particular, the property tax used to adjust the income of high-income group is only 4.4 percent. All are well below the average of OECD countries.

Table 2-3 **The Tax Structure of South American Countries (2019)**

Country	Individual Tax	Corporate Tax	Tax Cannot Be Distributed Between Individuals and Corporations	Social Security Tax	Property Tax	Value-added Tax	Consumption Tax Other Than VAT	Other Taxes
Argentina	7.07%	9.64%	1.25%	19.95%	9.14%	24.95%	27.28%	0.73%
Bolivia	0.74%	15.53%	0.00%	25.08%	0.75%	29.22%	19.77%	8.91%
Brazil	9.17%	8.64%	4.59%	25.71%	4.61%	21.18%	21.65%	4.45%
Chile	7.17%	23.41%	4.27%	7.31%	5.41%	39.88%	13.18%	-0.62%
Columbia	6.17%	24.47%	1.66%	9.51%	9.08%	29.63%	13.31%	6.17%
Ecuador	0.91%	6.05%	14.65%	27.13%	1.59%	30.26%	19.31%	0.10%
Guyana	14.09%	23.32%	0.36%	9.48%	1.97%	21.05%	28.88%	0.86%
Paraguay	1.88%	16.37%	0.00%	26.45%	1.34%	35.73%	17.62%	0.61%
Peru	11.52%	23.02%	2.00%	12.08%	2.39%	38.45%	8.73%	1.81%
Uruguay	14.97%	10.12%	1.05%	26.43%	7.70%	25.43%	13.69%	0.62%
LAC Average	8.86%	15.46%	2.73%	17.13%	3.83%	27.74%	22.02%	2.23%
OECD Average	23.96%	9.55	0.85%	25.71%	5.62%	20.45%	11.80%	2.05%

Source: https://taxfoundation.org/latin-american-tax-revenue-caribbean-tax-revenue/.

The tax structure of South American countries makes the tax stability and income regulation function relatively weak. According to the OECD, in the past decade, with the long-term downturn in economic growth after 2014, the proportion of tax revenue to GDP in most South American countries reached its peak in recent years around 2015, and then declined slightly. From 2010 to 2019, the only countries with relatively stable tax growth trends were Brazil, Chile, Guyana, and Uruguay. At the same time, the average proportion of regional tax to GDP has always been below 25 percent, with countries such as Venezuela, Paraguay, and Peru even accounting for only about 15 percent. In comparison, the tax revenue in OECD countries during the same period accounted for approximately one third of GDP, while in South America, only Brazil was able to reach this proportion (see Table 2-4). It can be seen that most South American countries have insufficient taxation and tax structure plays a relatively limited role in regulating income distribution.

Table 2-4 Proportion of Tax Revenue to GDP in South American Countries (%)

	2010	2011	2012	2013	2014	2015	2016	2017	2018	2019
Chile	19.6	21.1	21.3	19.9	19.6	20.4	20.1	20.2	21.1	20.7
Columbia	18.1	18.9	19.9	20.0	19.6	19.9	19.1	19.0	19.3	19.7
Argentina	29.1	29.3	30.6	31.2	31.1	31.5	30.7	30.0	28.9	28.6
Bolivia	22.9	25.1	25.9	26.7	27.9	29.5	27.9	25.9	25.0	24.7
Brazil	32.4	33.3	32.5	32.5	31.8	32.0	32.2	32.3	33.2	33.1
Ecuador	16.0	17.6	19.7	19.5	19.2	21.3	19.9	19.9	20.7	20.1
Guyana	16.0	16.4	15.8	16.4	17.8	18.1	18.4	19.5	22.2	23.2
Paraguay	12.1	12.9	13..4	12.7	13.9	13.7	13.4	14.0	13.8	13.9
Peru	17.8	18.4	19.0	18.9	19.2	17.4	16.2	15.3	16.5	16.6
Uruguay	26.3	26.7	27.0	27.5	27.4	27.4	27.8	29.0	29.2	29.0
Venezuela	11.8	13.4	14.1	14.4	—	—	—	—	—	—

continued

	2010	2011	2012	2013	2014	2015	2016	2017	2018	2019
LAC Average	20.2	21.2	21.7	21.8	22.7	23.1	22.6	22.5	23.0	23.0
OECD Average	31.9	32.2	32.7	33.0	33.2	33.3	34.0	33.7	33.9	33.8

Source: https://taxfoundation.org/latin-american-tax-revenue-caribbean-tax-revenue/.

2.1.3 Minimum Wage Plan

The minimum wage system began at the end of the 19th century, and the International Labour Organization formulated three Conventions (No.26, No.99, No.131) as well as Recommendations (No.30, No.89, No.135) on minimum wages in 1928, 1951, and 1970. In line with global development, South American countries have gradually established a minimum wage system since the early 20th century, and currently this system has covered all countries in the region.

In the past decade, in order to protect labors from the impact of the minimum wage and reduce wage inequality among lower income groups, most South American countries have continuously raised the minimum wage level. According to data from the United Nations Economic Commission for Latin America, except for Venezuela, the minimum wage index of other South American countries has maintained an overall growth trend. The growth rate of the minimum wage in most South American countries is higher than the average global growth rate. Among them, Bolivia and Uruguay have the fastest growth rate of the minimum wage, with an average annual growth rate of 8.8 percent and 7.7 percent, Chile, Peru, and Ecuador have an average annual growth rate of over 3 percent, which is generally consistent with the level of emerging economies worldwide, the average annual growth rate of the minimum wage in Brazil and Colombia is about 1.5 percent, while Uruguay is 0.3 percent, equivalent to developed economies (see Table 2-5).

Table 2-5 Average Minimum Wage Index in South American Countries

	2010	2011	2012	2013	2014	2015	2016	2017	2018	2019
Argentina	321.3	364.4	—	—	—	—	—	—	—	—
Bolivia	119.9	130.9	144.0	174.4	197.8	218.6	229.9	247.8	249.5	252.4
Brazil	182.1	182.1	197.5	202.7	203.6	203.3	208.7	214.8	211.0	212.7
Chile	127.7	129.8	133.5	139.9	145.3	149.1	156.5	161.2	165.0	171.7
Columbia	115.2	115.9	118.8	121.2	123.1	122.6	122.0	125.2	128.4	131.5
Ecuador	161.7	170.2	179.1	190.0	196.1	196.4	199.6	203.7	210.1	213.9
Paraguay	102.5	105.2	103.9	101.2	104.3	102.7	99.3	104.6	104.3	105.2
Peru	110.1	120.7	133.6	135.6	131.4	126.9	133.3	135.0	142.6	142.7
Uruguay	196.8	227.7	252.8	256.1	166.1	273.3	277.5	287.8	292.7	303.4
Venezuela	93.8	89.9	91.2	84.2	76.5	66.3	78.3	93.6	42.5	27.3

Note: Average Minimum Wage Index in 2000 is assumed to be 100.
Source: CEPALSTAT.

2.1.4 Wage Collective Bargaining Mechanism

A well-functioning collective bargaining mechanism helps to ensure the fair sharing of development achievements among the working class and reduce inequality. The minimum wage can also be determined through collective bargaining. In addition, it can produce a broader equal inducement effect by promoting a fair wage structure and other attributes of an inclusive labour market, including equal treatment, employee participation and skill development. Empirical evidence from developed countries shows that countries where collective agreements cover a large number of labors have a smaller degree of inequality.

Among South American countries, only Uruguay and Argentina have established relatively stable wage collective bargaining mechanism.① In Uruguay, the Single Union of Domestic Workers (SUTD) participates

① https://www.ilo.org/wcmsp5/groups/public/---americas/---ro-lima/documents/publication/wcms _ 534457.pdf.

in collective bargaining with the union of housewives, consumers, and users.[①] At the 2008 Wage Committee Conference, in addition to reaching an agreement on issues related to wage, all parties also were committed to working together to raise public awareness, establish seniority bonuses, design measures to create dignified working conditions, prohibit sexual harassment, and require the payment of partial severance when the working hours are reduced (Decree No. 670/008). At the 2013 Conference, the Wage Committee established a full attendance bonus and agreed to define the working nature of the department and employment contracts. In Argentina, the National Commission on Private Household Labour was established in September 2015, where trade union organizations, employer organizations and the Ministry of Labour conducted centralized negotiations on wages.

Bolivia has also carried out activities to promote social dialogue and collective bargaining in recent years. Since 2013, with the participation of representatives from the Ministry of Labor, Employment and Social Protection, Union of Housewives of Bolivia and La Federación Nacional de Trabajadoras del Hogar de Bolivia (FENATRAHOB), a tripartite round table has been organized to develop Individual Employment Contract and Wage, Social Security, and Occupational Safety Manual. A study on freedom of association and collective bargaining has been organized to provide baseline information for developing a tripartite action course.[②]

---

① Bastidas, M. (2014). Organización de las trabajadoras de hogar en las Américas. Buenas prácticas y desafíos en función de Convenio N° 189 de la OIT. Turin: ILO.

② Lexartza, L., Chaves, Maria J. and Carcedo, A., "Policies to Formalize Paid Domestic Work in Latin America and the Caribbean", Lima: ILO, *Regional Office for Latin America and the Caribbean*, 2016.

2.2 Social Redistribution

In addition to individual income tax, corporate income tax, property tax and other taxes, social redistribution policies in South American countries are mainly reflected in social security policies and transfer payment policies.

2.2.1 Social Security

Since the 1990s, South American countries have initiated structural pension reforms and implemented a series of different pension plans, including the traditional pay-as-you-go public system with defined benefit and the parallel and hybrid structure of individual capital accounts with defined contribution based on private sector management.

In terms of the coverage of pension, South American countries have established a pension system that covers the entire region. According to the OECD classification of the three levels of the pension system, half of South American countries have established the first-level public pension plans, which are mandatory and not related to income, specifically involving target pension, basic pension, and minimum pension. However, Brazil, Colombia, Paraguay, Peru, Uruguay, and Venezuela have not established such plans (see Table 2-6). Except for Suriname, which has not implemented the second type of mandatory individual savings pension system, other South American countries have implemented the mandatory, income linked second-level pension plans. Among them, most countries, similar to developed OECD economies, implement pay-as-you-go public pension plans with defined benefits, while Chile replaced the benefit-defined public pay-as-you-go plan with a mandatory, contribution-defined private accumulation plan in 1981 and Uruguay also established the mandatory, contribution-defined private accumulation plan as the supplement.

Table 2-6 Pension System in South America

	First-level Pension Plans			Second-level Pension Plans	
	Public Pension System			Public System	Private System
	Target Pension	Basic Pension	Minimum Pension	Categories	Categories
Chile	√		√		DC
Columbia				DB	
Ecuador	√			DB	
Guyana	√			DB	
Paraguay				DB	
Peru				DB	
Suriname		√			
Uruguay				DB	DC
Venezuela				DB	
OECD Countries					
Canada	√	√		DB	
France			√	DB+Points	
Germany	√			Points	
Portugal			√	DB	
Spain			√	DB	
UK	√	√	√	DB	
USA				DB	

Note: Defined Benefit Plan (DB Plan) is an accumulation plan with defined benefit, that is, a pay-as-you-go pension plan; Defined Contribution Plan (DC Plan) is an accumulation plan with defined contribution, which is a mandatory pension plan with individual accounts; Points refer to Points Schemes, where employees receive retirement points based on their income.

Source: OECD/IDB/The World Bank (2014), *Pensions at a Glance: Latin America and the Caribbean*, OECD Publishing.

In terms of the effectiveness of pension systems, pension plans in almost all South American countries are facing challenges. Among them, Brazil, Colombia, Guyana, Paraguay, Peru, and Venezuela adopted DC plans, while Argentina, Bolivia, Ecuador, Guyana, and Uruguay implemented hybrid plans. These two types of plans faced unsustainable risks as the left-wing government expanding pension commitments in the early 21st century without increasing contributions, making it difficult for continual fiscal subsidies. The DC plan adopted by Chile is unable to provide "sufficient" pension due to comprehensive factors such as insufficient coverage, low mandatory contribution rate, and relatively low retirement age.

2.2.2 Transfer Payment

Since the beginning of the 21st century, public policies in South America havetransformed the target of public expenditure, with greater emphasis on the social sector and public investment. Countries have actively used financial tools and made continuous innovation and efforts in areas such as transfer payment. Since the mid-1990s, Brazil has implemented Conditional Cash Transfer (CCT) Payment, which effectively reduces inequality in social distribution by linking transfer payment to education (e.g. enrollment of the recipients' child) or health (e.g. vaccination). Ecuador and Paraguay promoted the human development grant and a conditional cash transfer program called "Programa Tekoporâ" to provide additional subsidies for the disables who meet poverty standards①. Governments in such countries as Ecuador provide wheelchairs, hearing aids, visual aids, artificial limbs, as well as psychological and rehabilitation services. Servicio Nacional de la Discapacidad (SENADIS) in Chile offers free or subsidized assistive technology and rehabilitation services for children

① Duryea, S., Salazar Salamanca, J. P., Pinzon Caicedo, M. 2019. We the People: Inclusion of People with Disabilities in Latin America and the Caribbean. http://dx.doi.org/10.18235/0002010.

under 10 years of age whose income is below the threshold.

According to the United Nations Economic Commission for Latin America, public expenditure on social services in South America significantly increased between 2000 and 2005 and between 2010 and 2015, especially the share of expenditure on education, health and social security. Meanwhile, the expenditure on economic affairs covering most public investments, as well as investment in housing and community services also improved. The increase in these social expenditures and transfer payment has a direct impact on poverty alleviation and inequality reduction, endowing impoverished and vulnerable groups more opportunities to participate in the society.

In public crisis, South American countries reduce the impact of the COVID-19 on citizens' health, welfare and income through social security institutions, plans and services. For example, since the outbreak of COVID-19, social assistance in Argentina and Colombia has provided additional cash transfers to beneficiaries, Bolivia has introduced a school feeding plan, Peru has formulated new social assistance plans for cash transfers to poor and vulnerable families, and Brazil's conditional "Bolsa Familiade" cash transfer plan has expanded to one million families. According to the United Nations Economic Commission for Latin America, the estimated expenditure on emergency cash and physical transfers in South America in 2020 exceeded the combined ratio of CCT and social pension in 2018, with a difference of 0.75 percentage point. (see Chart 2-6).

Meanwhile, South American countries have promoted innovation in transfer payment tools and increased the coverage of social safety net. Countries such as Brazil and Colombia use social registration to promote the coverage of benefits to non-beneficiaries, while

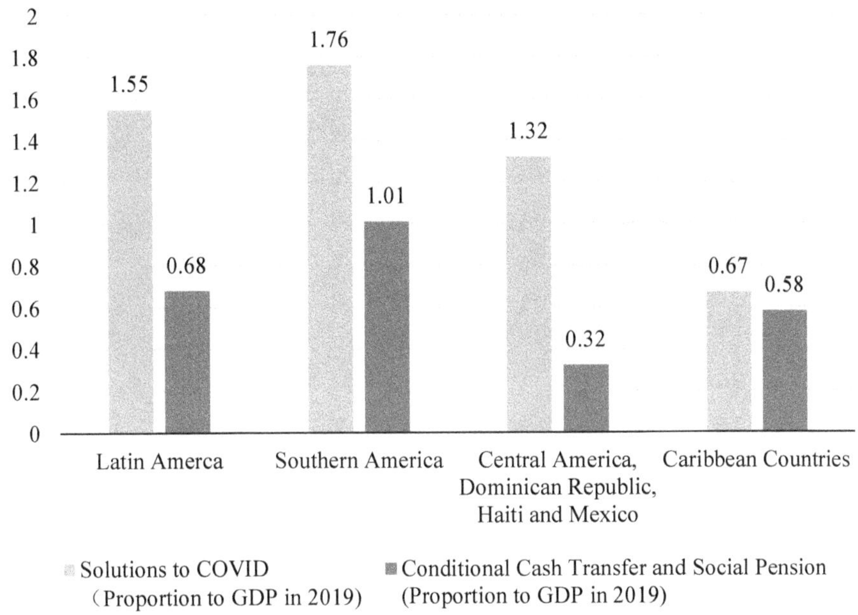

Chart 2-6 Estimated Expenditures for Emergency Cash and Physical Transfers in Latin America in 2020 and Conditional Cash Transfer Plans and Social Pensions in 2018

Source: Economic Commission for Latin America and the Caribbean (ECLAC), on the basis of official information from the countries; COVID-19 Observatory in Latin America and the Caribbean [online] https:// www.cepal.org/es/temas/covid-19 and Observatory on Social Development in Latin America and the Caribbean, "Social Development and COVID-19 in Latin America and the Caribbean" [on/line] https://dds.cepal.org/observatorio/socialcovid19/listamedidas.php.

Quote from: Economic Commission for Latin America and the Caribbean (ECLAC), 2021. Social Panorama of Latin America, 2020 (LC/PUB.2021/2-P/Rev.1).

most South American countries use beneficiary registers to provide supplementary benefits to safety net beneficiaries, and rely on social workers and social security program personnel to provide relief items to individuals under quarantine①. However, South American countries

① Williams, A. and Gonzalez, S.B. (2020). Towards adaptive social protection systems in Latin America and the Caribbean: A synthesis note on using social protection to mitigate and respond to disaster risk. The World Bank.

still face challenges in crisis response, including providing support to highly informal impacted workers, remaining regions where social registration is still not covered or with low coverage, and the payment mechanism inconsistent with the social distance is limited to cash payment.

2.3 The Third Distribution

2.3.1 Overseas Support

South American countries receive overseas support from both private and official channels. In private channels, overseas remittances have always been the main external source of funding for South American countries, making a certain contribution to regional economic development. Since 80 to 90 percent of overseas remittances are used to meet the basic needs of recipient households (food, health, and housing), a decline in remittances can have a significant negative impact on consumption and poverty in some countries. As the overseas remittance income of South American countries mainly comes from American and European countries, there is fluctuation in its stability. For example, affected by the COVID-19, in the first eight months of 2020, the South American countries with a year-on-year decrease in the inflow of overseas remittances include Bolivia (-26 percent), Peru (-22 percent), Paraguay (-16 percent) and Ecuador (-10 percent), which has had a particular adverse impact on the local economy, especially inhibit the expenditure on consumption of low-income people.

In official channels, the support and assistance from the international community to South America is also an important factor in its social development. For example, on September 9, 2019, Britain's Foreign Affairs Committee released its report on the 20th meeting of 2017-2019,

Global Britain and South America (HC 1617). [①] The report states that in September 2019, the UK Department for International Development announced at the United Nations General Assembly that in addition to the £ 14.5 million declared earlier in 2019, it will also provide more funds for Venezuela and the South America, totaling the UK's response expenditure to £ 44.5 million. Venezuela's neighboring countries (such as Colombia) had received a large number of immigrants and refugees escaping from the crisis, putting pressure on local services. The British government should also provide financial support to Colombia through mechanisms such as the World Bank Global Preferential Financing Fund (with a planned £ 8 million) to ensure necessary support for immigrants and refugees fleeing Venezuela.

In addition, the Inter-American Foundation (IAF) is an independent foreign aid agency of the U.S. government, established in 1969 to promote the citizen-led development in Latin America. IAF works directly with community organizations to help them identify and address issues, such as economic opportunities, family and social violence, social inclusion, and citizen participation. In 2020, IAF's expenditure on the COVID-19 reached a total investment of about USD 21.7 million, funding 151 regional organizations in 21 countries.[②] In addition, in 2020, IAF and community organizations in Latin American countries jointly invested approximately USD 64.5 million in developing regional projects, of which 28 percent was for sustainable agriculture and food security, 21 percent was invested for enterprise development and employment skills. In such rescue plans covering the entire region, South American countries

---

① https: //publications.parliament.uk/pa/cm5801/cmselect/cmfaff/669/66902.htm.

② IAF. (2020) Annual Report: 2020 in Review. Available at: https://www.iaf.gov/content/data-report/annual-report-2020-in-review/ (Access 11 August 2021)

have become the main recipients of aid.

2.3.2 Social Charity, Preferential Policy and Support

The development of philanthropy in South America is relatively backward. On the one hand, business leaders in South America (and even Latin America) are absent from regional and global philanthropy, and the wealthiest group in the region has not signed donation commitments, with only a few companies establishing relevant funds. On the other hand, with a few exceptions, donations from the global wealthiest group have not generated a culture of charity and responsible giving in South America (including Latin America).

3. Major Factors Restricting Latin America's Common Prosperity

In terms of social wealth distribution system, South American countries have established a distribution system of primary distribution, social redistribution and third distribution covering the whole region. However, in reality, most countries in the region still have a wide gap between wealth stock and common prosperity, and inequality in income increment is also very prominent. According to the World Bank, there are differences in the distribution of income from different sources in South America, based on the distribution of various income groups. The imbalance in the distribution of property income is the most significant, with high income groups accounting for 84 percent and middle and upper-income groups income groups accounting for 10 percent, while the total proportion of property income in the top three quintiles is only 6 percent. The imbalance in the distribution of pension income is also prominent, with high income groups accounting for 66 percent, middle and upper-income groups accounting for 21 percent, and middle income groups accounting for 9 percent, while lower-middle income and low income groups share 4 percent and 1 percent of the pension income. The distribution of labor income and other non-labor income is also significantly imbalanced, with high income groups accounting for 55 percent of each of these two incomes, middle and upper-income and middle income groups accounting for 20 percent and 13 percent, and lower-middle income and low income groups accounting for only 8 percent and 3 percent. The distribution of transfer income shows a certain balance, but the proportion of high income groups exceeds 25 percent, the proportion of middle income groups is around 20 percent, and the proportion of low income groups is only 15 percent.

The distribution gap of wealth stock and income increment in South America impedes the progress of achieving common prosperity in this region, and the formation and accumulation of contradictions include various structural factors.

Firstly, the growth of most countries in South America cannot create enough new social wealth. Since 2014, South American economic growth has slowed down, and the regional economic growth rate has been consistently lower than the world average, even lower than the average growth level of developed economies. In 2020, impacted by the COVID-19, South America experienced the worst economic recession in nearly a century, with a GDP growth rate of -7.3 percent, the regional unemployment rate exceeding 10 percent, and the regional poverty rate increasing significantly. According to the Economic Commission for Latin America, the economy of the Latin American region, including South America is estimated to recover to the levels of the 2010s until 2023, and the living standards of the impoverished population in the region have now dropped to the levels of the 1990s, while the extremely poor population has retreated to the levels of the 1980s. Under the severe economic and social crisis, South America lacks endogenous growth momentum, and total factor productivity growth has long lagged behind other emerging markets and developing economies. According to statistics, in the past decade, the average growth of South American countries has almost stagnated, and Venezuela, Argentina, Brazil, and Ecuador have also experienced varying degrees of decline (see Chart 2-7). In this case, the newly added wealth in South America is limited (even shrinking), and the distribution of wealth falls into the division of the original basic wealth, while the vulnerable groups cannot be fully protected during this period, and the regional wealth and income distribution trap into a vicious circle.

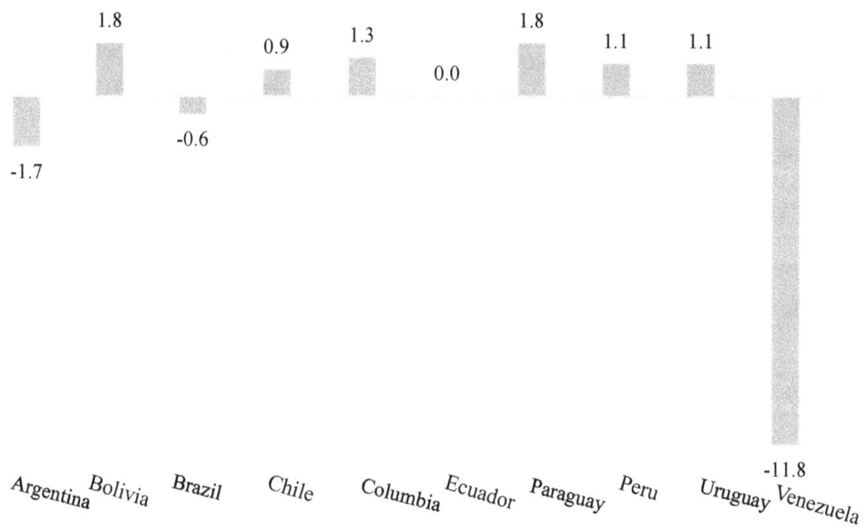

Chart 2-7 Per Capita GDP Growth Rate of Major South American Countries (2010-2020, %)

Source: CEPALSTAT.

Secondly, the coverage of social security needs to be improved. First of all, the increase in the working population and middle class in South America requires the provision of new employment and "decent employment" opportunities, while the current employment situation in Latin America is inconsistent with this demand and difficult to meet the changing social needs. In particular, most young people in South America (aged 15 to 24) are engaged in informal employment, and the open unemployment rate is much higher than the overall social unemployment rate. For example, in 2020, the unemployment rate of young people in Argentina, Brazil, Uruguay and other countries (over 30 percent) was more than three times the social unemployment rate, which was over twice in Bolivia, Chile, Peru and other countries, and young labors were not in employment, education, or training. In the second place, the increase in the elderly population requires an amplification in social security such as pensions, while various existing pension plans in Latin America face challenges. Thirdly, the emerging middle class has a clear understanding of the driving role of education in ensuring upward mobility, which is also a driving force for the significant improvement in education indicators such as enrollment in South America in the past decade. However, the quality of education in South America still needs to be improved. The latest edition of the OECD's (2018 edition) Programme for International Student Assessment (PISA) shows that Latin American students, including those from South America, have lower abilities in reading, science, and mathematics than the global average.

Thirdly, the social mobility stagnates. After 2002, with the significant increase in the per capita household income, the increasing proportion of the middle class population and income has not only significantly reduced poverty, but also reduced the size of the low-income class in general. This indicates that the gradual increase in per capita household income has promoted the process of economic mobility, allowing low-income groups to step in the next income class. However, affected by the stagnation of economic growth, especially the severe impact since the COVID-19, this upward flow has stopped in the past two years.[①] According to the Economic Commission for Latin America, from 2019 to 2020, the size of middle and upper-income group shrunk by 1 percentage point, and the size of the middle income group and lower-middle income group decreased by 3.5 percentage point, while the low-income group increased by 4.7 percentage point. At the same time, such decline has had an impact on structural imbalance, and vulnerable groups such as women and low-skilled labors have been severely impacted.

Fourthly, there are structural defects in the social distribution system. In the primary distribution system, the issue of income inequality is more prominent, and there is a certain mismatch between the tax structure dominated by consumption tax and value-added tax and the tax governance capabilities of South American countries. In reality, frequent tax avoidance and evasion incidents have led to limited government revenue capacity and inability to play a sufficient role in subsequent social distribution. In the social redistribution system, the proportion of income tax, property tax, and social security tax is relatively low, and the "correction" of the wealth gap is insufficient. The distribution system is constrained by the limited toolbox and prominent external fragility, making it difficult to further correct wealth inequality. At the same time, there are still shortcomings in the establishment of the distribution system in South American countries, such as inadequate national aid or unemployment insurance plans for two-thirds of Latin American countries. Among them, Argentina, Brazil, Chile, Colombia, Ecuador, Uruguay and Venezuela in South America implement public unemployment insurance plans, but

---

① https://repositorio.cepal.org/bitstream/handle/11362/46688/8/ S2100149_ en.pdf.

Paraguay and Suriname do not establish any unemployment protection mechanisms, while Bolivia and Peru only provide severance package to the unemployed. This has led to a lack of sufficient social safety nets as the "sound foundation" in South American countries during the crisis, resulting in the overall employment structure being affected by the crisis and the impossibility of vulnerable groups to receive sufficient protection.

Germany*

1. Basic Information

Germany is a large economy with relatively balanced development in Western countries, and its degree of social inequality is the lowest among major Western countries. In the field of social insurance, Germany is a pioneer, and Bismarck's social insurance model has significant influence worldwide. In many fields such as manufacturing, vocational and technical training, compulsory education system, and modern bureaucracy, Germany has a lasting and profound influence on countries around the world. Germany has become a role model of many countries to follow in many areas, such as industrial technology, social security, dual vocational training, etc. Meanwhile, Germany's social market economy model and social partnership also enjoy a high reputation, which has a significant impact on the economic system of the European Union, and also has a unique influence on international institutions, including the International Labour Organization. The research on the degree of common prosperity and the governance of common prosperity in Germany will provide an important reference for China's current cause of common prosperity.

---

* Author: LIU Tao, School of Public Affairs, Zhejiang University.

According to the World Bank, the per capita GDP of Germany has increased from USD 41,531 per year in 2010 to USD 45,723 per year in 2020①, and the per capita GNI in Germany has improved from USD 44,550 per year in 2010 to USD 46,980 per year in 2020②. This indicates Germany's per capita national product and per capita national income rank in the middle and upper reaches of developed countries. The current average life expectancy in Germany is 78.6 years old for males and 83.4

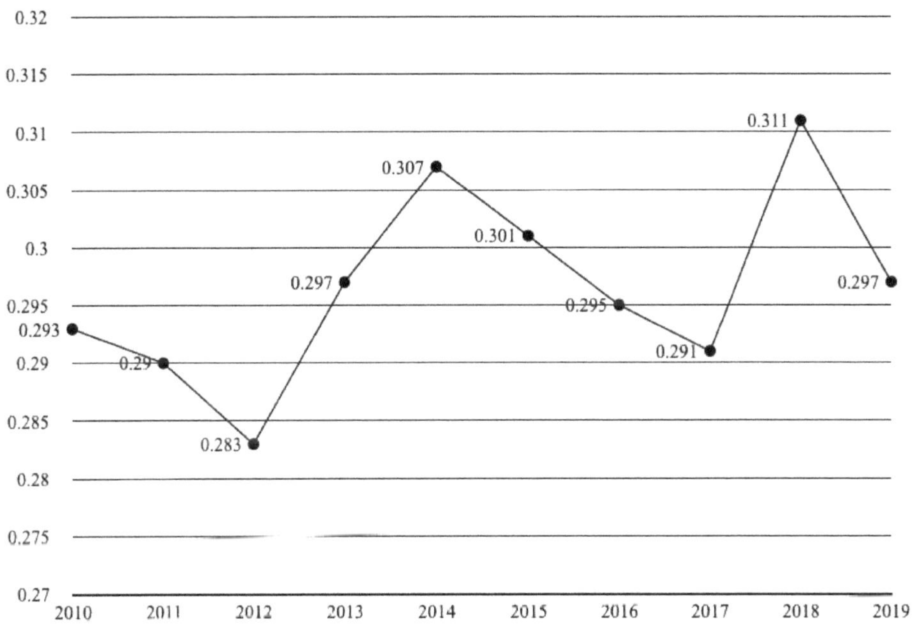

Chart 3-1 Development Trend of Gini Coefficient of Net Income in Germany (2010-2019)

Source: data from German Federal Statistical Office, refer to https://www.destatis.de/DE/Themen/Gesellschaft-Umwelt/Einkommen-Konsum-Lebensbedingungen/Lebensbedingungen-Armutsgefaehrdung/Tabellen/eink-ommensverteilung-silc.html#fussnote-2-114660.

---

① Refer to data from the World Bank on the per capita GDP of Germany, https://data.worldbank.org/indicator/NY.GDP.PCAP.CD? locations=DE.

② Refer to data from the World Bank on the per capita GNP of Germany, https://data.worldbank.org/indicator/NY.GNP.PCAP.CD? locations=DE.

years old for females①. The number of doctors per 1,000 inhabitants in Germany in 2018 was 4.25, which was 3.71 in 2010②. Furthermore, the number of hospital beds per 1,000 inhabitants in Germany decreased from 8.25 in 2010 to 8.0 in 2017.③ From the perspective of the Gini Coefficient, the main index reflecting the degree of domestic income inequality, the Gini Coefficient of Germany's net income has basically remained at a lower level in the past decade. Although in some years it has exceeded 0.3, most of the time, Germany's Gini Coefficient is lower than 0.3. In 2010, the Gini Coefficient of net income in Germany was 0.293, and in 2019, it was 0.297. Despite a slight increase, Germany has always maintained the lowest Gini Coefficient among the large developed economies, suggesting Germany is the country with the most equal income distribution among the western countries.

2.Primary Distribution

In 2020, the employment rate of the population aged from 20 to 64 in Germany was 80.1 percent, with male employment rate of 83.2 percent and female employment rate of 76.9 percent. As Germany resolutely carried out the labor market reform under the governance of Schröder's "Red-Green" Coalition (1998-2005), implemented a series of controversial reforms from "Hartz-Konzept I" to "Hartz-Konzept IV", and promoted to the active social

① Refer to the data from Statista on average life expectancy by gender and age group in Germany, https://de.statista.com/statistik/daten/studie/1783/umfrage/durchschnittliche-weitere-lebenserwartung-nach-altersgruppen/.

② Refer to the data from Statista, https://www.statista.com/statistics/236511/practicing-doctors-per-thousand-inhabitants-in-germany-since-1991/.

③ Refer to the data from the World Bank on the number of hospital beds per 1,000 inhabitants in Germany, https://data.worldbank. org/indicator/SH.MED.BEDS.ZS? locations=DE.

investment policy and favorable welfare state policy[①], the unemployment rate declined and the employment rate increased continuously. The total employment rate in Germany increased from 69.4 percent in 2005 to 80.1 percent in 2020 (see Chart 3-2) and the female employment rate during the same period improved from 63.1 percent to 76.9 percent, while the unemployment rate declined steadily from 11.7 percent in 2005 to 5 percent in 2019, which slightly rebounded to 5.9 percent in 2020 impacted by COVID-19 (see Chart 3-3). The Sustained work welfare tendencies are conducive to the prosperity of the job market and the growth of total national wealth.

Taxation in Germany can be mainly divided into three categories, taxation on corporate profits, consumption and assets. Corporate income tax is also known as corporate tax, the taxpayer of which is a corporation operating as a limited liability company with the tax base as the 15 percent of the corporation profits. A unified corporate income tax rate is implemented throughout Germany, with half of the corporate income tax revenue received by both the federal and state governments. Germany implements the progressive tax on individual income. According to different incomes,

---

① The highly controversial Hartz-Konzcpt IV within Germany has changed the previous loose design of unemployment insurance and social assistance system. It has tightened the payment conditions for employment groups and implemented active employment promotion and training measures. In particular, it has merged unemployment assistance and social assistance for the employment age group into "Unemployment Compensation No.2". It has sent a signal to the labor market of work welfare and active employment through radical measures such as reducing payment of benefit, shortening the duration for payment of benefit, conditional oayment of benefit and the combination of rewards and punishments. Although this reform is still a highly controversial topic in Germany today, there is no denying that Hartz-Konzept IV has significantly enhanced the work welfare and positive employment tendency in German society. Refer to Liu Tao's Reform of German Labor Market: The V-shaped Transition of Social Policy and the Neutralization of the Political Spectrum, *Chinese Journal of European Studies*, 2015(1).

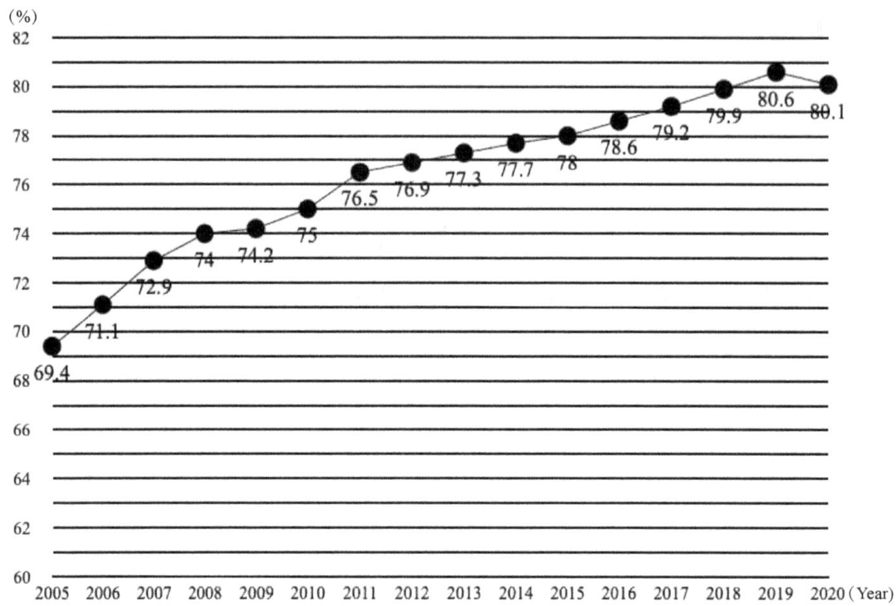

Chart 3-2 Changes in Employment Rate of People Aged From 20 to 64 in Germany From 2005 to 2020

Source: data from Statista, refer to https://www.statista.com/statistics/227005/unemployment-rate-in-germany/.

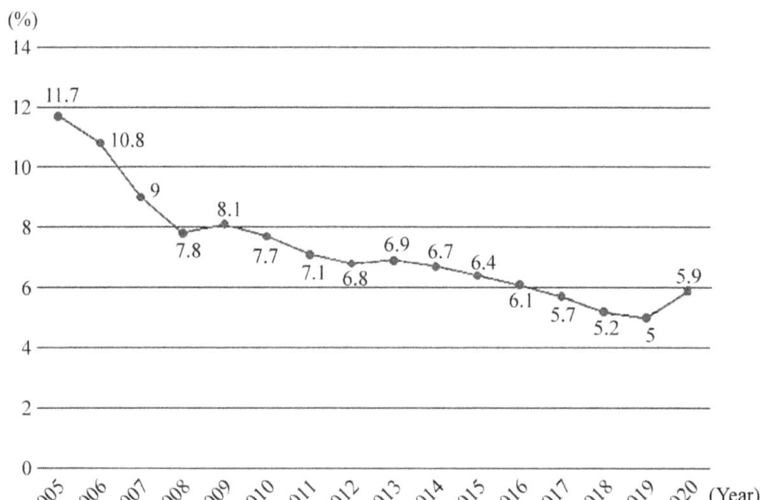

Chart 3-3 Changes in Unemployment Rate in Germany from 2005 to 2020

Source: The author creates the chart based on data from Statista, refer to: https://de.statista.com/statistik/daten/studie/198921/umfrage/erwerbstaetigenquote-in-deutschland-und-eu-nach-geschlecht/.

the individual income tax gradually varies from the lowest 14 percent to the highest 45 percent. In 2020, the individual tax exemption in Germany was EUR 9,08. In Germany, companies and individuals also need to pay an additional 5.5 percent solidarity tax, which is mainly invested in the eastern states to narrow the gap between the East and West regions of Germany.

Between 2010 and 2019, the ratio of the average income of the 20 percent richest to the 20 percent poorest in Germany slightly increased from 4.5 times to 4.9 times. The fluctuation is relatively slight on the whole, and the income difference between these two groups is mostly below 5 times in most years (see Chart 3-4). In the past decade, the average gap between 20 percent of the highest income group and 20 percent of the highest income group in Germany was 4.67 times.

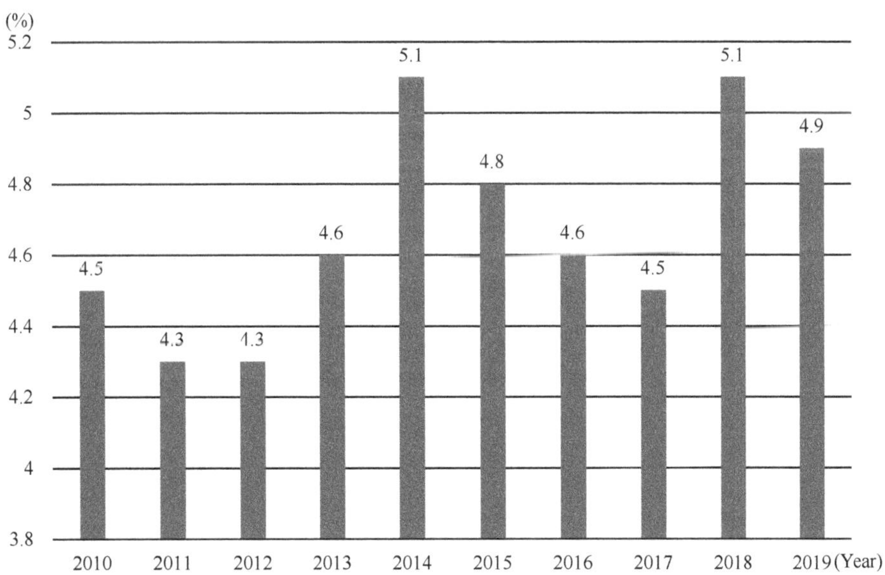

Chart 3-4 Changes in the Ratio of the Average Income of the 20 Percent Richest to the 20 Percent Poorest in Germany(2010-2019)

Source: data from German Federal Statistical Office in terms of income distribution in Germany, https://www.destatis.de/DE/Themen/Gesellschaft-Umwelt/Einkommen-Konsum-Lebensbedingungen/Lebensbedingungen-Armutsgefaehrdung/Tabellen/einkommensverteilung-silc.html#fussnote-2-114660.

According to the German Institute for Economic Research, the proportion of the middle-income group in Germany (income from 70 percent to 150 percent of the median) dropped from 64.5 percent in 1985 to 56.0 percent in 2016, indicating the shrinking of middle-income group in Germany. During the same period, the proportion of the high-income group (income over 150 percent of the median) increased from 15.3 percent to 19.7 percent and the proportion of the low-income group (income is below 80 percent of the median) rose from 20.2 percent to 24.4 percent. This suggests Germany features the M-Form Society commonly shared by Western countries, i.e., the proportion of extreme rich and the extreme poor increases but the proportion of middle class decreases. Overall, the middle class remains the mainstream of German society, and the olive-shaped social structure in Germany remains solid.

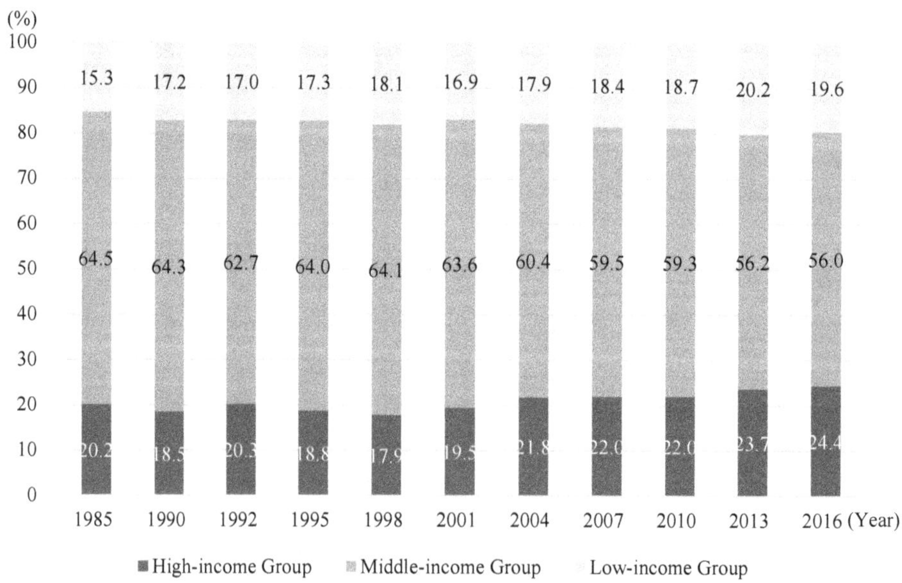

Chart 3-5 Changes in the Middle-income Group in Germany From 1985 to 2016 (%)

Source: The author creates the chart based on data from the German DIW; SOEPv34, German DIW.

From the perspective of disposable income, the proportion of disposable income to national income slightly increased from 66.8 percent in 2010 to 69 percent in 2018, showing a higher wage ratio became a significant component of Germany's national wealth in the primary distribution due to the unique collective bargaining mechanism. Industry unions and employers' associations in Germany determine the unified wage level and a package of collective agreements for the industry through collective bargaining and establish a high degree of social autonomy and self-management principle. The government only provides directional guidance and basic data on the labor market, and does not directly intervene in collective bargaining. This type of labor-capital relationship is named "social partnership".

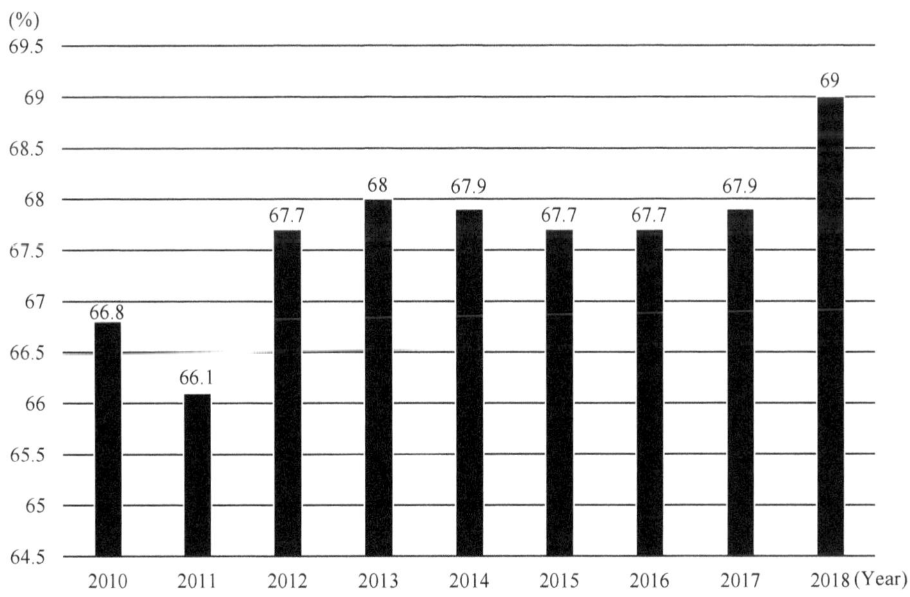

Chart 3-6 The Proportion of Labor Income to National Income in Germany From 2010 to 2018

Source: The author creates the chart based on data from Statista, refer to: https://de.statista.com/statistik/daten/studie/161378/umfrage/anteil-des-arbeitnehmerentgelts-in-deutschland/.

3. Social Redistribution

The core of the German "Sozialstaatlichkeit" system is the social insurance system. Four of the five major insurance systems in the world originated from Germany, namely pension insurance, medical insurance, industrial accident insurance and long-term care insurance, while the unemployment insurance system was initiated by France. As of 2018, a total of 56.09 million residents in Germany participated in statutory pension insurance[①], accounting for approximately 83 percent of the aged above 20. In 2020, Germany's statutory medical insurance (including statutory care insurance) covered a total of 73.36 million German residents[②], occupying about 88 percent of the total population. Including residents from high-income groups who choose to participate in private medical insurance (including private long-term care insurance), the medical insurance system in Germany (including long-term care insurance) is close to covering all residents. According to "German Social Accident Insurance" (DGUV), the highest agency of German industrial accident insurance, a total of 64.2 million people in Germany participated in industrial accident insurance in 2020 (including prevention of accident risks in kindergartens, schools and universities)[③], greatly exceeding the total number of employment in Germany (44.72

① Refer to the data from Statista on the number of participants in pension insurance, https://de.statista.com/statistik/daten/studie/6948/umfrage/anzahl-der-rentenversicherten-in-deutschland-seit-1965/.

② Refer to the data from Statista on the number of participants in medical insurance, https://de.statista.com/statistik/daten/studie/155823/umfrage/gkv-pkv-mitglieder-und-versichertenzahl-im-vergleich/.

③ Refer to the data from Germany on statutory accident insurance, https://www.dguv.de/de/zahlen-fakten/versicherte-unternehmen/index.jsp.

million). It is obvious that industrial accident insurance in Germany has surpassed the scope of traditional "industrial injury", and due to the strict social laws, unemployment insurance in Germany has covered almost all formal employment groups. The groups that do not participate in social insurance include flexible employees and immigration workers as well as employees in such fields as gig economy and platform economy.

The substitution rate for the standard pension in Germany is 67 percent. Assuming German employees work continuously for 45 years, they will meet the requirements of the standard pension career and receive the most generous pension, which is 67 percent of their income. However, facing the transformation of the post industrial society, it is relatively rare for people to meet a standard working term of 45 years. With the improvement of education level, the extension of education time, and the delay of people entering the job market, the total working time and years of the employment group continue to decrease. This change in the working life cycle is also reflected in the actual substitution rate of pension. According to statistics, the actual pension substitution rate in Germany in 2017 was only 48.2 percent, while it is estimated to decline to 44.5 percent[①]. To address the elderly pension problem and the elderly poverty problem, Germany complies with the global trend and encourages the construction of a multi-pillar pension insurance system, including the first pillar of statutory pension insurance, the second pillar of corporate pension insurance, and the third pillar of market pension insurance. The major reform is the Riester Pension Scheme (Riester Rente) established in Germany in 2001. Riester Pension is a market endowment insurance system encouraged and funded by the state, contributed by individuals

① Refer to the data from Federal Agency for Civic Education on pension payment level: https://www.bpb.de/politik/innenpolitik/rentenpolitik/290755/das-rentenniveau.

and accumulated by funds. It is assumed that the insured participate in Riester Pension with 4 percent of pre-tax income every year, who will receive a basic subsidy of EUR 175 per year from the German government and receive an additional subsidy of EUR 300 per year for each child. A maximum of EUR 2,100 can be offset against tax. As of the first quarter of 2021, a total of 16.314 million German residents signed Riester contracts and participated in Rieste. ① According to the data in 2019 from Statista, the promotion rate of corporate pension insurance in Germany is 53.9 percent, with a total of 18.2 million people participating in corporate pension insurance, while a total of 21 million people enjoy occupational pension benefits.② Starting from 2012, Germany has been gradually advancing the retirement age to 67 years old in 2029 through incremental reforms. Currently, there is a discussion in Germany about extending the retirement age to 69 years old.③

During the governance of Schröder's "Red-Green" Coalition (1998-2005), Germany conducted a significant institutional transformation and reform of the social assistance system. The single social assistance system in the Federal Germany was gradually split and transformed into several systems targeting different groups. The new system was renamed the Basic Living Security System (Grundsicherung), which can be divided into three categories. The first category is the basic living security for the elderly and disabled and the second category

---

① Refer to the data from Statista on the the number of participants in Reister Pension: https://de.statista.com/statistik/daten/studie/39412/umfrage/anzahl-der-abgeschlossenen-riester-vertraege/.

② Refer to: https://de.statista.com/statistik/daten/studie/628992/umfrage/verbreitungsquote-der-betrieblichen-altersversorgung-in-deutschland/.

③ Refer to the Frankfurt's report on the German Federal Bank's proposal to extend the retirement age to 69 years old: https://www.fr.de/wirtschaft/rente-bundesbank-fordert-anhebung-renteneintrittsalters-zr-13142429.html.

is basic living assistance, including assistance for some disables, children and social assistance during hospitalization treatment. The third category is basic living security for job seekers, including Unemployment Insurance No.2 and two social securities. The social assistance and relevant treatment of these three categories are the same but the payment conditions are different. For the elderly, disabled, and children, the application and review process is relatively simple. As mentioned above, for job seekers in the age group of employment, the rights and interests of social assistance are thoroughly linked to work benefits, so they need to undergo strict review by the national social assistance department. At the same time, they must regularly participate in job training and receive reasonable job positions provided by local employment centers. Those who violate job seeking regulations and requirements will be punished, and even their payments of benefits will be temporarily or permanently frozen. In summary, for the third category, Germany strictly adheres to the concept of a social investment country, using policy adjustments to encourage people to return to the labor market, and to some extent, it also creates a "shame effect" on the group at the employment age but receives social assistance. According to the federal government, the basic living security benefits for the one-person family in Germany in 2021 were EUR 446 per month and ERO 401 for couples per person per month. Other benefits include social assistance benefits for children (see Table 3-1). The above benefits are only essential ones. In addition to basic benefits, social assistance also includes subsidies for water, electricity, heating, and renting.

In terms of elderly security, Germany is the first country in the world to establish long-term care insurance, which has stimulated the stock and increment of social care demand, and has also become an important

Table 3-1 Basic Living Security (Social Assistance) Benefits in Germany in 2021 (Monthly)

Payment Objects	Benefits (EUR)	Grade
Single or Single-parent Group	446	Standard Treatment Grade 1
Per Person of the Couple	401	Standard Treatment Grade 2
Adults in Educational Institutions	357	Standard Treatment Grade 3
Unemployed Adults Below 25 Living with Parents	357	Standard Treatment Grade 4
Teenagers Aged from 14 to 17	373	Standard Treatment Grade 5
Children Aged from 6 to 13	309	Standard Treatment Grade 6
Children Aged from 0 to 5	283	Standard Treatment Grade 7

Source: translated and summarized by the author based on data from the Website of the German Federal Government, refer to: https://www.bundesregierung.de/breg-de/suche/regelsaetze-steigen-1 775798.

institutional driving force for the development of nursing homes and institutions. According to statistics, as of 2019, a total of 3.9997 million German residents have gained care benefits from long-term care insurance, 85,820,000 of which have received care in elderly care and nursing institutions, while 3.1414 million German residents have received care at home and obtained care benefits from statutory care insurance[①]. The German long-term care insurance system adheres to the principle of "family-care priority", strengthens the function of home care while establishing a statutory care insurance system, and provides cash subsidies to family members for home care. Despite encouraging family care as a priority, being stimulated by the system of nursing needs, there has been

① Refer to the statistics on "facts and data" of long-term care insurance in Germany, https://www.bundesgesundheitsministerium.de/fileadmin/Dateien/3_Downloads/Statistiken/Pflegeversicherung/Zahlen_und_Fakten/Zahlen_und_Fakten_der_SPV_Februar-202_bf.pdf.

a significant growth trend in nursing homes and nursing institutions in Germany. According to relevant statistics, there were a total of 11,712 nursing homes and nursing institutions in Germany in 2020, of which 43.6 percent were commercial nursing homes, 52.9 percent were nursing homes operated by public welfare organizations, while 3.5 percent are community nursing homes. From the perspective of agency attributes, nursing homes operated by commercial and public welfare organizations dominate the welfare market, while public nursing institutions account for an absolute minority.[①]

In the fields of maternal and child security, family and female social protection and welfare, Germany has a combination of policies at different levels, with some special cares that are beneficial to women and children across different social policy areas:

(1) The German statutory pension insurance system gives women who have children the right to pension insurance qualification. German women can obtain the right to pay for three years of pension insurance based on the local social average wage for every child they have, and the Riester Pension Scheme mentioned above also directly gives family members who have children a subsidy of EUR 300 per child;

(2) Germany's statutory medical insurance includes a generous "Familienversicherung" system, where children participate in the statutory medical insurance free of charge with the main insured members of the family. Couples with low or no income can also participate in the "Familienversicherung" free of charge with the main employer. This system greatly guarantees the medical rights and interests of children and women, and improves the overall health level of the German residents;

---

① Refer to the statistics on German insurance market, https://www.pflegemarkt.com/2016/10/28/anzahl-und-statistik-der -altenheime-in-deutschland/.

(3) According to the long-term care insurance system in Germany, insured individuals who have not given birth to offspring are required to pay an additional 0.25 percent of long-term care insurance premiums, implementing implicit redistribution policies in childless families and families with children;

(4) Germany implements an inclusive children benefits system. Any German residents and children of eligible foreign immigrants can receive children benefits. The current child benefits in Germany are as follows: resident with one child receives EUR 219 per month, EUR 219 per month for two children, EUR 225 per month for three children and EUR 250 for four children or above[①];

(5) In addition to the traditional maternity leave system, Germany has also promoted a "parental (upbringing) benefits" system since 2007, which stipulates that either parent can apply for this cash benefits after the birth of the baby, and both parents can apply for this benefits to fulfill their childcare responsibilities at home, which is 65 percent to 67 percent of their wage income, and the maximum payment period is 14 months. If the applicant is unemployed previously or is a housewife, she can directly receive a monthly subsidy of EUR 300;

(6) Other service facilities and measures related to child care and education are included in Social Law Act VIII (SGB VIII).[②]

According to the OECD, the proportion of public social expenditure to GDP in Germany in 2019 was 25.9 percent, significantly higher than the average level of 20 percent in OEC D countries, surpassing major Anglo American countries such as the United States (18.7 percent) and the

---

① Refer to statistics on the social benefits of families and children, https://www.arbeitsagentur.de/familie-und-kinder/kindergeld-anspruch-hoehe-dauer.

② Refer to SGB VIII, https://www.sozialgesetzbuch-sgb.de/sgbviii/1.html.

United Kingdom (20.6 percent), Canada (18 percent), and Australia (16.7 percent) as well as Sweden (25.5 percent) and Norway (25.3 percent), but lower than France (31 percent), Italy (28.2 percent), and some Nordic countries such as Finland (29.1 percent) and Denmark (28.3 percent) (see Chart 3-7).

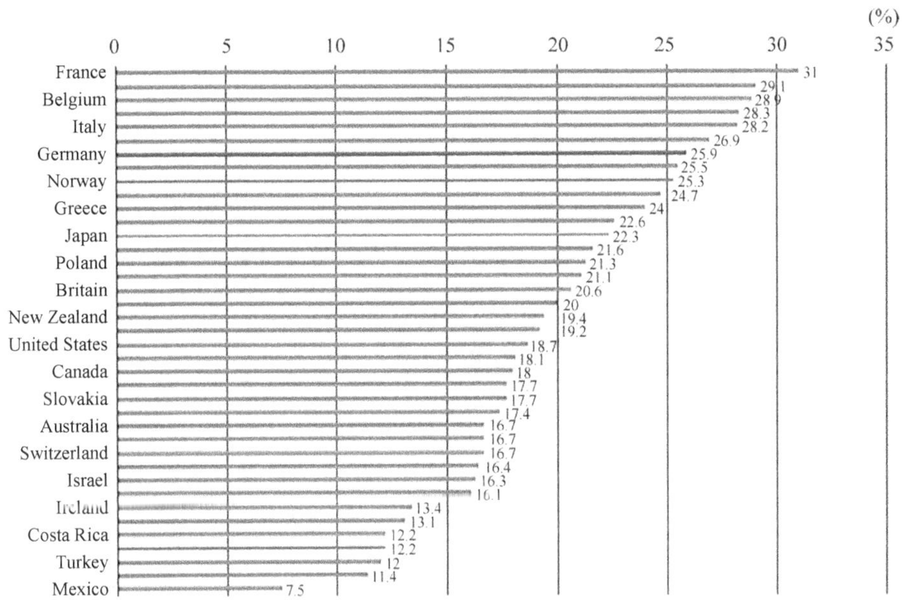

Chart 3-7 The Proportion of Public Social Expenditure to GDP in OECE Countries in 2019 (%)

Source: translated and summarized by the author based on data from OECD.

Data from: OCED Statistical Data on Public Social Expenditure, https://www.oecd.org/berlin/presse/aktuelle-zahlen-zu-oeffentlichen-sozialausgaben-23012019.htm

4. The Third Distribution and Others

According to Statista, German citizens donated a total of EUR 5.139 billion in 2019, of which 75.3 percent was invested in humanitarian aid, 5.9 percent was invested in animal protection, 3.5 percent was invested in the field of environment and natural conservation, 3.0

percent was invested in sports, 2.5 percent was invested in cultural and monument maintenance, and 9.9 percent was invested in other fields.① According to statistics on 2020 German social volunteer service, a total of 17.1 million German citizens participated in social volunteer services, accounting for 21.2 percent of the total population of Germany. Among them, 27 percent of the employed population provide additional social volunteer services in addition to their own jobs.② The young population has become an important supplementary source of nursing social workers in charitable, public welfare, and social institutions. An investigation on German civil society organizations and associations in 2017 indicated there were over 600,000 public welfare institutions in Germany, 95 percent of which exist in the form of associations, foundations, cooperative associations, and other organizations.③ Public welfare organizations can be exempt from corporate income tax as long as they serve the purposes related to their charters (i.e., engage in non-profit public welfare undertakings). However, tax exemption does not apply to economic corporations, such as public welfare sports clubs that operate restaurants in the clubhouse and profit from it, which must pay taxes for their catering industry. Non-profit corporations are required to pay value-added tax at a preferential tax rate of 7 percent.

From the perspective of urban-rural and regional inequality, Germany

---

① Based on data provided by the German Endowment Commission, https://de.statista.com/infografik/8596/spendenvolumen-und-spendenzwecke-in-deutsch-land/.

② Refer to data from Statista on German social volunteer services, https://de.statista.com/themen/71/ehrenamt/.

③ Refer to the introduction to the Bertelsmann Stiftung on the development of public welfare institutions in Germany, https://www.bertelsmann-stiftung.de/de/unsere-projekte/zivilgesellschaft-in-zahlen/projektnachrichten/ziviz-survey-2017/.

has also taken a series of actions to eliminate regional and urban-rural inequality. Since the 1960s, Germany has also taken a package of measures in the field of public policy to revitalize rural areas and small and medium-sized cities. In addition to implementing a strategy of spatial equalization and urban-rural equalization, Germany also introduced laws specifically targeting spatial equality and equalization development. In 1997, the German Parliament passed the *Spatial Planning Law (Raumornungsgesetz)* to regulate the equalization of development between regions, large, small, and medium-sized cities, as well as between urban and rural areas, with the main purpose to promote balanced migration flows and spatial population distribution through public policies. It aimed to promote reasonable migration flows through balanced economic, social, and ecological policies to prevent excessive migration and urban expansion towards a certain destination. Germany is the only major industrialized country without megacities, which is also related to Germany's promotion of urban population diversion through universal public services and the "decentralized perspective" under Germany's Federalism culture.

5. The Eastern Construction after Unification of Germany

After the unification of Germany in 1990, the German Federal Government faced a knotty problem. Although the former Democratic Germany was one of the most developed countries in the Soviet Union and Eastern Europe with the highest living standards, there was still a wide gap in productivity and living standards between East Germany and West Germany. At that time, the per capita national product of East Germany was only one third of that of West Germany, and the productivity of East Germany was only more than 40 percent of that of West Germany. Furthermore, the external debt of the East German government is as high as nearly USD 10 billion, and the gap between East and West Germany is comprehensive. At the same time, due to the massive gap between East and West Germany in the fields of economic system, social system, and social security system, the unified Germany faces a heavy task to fill the "West-East Divide" in Germany and unify the system.

In the 1990s, the Federal Government implemented the overall planning and design of the transformation for the economic system and reform of East Germany. At the same time, the German government also invested significantly in backward infrastructure such as railways, highways, bridges, urban infrastructure, communication equipment and facilities in East Germany in the 1990s. By 2000, The popularizing rate of telephone and digital communication level in the former East Germany region have already reached and caught up with the former West Germany region. Germany has taken a very rare tax measure for the unification of Germany, that is, the German employees mentioned above need to pay a "solidarity tax" for the unification of Germany. This tax has been formally collected since 1995, and it has accounted for 5.5 percent of individual income and corporate income since 1998, which is fully owned by the federal government and used for long-term transfer payments for German unification. In 2020 alone, the solidarity tax reached EUR 18.7 billion in Germany[①], while during the entire stage of German unification, the federal government's transfer payments to the East (including those in the

---

① Refer to the data from Statista on the solidarity tax in Germany, https://de.statista.com/statistik/daten/studie/30376/umfrage/steuereinnahmen-des-bundes-durch-den-solidaritaetszuschlag/.

field of social security) amounted to EUR 2 trillion[1].

In the process of continuously promoting the "construction of the east", the infrastructure of the eastern states of Germany has been constantly improved. Hardware facilities of some universities in the eastern region, such as Humboldt University, Leipzig University have ranked in the forefront of Germany, attracting a large number of students from West Germany to reverse flow to East Germany[2]. According to the German DIW, since 2009, German residents who moved from the east to the west have begun to fall back, and the gap between the western and eastern immigration balance has begun to narrow. From 2017 to 2019, the number of residents who moved into East Germany exceeded the number of residents who moved out of East Germany for the first time[3]. Since the unification of Germany, the eastern German federal states have become net surplus areas for immigrants for the first time, indicating that the attractiveness of the eastern federal states is on the rise. According to the data from German Federal Ministry of Finance, German DIW and German Institute for Economic Research in 2020, the proportion of the per capita GDP of eastern German residents to that in West Germany increased from 33 percent in 1991 to 69 percent in 2019, the proportion of the net household income of East Germany to that in West Germany rose from 54 percent in 1991 to 82 percent in 2019. Meanwhile, the proportion

---

① Refer to the data from Federal Agency for Civic Education on different estimates of solidarity tax in Germany, https://www.bpb.de/geschichte/deutsche-einheit/zahlen-und-fakten-zur-deutschen-einheit/212659/die-frage-nach-den-kosten-der-wiedervereinigung.

② Refer to the data and report from German DIW: "30 Years After the Fall of the Berlin Wall: East Germany becomes attractive to students in the West", https://www.destatis.de/DE/Presse/Pressemitteilungen/2019/09/PD1 9 _378_213. html.

③ Refer to the data from Federal Agency for Civic Education on internal immigration in Germany, https://www.bpb.de/nachschlagen/zahlen-und-fakten/soziale-situation-in-deutschland/313837/binnenwanderung.

of employee wages in Eastern Germany to that in Western Germany increased from 49 percent in 1991 to 82 percent in 2019, while the proportion of the actual domestic product (used to measure productivity) of employees improved from 42 percent in 1991 to 2019. The proportion of unit labor costs in East Germany to that in West Germany decreased from 119 percent in 1991 to 102 percent in 2019, while the proportion of assets owned by residents increased from 38 percent in 1991 to 78 percent in 2019 and the proportion of the asset stock of employees climbed from 40 percent in 1991 to 89 percent in 2019 (see Chart 3-8). The above data fully shows that in about 30 years after the unification of Germany, the gap between living standards and economic productivity between the East and the West has been significantly reduced, and there has been a

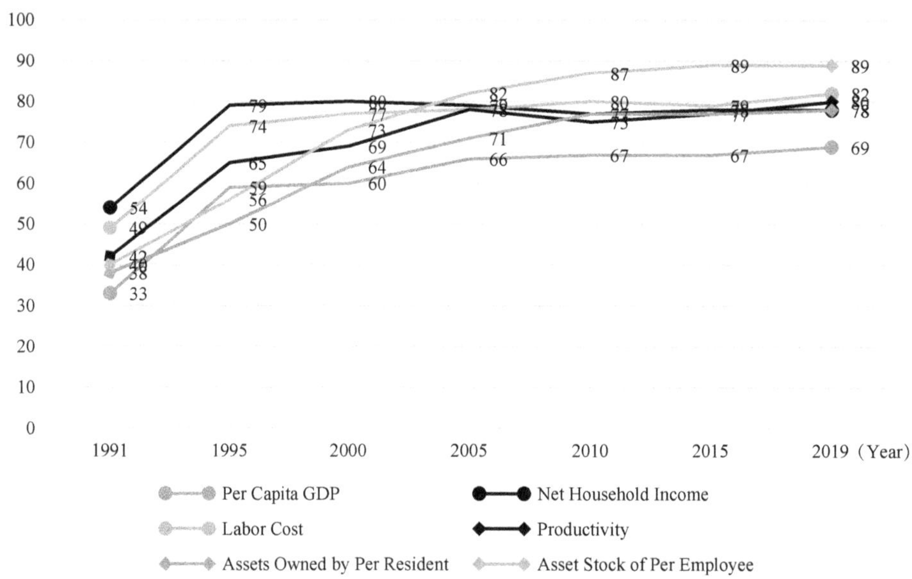

Chart 3-8 The Development Trend of Major Economic Indicators in East Germany Compared to West Germany (100 as the West Germany Standard)

Material Source: The author creates the chart based on data from BMF and DIW.

Data Source: Röhl, K. H. (2020). 30 Jahre Wiedervereinigung: Ein differenziertes Bild. IW-Trends-Vierteljahresschrift zur empirischen Wirtschaftsforschung, 47(3), 93-111.

trend of convergence in the development of the East and West regions of Germany. Although the gap between the East and West still exists to some extent, such a gap has become increasingly smaller. The significant convergence trend of the East-West gap in Germany in recent years has also had a profound and immeasurable impact on the immigration pattern within Germany. After the unification, Germany experienced a balanced domestic population migration for the first time, and the "hollowing-out of East Germany" trend of concern in the early stages of unification did not occur. This is closely related to Germany's great efforts in eastern construction and narrowing the East-West gap.

France*

1. Basic Information

France is a model of Western countries that values equality over efficiency, with a high level of social equality, much higher than the United States and Britain, which pursue economic liberalism. To some extent, its social equality is also higher than that of Germany, which pursues a social market economy. According to the OECD, in 2019, the poverty rate in France was 8.5 percent, lower than Germany (10.4 percent) and the United Kingdom (11.7 percent), which is at a lower level among OECD countries (see Chart 4-1). France has a generous social security system with wide coverage, providing citizens with good protection from the beginning to the end of life. However, France's economic development is relatively slow and lacks vitality among developed Western countries. The state-owned sector in economy is relatively high, and industries related to the national economy and people's livelihood such as transportation, energy, and military sector are mostly state-owned or quasi state-owned (state controlled). Large enterprises, especially state-owned enterprises, are the main driving force of the French economy, while small and medium-sized enterprises lack vitality.

---

* Author: PENG Shuyi, Institute of European Studies, Chinese Academy of Social Sciences.

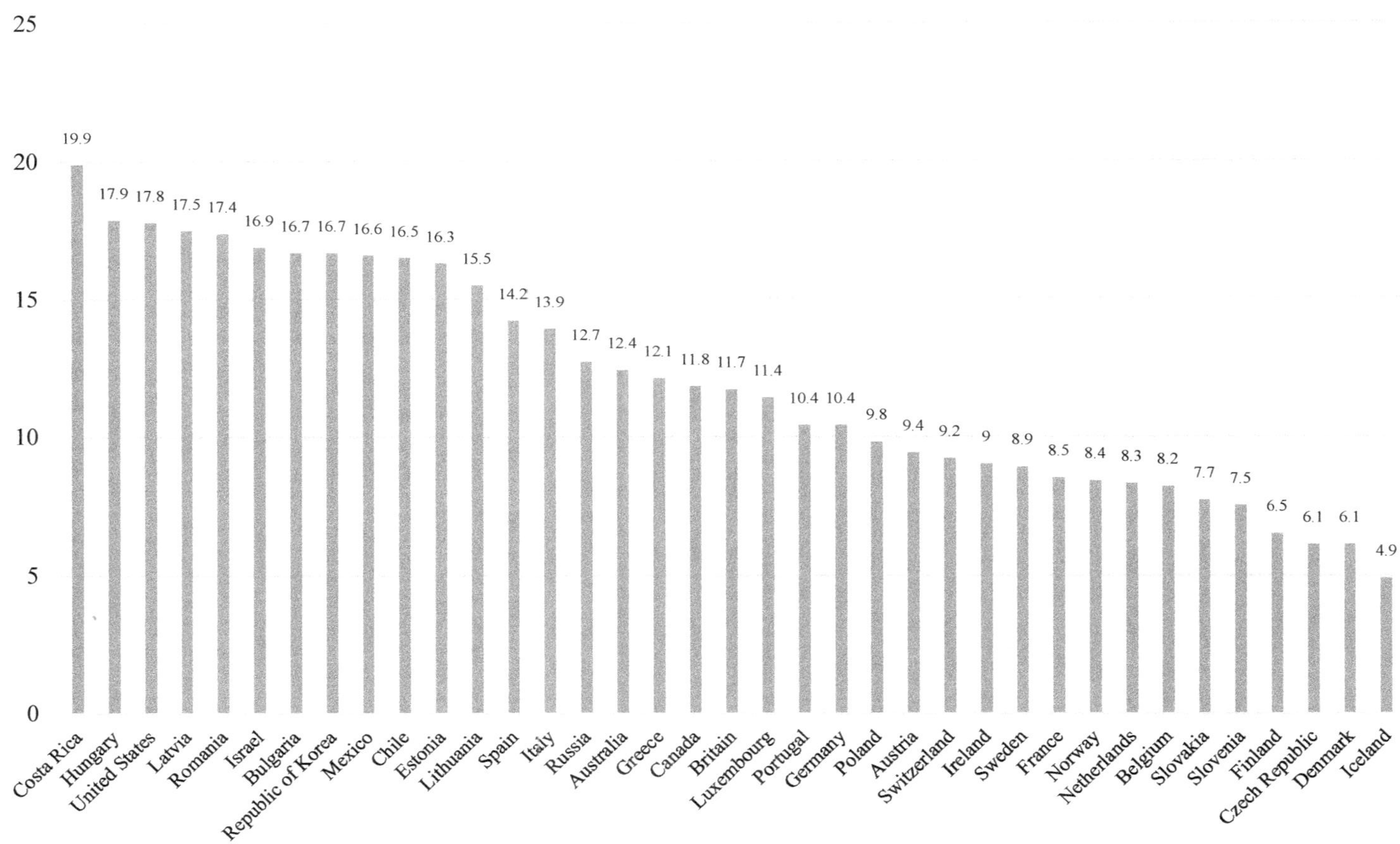

Chart 4-1 Comparison of Poverty Rates in OECD Countries

Source: https://www.statista.com/statistics/233910/poverty-rates-in-oecd-countries/.

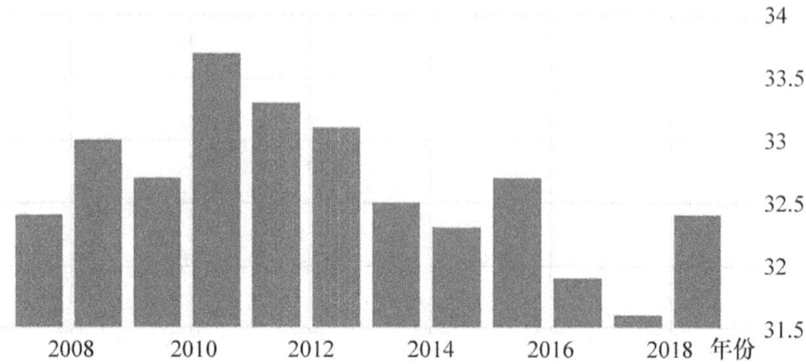

Chart 4-2 Gini Coefficient in France (World Bank)

Source: https://tradingeconomics.com/france/gini-index-wb-data. html.

According to data from the World Bank, the per capita GDP of France increased from USD 21,794 in 1990 to USD 45,334 in 2008, with subsequent declines and fluctuations, reaching USD 38,625 in 2020.[①] The per capita GNI increased from USD 20,640 in 1990 to USD 44,350 in 2011, followed by declines and fluctuations, up to USD 42,290 in 2019.[②] Both indicators are above average among developed countries.

In 2009, the average life expectancy in France was 79.9 years for men and 85.6 years for women[③], with the infant mortality rate at 3.8 percent, which remained basically stable in the past 15 years. In 2020, the number of hospital beds per 1,000 inhabitants in France was 5.8[④], which was the result of France's continuous reduction in hospital beds and encouragement to replace hospitalization with daytime outpatient surgeries to cut down medical insurance expenses in the last decade. For a decade, France's Gini Coefficient (see Chart 4-2) has remained at a low level from 0.31 to 0.34 and its net Gini Coefficient has been even

---

① https://data.worldbank.org/indicator/NY.GDP.PCAP.CD?locations=FR.

② https://data.worldbank.org/indicator/NY.GNP.PCAP.CD?locations=FR.

③ https://www.insee.fr/fr/statistiques/4277640?sommaire=4318291.

④ https://fr.statista.com/infographie/12883/lits-hopitaux-disponibles-par-pays/.

lower, at no more than 0.3. The disposable income of French households accounts for 70 percent of GDP, which is at a high level among major developed countries.

2. Primary Distribution

In 2019, the employment rate of the population aged 15-64 in France was 65.5 percent, lower than the average level of 28 EU countries of 69.3 percent and ranked sixth from the bottom in the EU, only better than Belgium, Spain, Croatia, Italy, and Greece. The employment rate was 68.8 percent for male and 62.4 percent for female (see Chart 4-3) ①. Since 2008, the employment rate in France has not fluctuated much, stabilizing

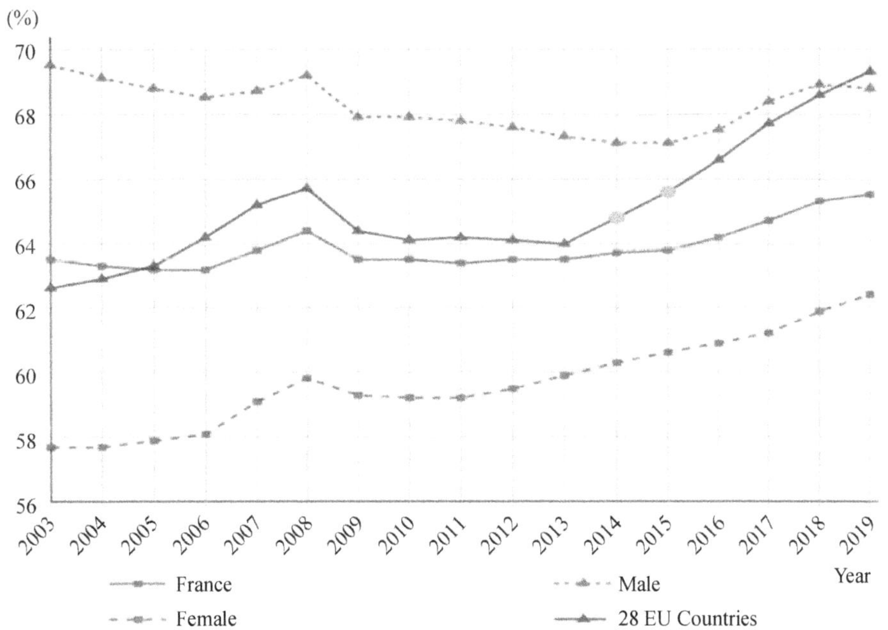

Chart 4-3 Employment Rate in France (compared to the EU)

① https: //www.insee.fr/fr/statistiques/3281596?sommaire=3281778.

at 63 percent-64 percent from 2008 to 2016, with a significant increase after 2016. Nevertheless, France, like other southern European countries, has consistently maintained a low employment rate in the EU. On the contrary, France's unemployment rate is relatively high (see Table 4-1), remaining at a high level of 9 percent-10 percent for a long time. The unemployment rate of the youth is exceptionally high, consistently above 20 percent, many of which become unemployed as soon as they graduate.

Table 4-1 List of Unemployment Rate in France(%)

Year	2008	2010	2012	2014	2015	2016	2017	2018
Unemployment Rate	7.4	9.3	9.8	10.3	10.4	10.1	9 .4	9.1
Female	7.8	9.5	9.7	10.0	9.9	9.9	9.3	9.1
Male	7.1	9.1	9.8	10.5	10.8	10.2	9.5	9.0
15-24 Years Old	19.0	23.3	24.4	24.2	24.7	24.6	22.3	20.8
25-49 Years Old	6.7	8.4	9.1	9.7	9.7	9.3	8.8	8.5
50-60 Years Old	4.4	5.6	6.1	6.9	7.0	6.9	6.6	6.4

Source: https://www.insee.fr/fr/statistiques/3281596?sommaire=3281778.

The main reasons for this situation are as follows. France also has a collective bargaining mechanism for labor and capital, but unlike Germany, both labor and capital can sit down calmly to negotiate and find a compromise solution. On the contrary, inheriting the radical political and cultural traditions since the Great Revolution, embedded with a deep-rooted concept of equality, the France Trade Union is skilled in street struggles, prone to street demonstrations, perseveres in defending labor interests, and ridicules the lack of backbone among Germans, who easily compromise. Based on the above backgrounds, France has better protection for workers, prohibiting arbitrary layoffs (layoffs should have sufficient reasons, be arbitrated by relevant institutions, and high compensation should be paid), and disallowing bankruptcy without authorization. This makes it difficult for employees to be dismissed once hired, and the labor market becomes rigid, causing companies unable to inject new employees. Therefore, companies are not willing to hire new employees without work experience, who can not be easily laid off if they are unsuitable, accounting for the high unemployment rate among young people.

France opposes measures like Germany that increase the flexibility of the labor market and does not encourage flexible employment methods such as "small and micro employment". The French believe that small and micro employment poses a risk of permanently pinning labors in low skilled, low payment, and unprotected informal employment positions. Therefore, France has introduced two measures. On the one hand, in response to the situation of a proliferation of short-term contracts and a serious shortage of long-term contracts, legislation has been introduced to crack down on informal employment. Macron, President of France, has introduced a bill that stipulates that enterprises with more than 11 employees which possess too many short-term contracts, temporary workers, hourly workers, and other unstable employment will be punished by paying an additional 1 percentage point of unemployment insurance contribution. On the contrary, the more long-term contracts a company has, the less it pays (1 percentage point less). This measure is mainly aimed at hotels, catering and other departments where short-term contract workers are concentrated.[1] Under the intense opposition from the trade union, this rule is temporarily not applicable to the construction and healthcare industries with numerous short-term contracts.

For the long run, in order to increase long-term employment rates,

---

① These two industries are currently not applicable to this measure.

France has shifted from social security to social investment, starting with education and training, and strives to provide citizens with high-quality and sustainable lifelong employment. For example, the French Government provides employment training and helps young people get employed who fail to enter university after high school graduation. It bridges between businesses and individuals to help solve employment problems. At the same time, it strengthens the provision of social services for special groups, such as establishing kindergartens with vocational integration functions, and providing care and other services for those seeking employment, especially single mothers, so that they can free up time to find jobs.

The taxes in France are mainly divided into four categories: corporate tax, individual income tax, consumption tax, asset tax, etc.

The main types of corporate taxes (Fiscalité des enterprises) include corporate taxes (L'impôtsur les sociétés, IS) and various social security contributions (see below). The company tax rate is classified into several levels based on the size of the turnover, ranging from 15 percent to 33 percent overall. The higher the turnover, the higher the tax rate.[①] The contribution rate of social insurance (unemployment, pension, work-related injury, medical and family benefits) currently only includes pension insurance, which is jointly paid by employees and employers. The other four items, family benefits, work-related injury insurance, and medical insurance are all paid by employers unilaterally. Medical insurance and unemployment insurance were originally co-paid by employers and employees. Since 2018, France has abolished employee contributions and compensated for the losses by increasing the "generalized social contribution tax" rate used to repay social security deficits. The "Generalized Social Contribution"

---

① https://www.impots.gouv.fr/portail/international-professionnel/ impot-sur-les-societes.

(contribution social généralisée; CSG) is a tax type introduced in the 1990s based on the total income of individuals, specifically designed to compensate for the shortfall in social security expenditures. Overall, the burden on French enterprises is relatively heavy.

The consumption tax is mainly value-added tax (TVA), with a standard tax rate of 20 percent. Some goods and services can be as low as 10 percent, 5.5 percent and 2.1 percent. Individual income tax is a progressive system, with tax rates ranging from 0 percent to 45 percent in 2021, divided into five levels (see Table 4-2).

Table 4-2 Individual Income Tax Rate

Tax Amount	Tax Rate
Below EUR 10,084	0
EUR 10,085-25,710	11 percent
EUR 25,711-73,516	30 percent
EUR 73,517-158,122	41 percent
EUR 158,123	45 percent

After tax, the income of French is relatively average, with a majority in the middle class and a minority in both the poor and the rich, showing as an olive-shaped society. According to statistics from 2018, the median income of France was EUR 21,250 per year, with the lowest 10 percent being below EUR 11,210 per year and the richest 10 percent at EUR 39,130 per year. The income ratio of the top and bottom 10 percent of the population is 3.5.[①] In 2018, 9.3 million people in France lived below the

① http://ses.ens-lyon.fr/actualites/rapports-etudes-et-4-pages/en-2018-les-inegalites-de-niveau-de-vie-augmentent-insee- septembre-2020 (Le rapport interdécile (D9/D1) est le rapport entre le niveau de vie plancher des 10% les plus aisés et le niveau de vie plancher des 10% les moins aisés. Il est de 3, 5 en 2018).

poverty line (EUR 1,063), with a relative poverty rate of 14.8 percent.[①]

3. Social Redistribution

France mainly redistributes society through a sound welfare system, transfers social wealth, helps vulnerable groups, and narrows the income gap.

3.1 The Social Security System from the Beginning to the End of Life

France has a well-established and generous social security system from the beginning to the end of life (see Chart 4-4 for details).

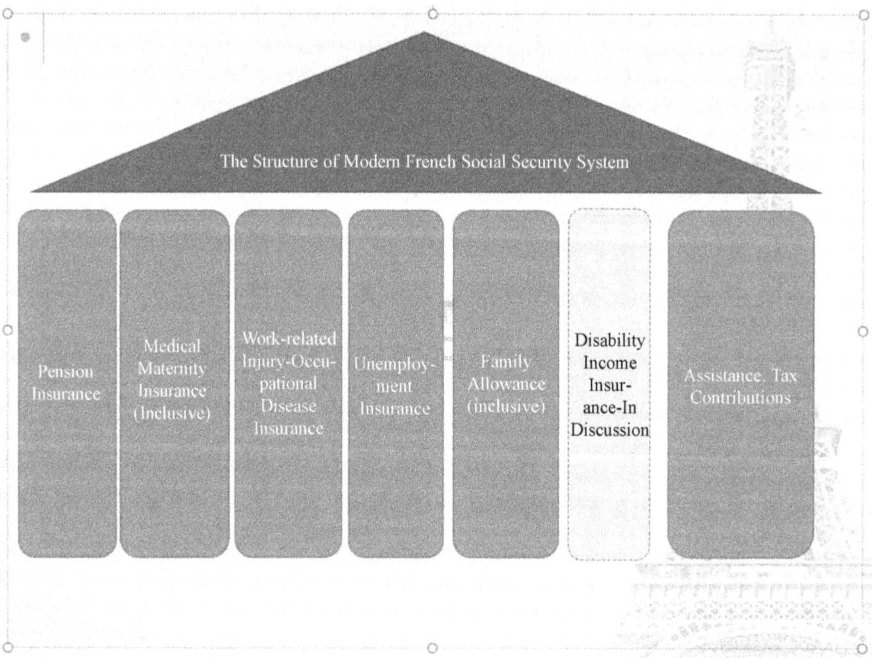

Chart 4-4 French Social Security System

① http://ses.ens-lyon.fr/actualites/rapports-etudes-et-4-pages/en-2018-les-inegalites-de-niveau-de-vie-augmentent-insee-septembre-2020.

The statutory pension insurance system is jointly paid by employers and employees, and the financing method is pay-as-you-go. The insufficient part is supplemented by the national finance, with the main focus on national responsibility and market plays a negligible role, with an average substitution rate of 60-70 percent. In France, more than two-thirds of the elderly's income comes from statutory pension insurance. Medical insurance is inclusive, with funds previously mainly coming from contributions from employers and employees. Currently, a considerable proportion of "Generalized Social Contribution" has been disbursed. Employee contributions were canceled in 2018, covering all citizens and eligible foreigners, with a focus on economically and health vulnerable groups. Major and long-term chronic diseases are fully reimbursed, without the need for patients to bear the burden, and those with incomes below a certain level is fully covered by the country. This system has long been rated by the World Health Organization as one of the best comprehensive healthcare systems in the world, which can effectively prevent people from becoming poor due to illness. In the context of aging, the French medical insurance system is keeping up with the times and plans to include items such as dentures, glasses, and hearing aids that were not previously included in medical insurance. Currently, France is discussing whether to follow Germany's example and establish disability income insurance.

France was the pioneer in establishing family policies, and as early as the early 20th century, a "family policy" with support for mothers and children as the main content emerged to ensure an increase in fertility rates and the regeneration of the workforce. At present, France has a family allowance system that is unilaterally funded by employers, providing a wide range of allowances for children and families, such as basic family allowance (inclusive, for all French families with children), maternity allowance, parenting allowance, care allowance, start of school allowance (for purchasing stationery during the start of school season), disabled children's allowance, etc., almost covering all the needs of a child from birth to adulthood. The system was initially inclusive and the benefits increased infinitely with the increase of the number of children. In recent years, after reforms, most of the benefits have transformed into means test based, only targeting groups below a certain income level, and a ceiling has been set for the amount of benefits, no longer increasing indefinitely with the increase of the number of children. France has corresponding assistance policies for the elderly, disabled, low-income and other socially disadvantaged groups.

France's public expenditure as a proportion of GDP has long been among the top globally. In 2018, France's public social expenditure accounted for 30 percent of GDP, far higher than the OECD average of 21 percent.

3.2 The Effectiveness of Social Redistribution

France divides the income of all residents into 10 levels, with the first three levels belonging to the low-income class, accounting for 30 percent of the total population. The highest proportion of their income comes from social subsidies (i.e. transfer payments), and the first level, which is the lowest income level, receives nearly half of their disposable income from social subsidies. Level 4-7 belong to the so-called middle class, with an average annual disposable income of EUR 21,600-50,950. The income of this group is mainly based on economic activities, namely wages, and the proportion of social subsidies (i.e. social transfers) significantly decreases. On the contrary, taxes account for 10-17 percent of their wages. The 8th and 9th levels belong to the affluent class, with an average annual disposable income of EUR 50,090-63,870. Their income mainly comes from economic activities, and the portion from social transfer is not only small but also mainly from basic family allowances (inclusive). The 10th level is for high-income individuals, with an average annual disposable income of over EUR 63,870. Property income accounts for a large proportion of this group's income (22 percent), much higher than the French average of 5 percent. This group has the heaviest tax burden, up to 30 percent, and at the same time, receives the least transfer payments, close to none. After the transfer payment, the income gap in France is significantly narrowed (see Table 4-3 and Chart 4-5), which clearly indicates the nature of French society, i.e. the redistribution of wealth from rich to poor.

Table 4-3 The Income Situation and Composition of France

Low-income Class	Middle Class	Affluent Class	High-income Class
Level 1-3 Monthly living standards below EUR 1,371 (EUR 16,459 per year)	Level 4-7 Annual average disposable income of EUR 21,600-50,950	Level 8&Level 9 Annual disposable income of EUR 50,090-63,870	Level 10 Annual disposable income above EUR 63,870
30 percent of the total population	50 percent of the total population	10 percent of the total population	10 percent of the total population
Monthly disposable income is less than EUR 1,800 euros, and annual average income is less than EUR 21,600	Monthly disposable income of EUR 2,859, with an average annual income of EUR 34,307	Monthly disposable income of EUR 4,787, with an average annual income of EUR 56,980	

continued

Low-income Class	Middle Class	Affluent Class	High-income Class
Level 1: social subsidies account for 47 percent Level 3: social subsidies account for 13 percent and property income accounts for 3 percent	Economic activity income accounts for 67-80 percent of disposable income, while social subsidies account for 1.8-7.5 percent and direct tax accounts for 10-17 percent of disposable income	Economic activity income accounts for 80 percent of disposable income, social subsidies account for very low proportion, mainly from family allowances(1.2 percent), and direct taxes account for 19 percent of disposable income	Asset income accounts for 22 percent, direct taxes account for 30 percent of disposable income, and social subsidies only account for 0.5 percent

Source: https://www.lafinancepourtous.com/decryptages/finance-perso/revenus/niveau-et- composition-des-revenus-moyens-en-france/.

From Chart 4-5, it can be seen that the social redistribution in France is significantly effective. The left figure shows the living standards of the 10 percent population with the lowest income. In this figure, the solid line segment represents the living standards before redistribution, and the dashed line represents the living standards after redistribution. Taking the 2008 global economic and financial crisis as the watershed, which was a heavy blow to low-income group, after redistribution, the living standards of low-income group was significantly improved, and the gap with the median living standards (in the middle figure) was dramatically narrowed. Meanwhile, the median living standards in the middle figure decreased after redistribution. The figure on the right shows the top 10 percent of the population with the highest income, and their living standards have also decreased after redistribution. This is also the main

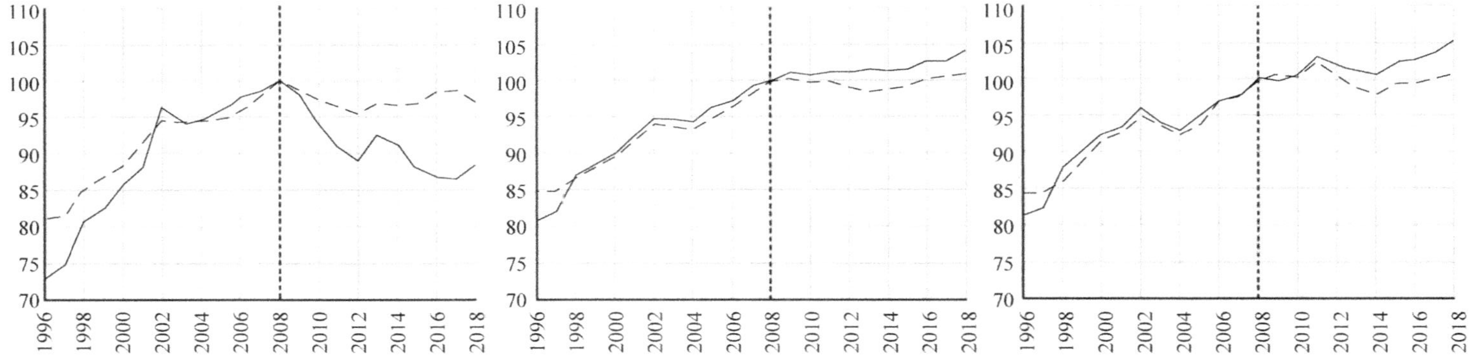

(a)Low-income Group (b)Middle-income Group (c)High-income Group

Chart 4-5 Development and Evolution of Living Standards of Low-income, Middle -income and High-income Groups in France (1996-2018)

Solid line segment: before redistribution; dashed line segment: after redistribution

Note: 100 for Year 2008

reason why the poverty reduction effectiveness of France's social security system is much better than that of countries such as the UK. The poverty rate in France is one of the lowest in both EU and OECD.

4. The Third Distribution and Others

There are serious regional differences in France's economy and development. Overall, Paris stands out alone, concentrating on the human and material resources. In addition to a few major cities, there is a significant gap between the capital cities and other regions in terms of infrastructure construction, culture, and social resources. Fortunately, the degree of nationalization of the French economy is high, and industries such as transportation and energy are mostly operated by the state, ensuring that railways and postal services can be extended to remote areas where capital is unwilling to intervene due to the lack of profitability. In other words, the "Green Train" operated by the French state-owned railway corporation in debt, as well as La Poste and Electricite De France guarantee the provision of essential public services to remote areas. At the same time, the government also transferred some cultural resources to the region to drive local economic development, such as the construction of the branch of Louvre Museum in Reims. Under relevant EU laws and regulations, France will also open up the public service market and introduce foreign investment for operation, such as carrying certain railway lines. At that time, whether some heavily losing branch railways will disappear has attracted attention from French society.

5. Conclusion

France is a model among developed countries that values equality over efficiency, and can be described as a model of redistribution of wealth from rich to poor to realize common prosperity. Its economic and social model is characterized by a high proportion of state-owned economic costs, high taxes, and sound welfare. The concept of equality is deeply rooted in citizen's hearts, and it attaches great importance to narrowing income disparities through social redistribution, earning it the title of "French Socialism". The advantages of such a model are as follows: prominent equality, balanced social development, small income gap among all social classes (although there has been a trend of widening in recent years), no extreme poverty and very few wealthy individuals, low living burden for the public -without difficulties in housing, getting medical service, and education as the impoverished group has social security housing and low-cost housing, medical treatment basically does not cost money, there's free for education and the distribution of educational resources is relatively balanced.

However, its drawbacks are also apparent.

Firstly, the country has a heavy financial burden, which is vividly described as "spraying money recklessly". In this way, the deficits in healthcare and pension insurance are huge, and fiscal sustainability gets worse. For this reason, the French Government introduced a new tax-Generalized Social Contribution-to compensate for the social insurance deficit, imposed taxes on harmful consumption behaviors such as alcohol and tobacco, i.e., tobacco tax and alcohol tax, levied on pharmaceutical companies to make up for medical insurance deficits, required individuals who have the potential to increase the risk of medical expenses (such as smokers and drinkers) and enterprises with health as their profit goals to take on more responsibilities. Secondly, the motivation is weak, and people's enthusiasm for creating wealth is not high. Moreover, enterprises have a heavy burden, high labor costs, weak international competitiveness, resulting in slow economic development and insufficient employment. Finally, the intensive state-owned enterprises in the economy inhibits the development of small and medium-sized enterprises, which are the main contributor to the employment. In this regard, the difference between France and Germany is obvious.

The greatest inspiration of the French model is that while attaching importance to equality (France's emphasis on the equality should be highly valued), enterprises should be appropriately deregulated to invigorate the economy. The healthy economic development and full employment are necessary prerequisites for common prosperity.

Northern Europe*

1. Basic Information

Since World War II, western developed industrialized countries have learned from the painful impact of two World Wars, changing the path of major powers competing for power and military strength since the end of the 19th century, and moving towards a people-oriented development direction for welfare states. This change was supported by the experience of wartime economy and Keynesianism that advocated state intervention, as well as by the progressive social trend that prevailed after World War II. Therefore, the concept of the welfare state is a special historical product formed after World War II, which draws on the concepts of state intervention and socialist, integrating these ideological elements into the economic foundation of the market economy. It seeks to reform the liberal capitalist system and form a path of "social capitalism" or "European social model". As a theoretical basis, European welfare states adopted Fabian socialist policies and the ideological line of social democracy, breaking the bipolar opposition between market liberalism and socialist public ownership, and seeking for the third path.

As a political foundation, the growth of social democratic parties

---

* Author: LIN Ka&LIU Zhan, Zhejiang University.

in various European countries has provided political power for the development of welfare states. After World War II, the forces of socialist political parties (including the Labour Party, Social Democratic Party, Socialist Party, etc.) in countries such as Britain, France, Germany, Sweden, and Denmark entered (or controlled) government cabinets and parliamentary organizations through elections, formulated a series of social policies and public service projects to ensure people's livelihoods, striving to achieve a fair and just society. These political activities also receive support from the working class and various left-wing political forces, establishing consensus politics through class coordination, making the goal of developing a welfare state supported by all the people and promoting social progress. Therefore, left-wing political parties have played a leading role in the development of the European welfare state system. For example, the Swedish Social Democratic Party has been in power for over half a century and has a significant influence in shaping relevant social policies, the Norwegian Labour Party has always held a leading position in the government, the Danish Social Democratic Party has possessed a central position in the government and the Finnish Social Democratic Party has also maintained a majority of seats in parliament. These practical situations all reflect the policy concepts and political foundations adopted by the Nordic leftist political parties, which play a crucial role in the development of Nordic welfare states. On this basis, the socialist concept is effectively combined with a liberal market economy, forming a social democratic welfare state marked by inclusive social policies.

The Nordic welfare states mainly refer to four countries with very similar socio-economic systems, i.e., Sweden, Norway, Denmark, and Finland. Since the 1990s, the social system and policies of neighboring

Iceland have gradually moved closer to the above-mentioned four countries, known as the “Five Nordic Countries”. Therefore, this study also includes Iceland. The total GDP and per capita GDP of the five Nordic countries are at a developed level in international comparisons, and their social welfare development is also at a leading position internationally. The five countries have developed technological levels and enormous potential for economic development. The population size of Nordic countries is relatively small, with a total population of 2.635 million people in the five countries, while the land area is large. Among these five countries, the population of Sweden is 9.69 million, Denmark is 56.4 million, Finland is 5.55 million, Norway is 51.4 million, and Iceland is 33000. The life expectancy varies among countries (see Table 5-1), but the average life expectancy of male and female in each country is over 80 years old. Taking Finland as an example, its male life expectancy is 78.8 years old, female life expectancy is at the age of 84.35, and the average value of both is 81.57 years old. Due to the relatively small population of the five Nordic countries, this is the main reason why their per capita GDP ranks among the top in the world (see Table 5-2). These countries have historically been impoverished areas in Europe, with severe population outflows. After entering the construction of welfare states, the social and economic life of these countries was significantly improved, with remarkable results in social construction and receiving high attention from the international community.

The welfare state model of Nordic social democracy has obvious characteristics compared to the liberal model of the United States, Britain, and the conservative model of the Continent. The Nordic countries have not only achieved a high level of economic development, but also successfully achieved social equality and justice. The poverty rate in

Table 5-1 **Life Expectancy**

		2010	2011	2012	2013	2014	2015	2016	2017	2018	2019	2020
Denmark	Male	77.2	77.8	78.1	78.3	78.7	78.8	79.0	79.2	79.1	79.5	79.6
	Female	81.4	81.9	82.1	82.4	82.8	82.7	82.8	83.1	82.9	83.5	83.6
Sweden	Male	79.6	79.9	79.9	80.2	80.4	80.4	80.6	80.8	80.9	81.5	80.7
	Female	83.6	83.8	83.6	83.8	84.2	84.1	84.1	84.1	84.3	84.8	84.2
Finland	Male	76.9	77.3	77.7	78.0	78.4	78.7	78.6	78.9	79.1	79.3	79.4
	Female	83.5	83.8	83.7	84.1	84.1	84.4	84.4	84.5	84.5	84.8	85.0
Norway	Male	79.0	79.1	79.5	79.8	80.1	80.5	80.7	81.0	81.1	81.3	81.6
	Female	83.3	83.6	83.5	83.8	84.2	84.2	84.2	84.3	84.5	84.7	84.9
Iceland	Male	79.8	80.7	81.6	80.5	81.3	81.2	80.4	81.1	81.3	81.7	81.7
	Female	84.1	84.1	84.3	83.7	84.5	83.8	84.1	84.3	84.5	84.7	84.5

Source: http://pxweb.nordicstatistics.org/pxweb/en/Nordic%20Statistics/Nordic% 20Statistics __Health__Life%20expectancy/LIFE01.px/table/tableViewLayout2/?rxid= 4bd7ba15-3c4a-4793-8711-6dblfc878223.

Table 5-2 **Per Capita GDP (2010-2019)**

	2010	2011	2012	2013	2014	2015	2016	2017	2018	2019
Denmark	32900.0	33500.0	33900.0	34300.0	35300.0	36900.0	37100.0	38700.0	39700.0	41400.0
Finland	29800.0	30900.0	30900.0	30500.0	30800.0	31900.0	32100.0	33200.0	34400.0	35400.0
Norway	44300.0	46800.0	49400.0	49200.0	48600.0	45400.0	42100.0	44800.0	47800.0	46600.0
Sweden	32300.0	33700.0	34300.0	34000.0	34800.0	36900.0	36000.0	36300.0	37000.0	37800.0
Iceland	30300.0	30800.0	31700.0	32400.0	33700.0	36700.0	37900.0	38500.0	39500.0	40200.0

Source: http://pxweb.nordicstatistics.org/pxweb/en/Nordic%20Statistics/Nordic%20Statistics__Economy__Economic%20structure/KEY01.px/?rxid=4bd7ba15-3c4a-4793-8711-6dblfc878223.

Nordic countries is generally low, and the wealth gap is small, with a Gini Coefficient of between 0.23 and 0.28, significantly lower than the EU average of 0.30-0.31 (see Table 5-3).

Table 5-3 Gini Coefficient of Nordic Countries (2010-2020)

	2010	2011	2012	2013	2014	2015	2016	2017	2018	2019	2020
Denmark	0.27	0.27	0.27	0.27	0.28	0.27	0.28	0.28	0.28	0.28	0.27
Finland	0.25	0.26	0.26	0.25	0.26	0.25	0.25	0.25	0.26	0.26	0.27
Iceland	0.26	0.24	0.24	0.24	0.23	0.25	0.24	0.25	0.23	-	-
Norway	0.24	0.23	0.23	0.23	0.24	0.24	0.25	0.26	0.25	0.25	-
Sweden	0.26	0.26	0.26	0.26	0.27	0.27	0.28	0.28	0.27	0.28	-
EU	0.30	0.31	0.30	0.31	0.31	0.31	0.31	0.31	0.30	0.30	-

Source: http://pxweb.nordicstatistics.org/pxweb/en/Nordic%20Statistics/Nordic%20 Statistics__Social%20integration%20and%20income__Poverty/GINI01.px/table/tableView Layout2/?rxid=4bd7ba15-3c4a-4793-8711-6dblfc878223.

This study focuses on the progress made in social security and fair services in these countries and engages in policy discussions. It starts with the primary distribution of income, social redistribution, and the third social distribution, while paying attention to the issues of income distribution and accessibility to public services, and discusses the impact of Nordic socio-economic prosperity and social stability on enhancing citizens' humanistic spirit and social solidarity awareness. The discussion also involves economic development and innovation orientation, in response to the core topic of equality and efficiency in the field of welfare state research.

2. Primary Distribution and Related Policies

The primary distribution of social wealth refers to the distribution of gross national income directly related to factors of production, which include labor, capital, land, and technology. This kind of distribution is the process of people giving rewards to the contributors of various production factors based on their contributions made in the production process. These returns are not only for paying wages to workers, but also for the providers of factors such as capital, technology, management, production materials, information, market, and sales. This involves the distribution of class interests and resources. Therefore, the key issue of the primary distribution is to address the coordination of various stakeholders in the market, and to discuss the methods and degrees of interest distribution among all parties.

The economic structure of Nordic countries is mainly private economy, and they are market economy countries. Taking Sweden as an example, most of the means of production are privately owned, state-owned enterprises account for a small proportion in the industrial sector, and commerce is mostly operated by private enterprises. The labor force employed by private enterprises accounts for over 80 percent of the total labor force. Nordic countries rely on the tripartite negotiation mechanism developed since the 1950s to coordinate labor relations. Tripartite negotiation mechanism has played an important role in determining labor remuneration, labor conditions, employment conditions, enterprise development planning, and ensuring employee welfare benefits. The trade unions in Nordic countries have solid organizational strength and play a vital and protective role in employment. At the same time, Nordic countries have made specific regulations in setting minimum wage standards, industry guidance standards and other aspects with a high threshold. In the operation of Nordic enterprises, both employers and employees have strong legal awareness, and they form a contractual consensus on the basis of labor contracts. Even in private employment, work relationships are more formal. On the one hand, the employment relationship of employees is protected by law, such as their rights in cases of illness, parturition, or unexpected work-related injuries. On the other hand, enterprises do not have to bear too much social and public responsibility in terms of employee welfare.

In recent years, the labor market in Nordic countries has developed steadily. The economies of Nordic countries continue to grow at a low speed. At the same time, the inflation rate is also relatively low. Comparing these two sets of data reveals the sustainable growth of Nordic countries. On the other hand, Nordic countries have adopted active labor policies to promote employment since the 21st century. In the past decade, its employment rate has remained above 70 percent, with a registered unemployment rate of only 3-8 percent. In the formulation of legal norms regarding employment and related wages and remuneration, Nordic countries have played a critical role in protecting labors' interests. The government formulates and strictly implements the minimum wage standard, various social insurances are contributed by enterprises for employees, and the wage level of employees in the primary distribution is not low.

Table 5-4 Economic Growth Rate of Nordic Countries (2010-2020)

Unit:%

	2010	2011	2012	2013	2014	2015	2016	2017	2018	2019	2020
Denmark	1.9	1.3	0.2	0.9	1.5	2.3	2.8	2.2	2.8	-2.7	
Sweden	6.0	3.2	-0.6	1.2	2.7	4.5	2.1	2.6	2.0	2.0	-2.8
Finland	3.2	2.5	-1.4	-0.9	-0.4	0.5	2.8	3.2	1.3	1.3	-2.8
Norway	0.7	1.0	2.7	1.0	2.0	2.0	1.1	2.3	1.1	0.9	-0.8
Iceland	-2.8	1.8	1.1	4.6	1.7	4.4	6.3	4.2	4.7	2.6	-6.6

Source: http://pxweb.nordicstatistics.org/pxweb/en/Nordic%20Statistics/Nordic%20 Statistics__Economy__Economic%20structure/KEY01.px/table/tableViewLayout2/?rxid =4bd7ba15-3c4a-4793-8711-6dblfc878223.

Table 5-5 Inflation Rate of Nordic Countries (2010-2020) Unit:%

	2010	2011	2012	2013	2014	2015	2016	2017	2018	2019	2020
Denmark	2.3	2.8	2.4	0.8	0.6	0.5	0.2	1.1	0.8	0.8	0.4
Iceland	5.4	4.0	5.2	3.9	2.0	1.6	1.7	1.8	2.7	3.0	2.8
Norway	2.4	1.3	0.6	2.1	2.1	2.1	3.6	1.8	2.7	2.2	1.3
Sweden	1.2	8.0	0.9	0.0	-0.2	0.0	1.0	1.8	2.0	1.8	0.5
Finland	-	-	-	-	-	-	0.3	0.7	1.1	1.0	0.3

Source: http://pxweb.nordicstatistics.org/pxweb/en/Nordic%20Statistics/Nordic%20 Statistics__Economy__Economic%20structure/KEY01.px/table/tableViewLayout2/?rxid =4bd7ba15-3c4a-4793-8711-6dblfc878223.

Nordic countries also attach importance to safeguarding the interests of employers. Countries protect the legitimate rights and interests of private owners who operate normally, encourage enterprise innovation, respect the operational laws of the market economy system and provide public services for the regular operation of enterprises within the legal framework. The tax rate paid by Nordic companies is set at 20-25 percent. These countries experienced a significant decrease in corporate tax rates from 2012 to 2014 (see Chart 5-7) to encourage innovation and entrepreneurship among enterprises. Nordic countries protect private property by the law, and the interests of investors are also protected by law. Land, farm, and enterprise transactions can be carried out in accordance with market laws. On an economic basis, the private economy of Nordic countries holds a dominant position in the national economy. Industry, agriculture, commerce, and private enterprises have become the main components of the national economy, while the proportion of state-owned enterprises is low. In the operation of Nordic enterprises, emphasis is placed on the autonomous operation of the market economy. In the 1980s, Sweden conducted experiments

Table 5-6

Employment and Unemployment (2010-2020)

			2010	2011	2012	2013	2014	2015	2016	2017	2018	2019	2020
Denmark	Male/Female from Age 15 to 64	Unemployment Rate	7.9	7.9	8.0	7.6	7.1	6.5	6.2	6.0	5.3	5.1	5.8
		Employment Rate	71.6	21.3	70.7	70.5	70.9	71.7	72.4	73.0	73.9	74.8	74.1
Sweden	Male/Female from Age 15 to 64	Unemployment Rate	8.8	8.0	8.1	8.2	8.1	7.6	7.1	6.9	6.5	7.0	8.5
		Employment Rate	72.1	73.6	73.7	74.4	74.9	75.5	76.1	76.9	77.4	77.2	75.5
Finland	Male/Female from Age 15 to 64	Unemployment Rate	8.5	7.9	7.8	8.3	8.8	9.6	9.0	8.8	7.5	6.8	7.0
		Employment Rate	67.9	68.6	69.0	68.5	68.3	68.1	68.7	69.6	71.7	72.6	71.6
Norway	Male/Female from Age 15 to 64	Unemployment Rate	3.6	3.3	3.2	3.5	3.6	4.4	4.8	4.3	3.9	3.8	4.5
		Employment Rate	75.1	75.1	75.6	75.2	75.0	74.6	74.1	73.8	74.6	75.1	74.4
Iceland	Male/Female from Age 15 to 64	Unemployment Rate	7.7	7.2	6.1	5.5	5.1	4.1	3.1	2.9	2.7	3.6	5.7
		Employment Rate	74.6	74.8	75.4	77.0	77.9	79.5	80.9	80.4	79.8	79.1	75.5

Source: http://www.nordicstatistics.org/labour-market/.

on corporate socialism, and some companies spontaneously adopted the idea of giving every employee a stake in the enterprise, encouraging each of them to work for their own enterprise. But this experiment of socialist transformation based on cooperative enterprise property rights did not become popular later on.

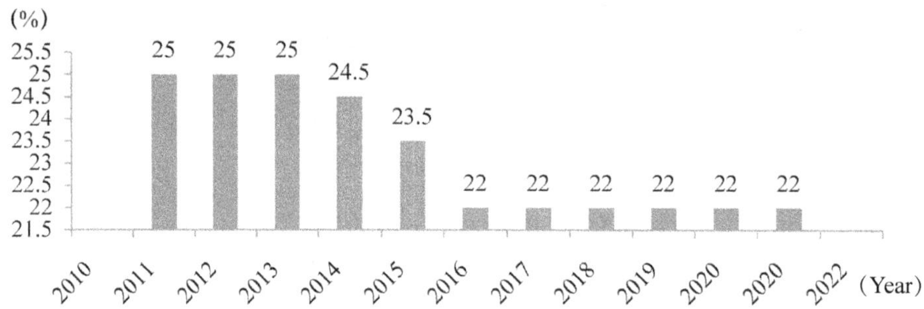

(a)Corporate Tax Rate in Denmark

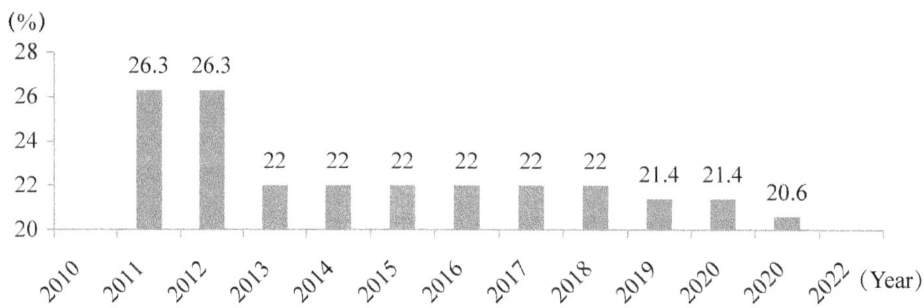

(b)Corporate Tax Rate in Sweden

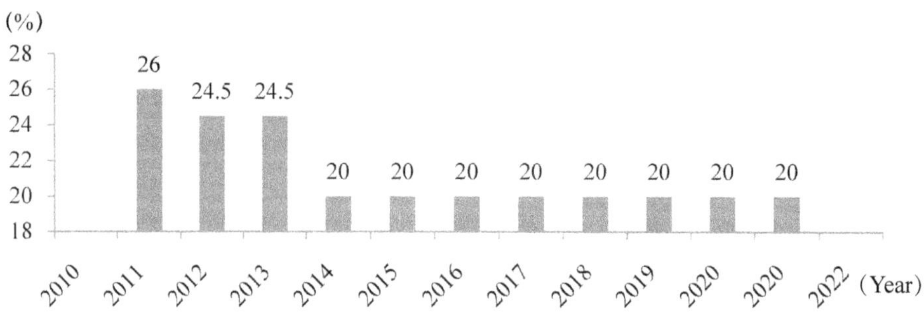

(c)Corporate Tax Rate in Finland

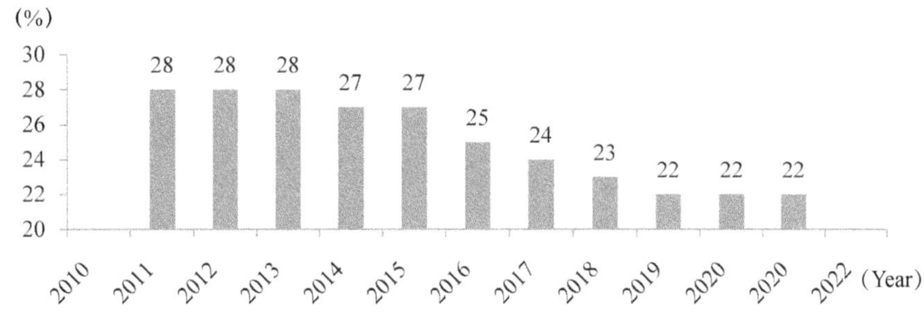

(d)Corporate Tax Rate in Norway

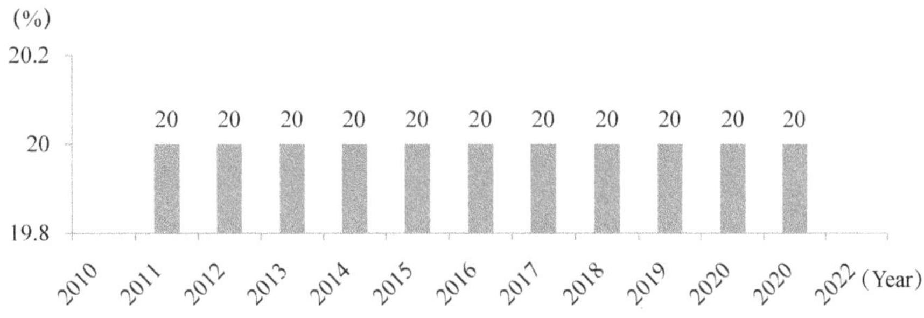

(e)Corporate Tax Rate in Iceland

Chart 5-1 Income Tax Rate of Nordic Countries

Sources: http://tradingeconomics.com/.

At the same time, all members of society are required to pay income tax to the state, and for high-income individuals, the tax rate is set at over 40 percent (see Chart 5-8). Norway and Iceland often have tax rates above 40 percent, while individual income tax in Denmark, Sweden, and Finland is above 50 percent (except for 2020, influenced by COVID-19). This high tax rate provides the foundation for the public financial supply of welfare states and material conditions for the formation of a middle-class society. The tax rate of such individual income tax is almost twice that of the corporate tax rate, reflecting the support of the government's economic policies for the operation of enterprises. On the other hand, the wage level of employees is also very high, even one of the highest in the global comparison. However, even after tax, the per capita income of Nordic countries still remains high.

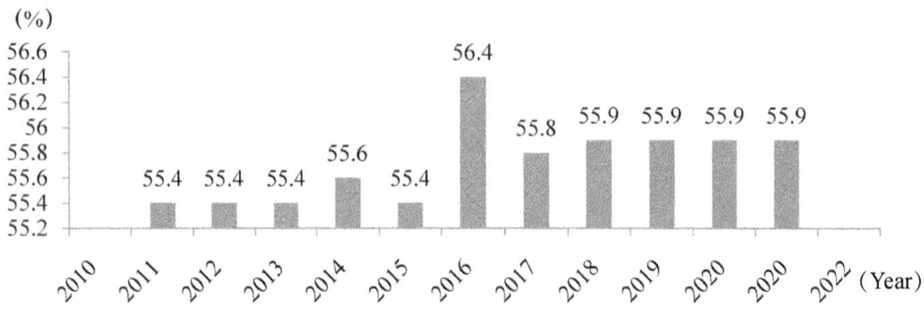

(a)Individual Income Tax Rate in Denmark

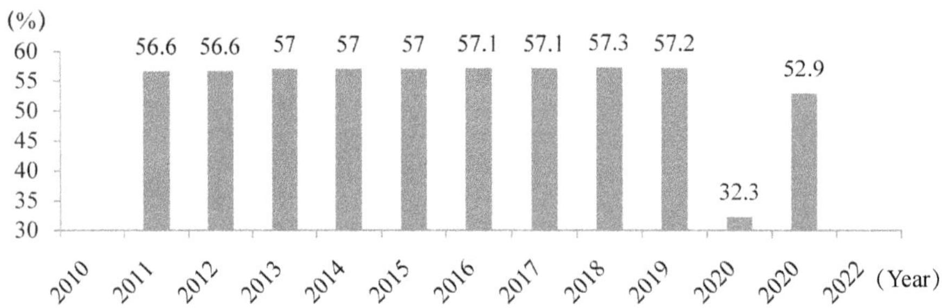

(b)Individual Income Tax Rate in Sweden

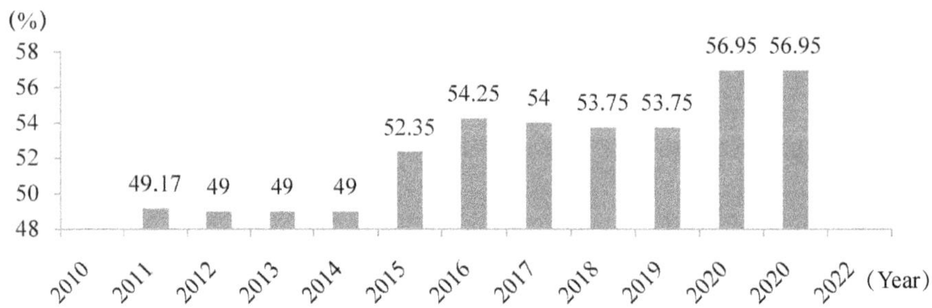

(c)Individual Income Tax Rate in Finland

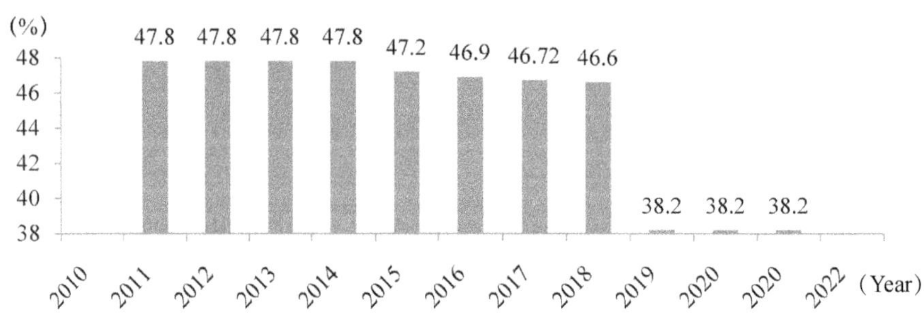

(d)Individual Income Tax Rate in Norway

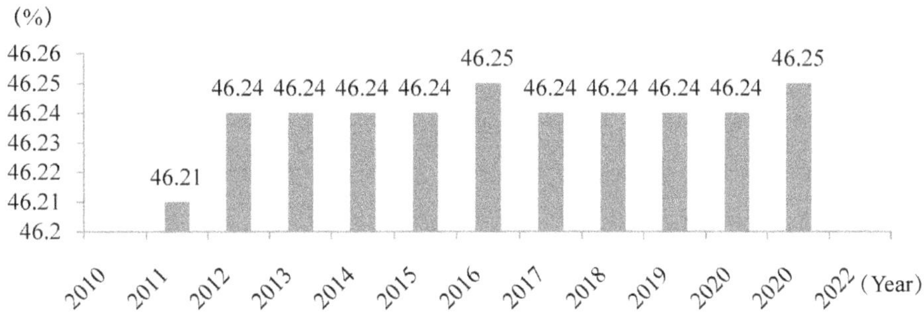

(e)Individual Income Tax Rate in Iceland

Chart 5-2 Individual Income Tax Rate of Nordic Countries

Sources: http://tradingeconomics.com/.

3. Social Redistribution and Related Policies

Based on the concept of social democracy and the spirit of social solidarity, the Nordic welfare countries pursue social equality and justice, thus developing various social projects in social security and services for social redistribution. In these projects, public finance indicators become the basic indicator of the overall situation of income transfer. Therefore, examining the status of public finances and expenditures on various social security measures in Nordic countries can reflect the redistribution effect of Nordic countries. Table 5-9 shows the overall situation of public expenditure and social welfare in the five Nordic countries. In 2020, among the five Nordic countries, in Denmark, Finland, Norway and Sweden, the proportion of government public expenditure to GDP was 54.0 percent, 56.7 percent, 58.4 percent and 52.9 percent respectively. These data are close to the average of 52.9 percent for EU countries, while Iceland showed a slightly lower proportion of 49.7 percent.

In terms of the composition of public expenditure, the metric of "the compensation for employees" (social insurance, etc.) in Denmark,

Finland, Norway, and Sweden is 15.4 percent, 12.8 percent, 16.5 percent and 13.1 percent, while the value is 16.1 percent in Iceland and 11.0 percent in EU. In terms of the "non-physical social allowances", the data for Denmark, Finland, Norway, and Sweden is 16.6 percent, 19.5 percent, 17.0 percent and 13.0 percent, and only 9.9 percent for Iceland, with the average of 18.7 percent for EU countries. If add up the compensation for employees and the cash payment for social allowances, we can obtain the basic expenses (incomplete ratio) spent by these countries on social welfare and social security. Among Denmark, Finland, and Norway, the result is 32 percent, 32.3 percent and 33.5 percent respectively, while 26 percent and 26.1 percent for Iceland and Sweden. Compared to the EU average of 29.7 percent, Denmark, Finland, and Norway are above the average, while Iceland and Sweden are below the average. From this, it can be seen that Denmark, Finland, and Norway spend about one-third of their GDP on social security and welfare, while Iceland and Sweden account for over a quarter of their GDP.

In addition to examining the level of social security and welfare in Nordic countries through the status of social expenditure, it is also necessary to summarize the characteristics of the institutional models of Nordic countries through different types of social policy projects. Among various social policy projects, the most representative one in Nordic countries is reflected in social allowances. Nordic countries have been developing child allowances since the 1930s, opening up the earliest Nordic inclusive policy projects. At present, children in Nordic countries can receive allowance as long as they have the local legal residency rights. After the 1980s, with the development of feminism, the welfare treatment of Nordic mothers also further improved. In addition, there are housing allowances, domestic service allowances, student allowances,

Table 5-7 The Composition of General Government Expenditure in Nordic Countries Unit:%

Country	Indicator	2010	2011	2012	2013	2014	2015	2016	2017	2018	2019	2020
Denmark	General Government Total Expenditure	56.7	56.4	58.0	55.8	55.2	54.5	52.5	50.5	50.5	49.2	53.9
	Employee Compensation (payable)	17.3	16.8	16.6	16.4	16.2	16.0	15.5	15.2	15.1	14.9	15.4
	Social Welfare Beyond Physical Social Transfer (payable)	17.1	17.2	17.3	17.4	17.2	17.0	16.5	16.1	15.8	15.6	16.6
	Physical Social Transfer-Market Production of Purchases (payable)	1.7	1.6	1.6	1.5	1.5	1.5	1.5	1.4	1.4	1.4	1.4
	Other Frequent Transfers (payable)	3.4	3.2	3.4	3.4	3.0	3.1	2.9	3.0	3.1	3.0	3.3
Finland	General Government Total Expenditure	53.9	53.7	55.4	56.8	57.3	56.5	55.6	53.6	53.4	53.2	56.7
	Employee Compensation (payable)	14.0	13.9	14.2	14.3	14.1	13.8	13.2	12.4	12.4	12.5	12.8
	Social Welfare Beyond Physical Social Transfer (payable)	17.4	17.1	17.9	18.8	19.5	19.7	19.4	18.8	18.4	18.2	19.5
	Physical Social Transfer-Market Production of Purchases (payable)	2.5	2.6	2.6	2.7	2.7	2.8	2.8	2.8	2.8	2.9	3.1
	Other Frequent Transfers (payable)	2.8	2.8	2.8	2.9	2.9	2.7	2.6	2.3	2.4	2.4	2.8
Iceland	General Government Total Expenditure	48.9	50.7	47.9	46.1	45.9	43.6	46.5	44.5	44.0	43.4	49.7
	Employee Compensation (payable)	13.2	13.2	13.3	13.2	13.5	13.5	13.5	14.1	14.2	14.2	16.1
	Social Welfare Beyond Physical Social Transfer (payable)	7.2	7.8	7.3	6.8	6.7	6.1	5.9	6.5	6.6	7.3	9.9
	Physical Social Transfer-Market Production of Purchases (payable)	-	-	-	-	-	-	-	-	-	-	-
	Other Frequent Transfers (payable)	1.8	1.6	1.5	1.5	1.5	1.4	1.6	1.6	1.7	1.7	2.0

continued

Country	Indicator	2010	2011	2012	2013	2014	2015	2016	2017	2018	2019	2020
Norway	General Government Total Expenditure	45.4	44.2	43.3	44.4	46.3	49.3	51.5	50.5	48.8	51.5	58.1
	Employee Compensation (payable)	13.4	13.2	13.2	13.5	13.9	14.7	15.3	15.1	14.6	15.3	16.3
	Social Welfare Beyond Physical Social Transfer (payable)	13.4	13.2	13.2	13.3	13.8	14.8	15.4	15.0	14.2	14.7	16.9
	Physical Social Transfer-Market Production of Purchases (payable)	2.1	2.0	2.0	2.0	2.1	2.2	2.3	2.2	2.1	2.2	2.4
	Other Frequent Transfers (payable)	2.5	2.4	2.3	2.4	2.6	2.8	2.9	2.8	2.7	2.9	3.4
Sweden	General Government Total Expenditure	50.4	49.7	50.9	51.6	50.7	49.3	49.7	49.2	49.8	49.3	52.9
	Employee Compensation (payable)	12.2	12.1	12.5	12.7	12.6	12.4	12.6	12.6	12.7	12.7	13.1
	Social Welfare Beyond Physical Social Transfer (payable)	13.8	13.2	13.8	14.1	13.7	13.2	13.1	12.8	12.6	12.3	13.0
	Physical Social Transfer-Market Production of Purchases (payable)	3.1	3.2	3.3	3.4	3.5	3.6	3.9	3.7	3.6	3.5	3.7
	Other Frequent Transfers (payable)	2.8	2.6	2.6	2.8	2.7	2.6	2.3	2.4	2.7	2.6	3.2
EU	General Government Total Expenditure	50.5	49.2	49.7	49.6	49.0	48.1	47.3	46.7	46.6	46.6	53.4
	Employee Compensation (payable)	10.9	10.6	10.6	10.6	10.5	10.3	10.2	10.1	10.1	10.1	11.0
	Social Welfare Beyond Physical Social Transfer (payable)	16.7	16.4	16.7	16.9	16.9	16.6	16.5	16.2	16.1	16.2	18.7
	Physical Social Transfer-Market Production of Purchases (payable)	5.2	5.1	5.1	5.2	5.3	5.2	5.3	5.3	5.2	5.3	5.7
	Other Frequent Transfers (payable)	2.3	2.2	2.3	2.4	2.3	2.2	2.2	2.1	2.2	2.2	2.6

Source: http://pxweb.nordicstatistics.org/pxweb/en/Nordic%20Statistics/Nordic%20Statistics__Public%20finance__Public%20expenditure/PUBS11.px/table/tableViewLayout2/?rxid=4bd7ba15-3c4a-4793-8711-6dblfc878223.

etc. The effective implementation of various social allowance programs can ensure that the people have a dignified life, as well as enhance civic awareness and social cohesion.

In various social expenditure projects, an overview of the status of social security and social service support can be concluded. Firstly, anti-poverty and social assistance projects are the most fundamental components of the social security system. In the public financial investment of social assistance projects in Nordic countries, the situation has remained basically stable. Secondly, social spending on projects for families and children has remained stable in other Nordic countries, except for Denmark, which has decreased. In terms of employment support policies, there have been significant fluctuations, especially after the US financial crisis and the European debt crisis from 2008 to 2009, social spending rapidly increased and then gradually decreased. In terms of medical insurance and pension insurance, expenditures in various countries have also remained stable, reflecting the strong sustainability of the system.

4. Social Services

To maintain people's basic living conditions and achieve social security, capital alone is far from enough. The development of Nordic welfare countries is not only reflected in income transfer and income security, but also in social services, especially for vulnerable groups such as the elderly, women, children, and people with disabilities (see Chart 5-10). The welfare service system of Nordic countries has gradually developed since the 1970s. In this process, Nordic countries first strengthened children's right to education and child benefits, and then developed allowances for mothers to take care of their children. Since the 21st century, Europe has

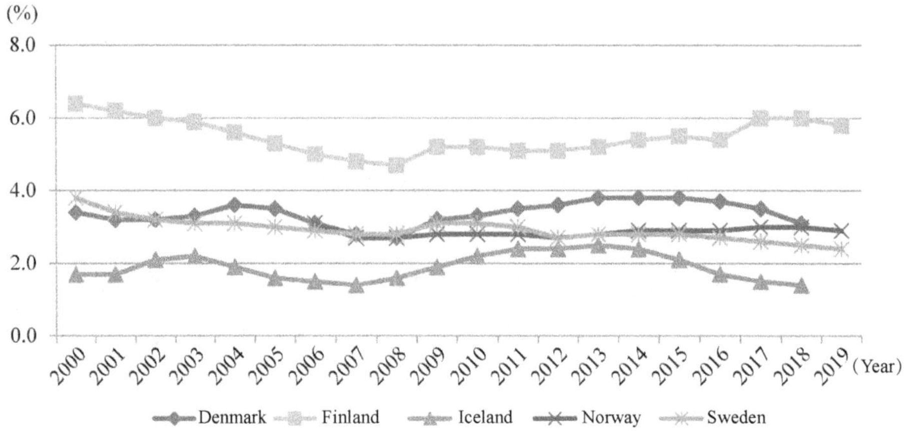

(a) The Proportion of Social Expenditure for Unemployment to GDP(%)

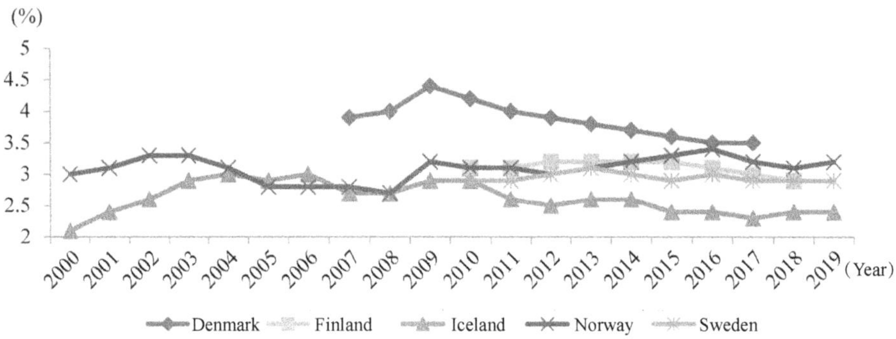

(b) The Proportion of Social Expenditure for Households and Children to GDP(%)

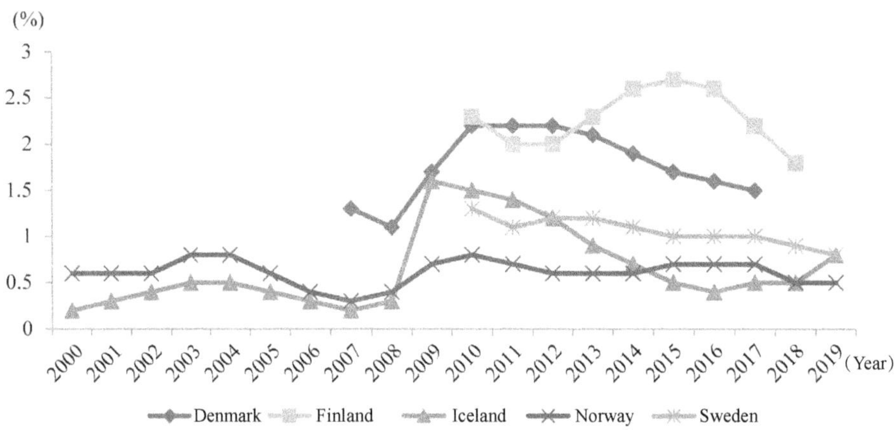

(c) The Proportion of Population Receiving Social Assistance in Cash Payments(%)

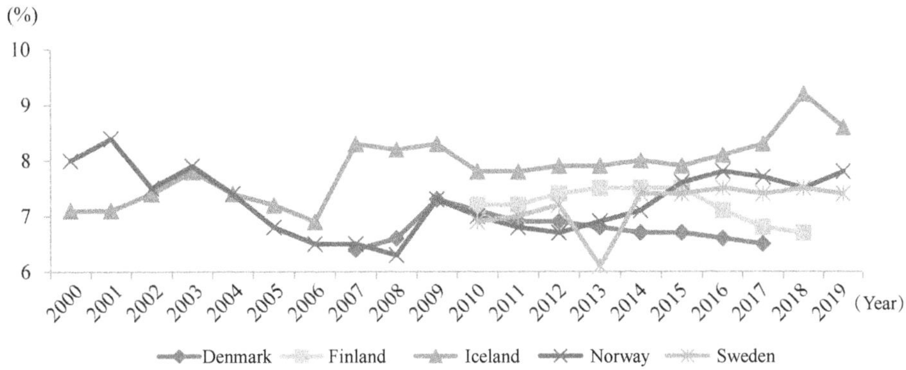

(d) The Proportion of Expenditure for Old-age Pension to GDP(%)

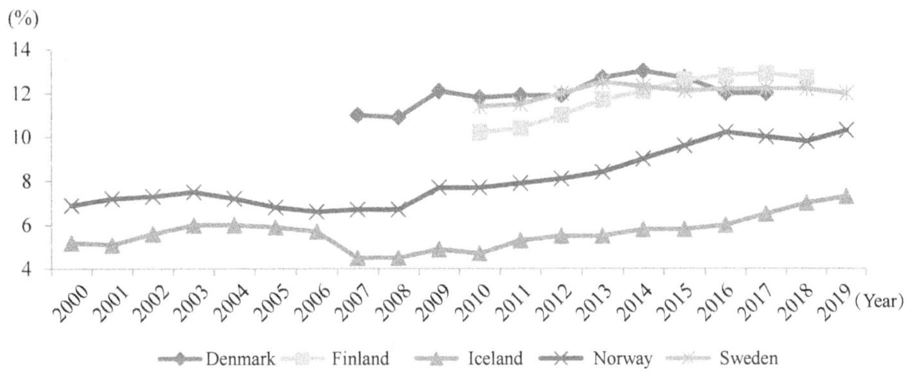

(e) The Proportion of Social Expenditure for Medical Insurance to GDP(%)

Chart 5-3 The Proportion of Various Social Welfare to GDP in Nordic Countries(%)

http://www.nhwstat.org/.

gradually entered a deep aging population. Under the pressure of aging, Nordic countries have made the development of elderly care services a focus of welfare services. In elderly care services, local governments in Nordic countries undertake public medical services such as hospitalization and home care for the elderly, and also evaluate the necessity of service levels and quantities through professional institutions.

Due to the wide range of social services, education and healthcare will be used as basic indicators to reflect the basic situation. In terms of education, Nordic countries regard strengthening education as a basic means to enhance their competitiveness, attach importance to investment in human capital, and improve the quality of their citizens and their scientific literacy. The proportion of investment in education or scientific research to GDP in Nordic countries is the highest in the world and the proportion of Nordic countries with a university degree between the age of 25 and 39 is higher than the average in the European Union. The high level of knowledge, culture, and education possessed by these citizens provides a foundation for these countries to become innovative countries, and provides a basic way for young people to alleviate the employment pressure. At the same time, it also provides human and intellectual resources for developing enterprises. It is precisely because of the high emphasis on education and scientific research that numerous industry leaders such as Ericsson, Nokia, Skype, Spotify, LEGO, IKEA, Volvo, and others have emerged in these small countries, all of which have demonstrated strong Nordic competitiveness in the global market.

Regarding healthcare, Nordic countries have mainly established public service systems in the development of medical service systems, with a large number of doctors, nurses, and hospital beds. According to the OECD, from 2012 to 2019, the number of doctors per 1,000 inhabitants in Denmark increased from 4.04 to 4.45 and the number of nurses grew from 10.87 to 11.45. In Sweden, the number of doctors per 1,000 inhabitants in the same period increased from 4.09 to 4.53 and the number of nurses was from 11.42 to 11.49. The number of doctors in Finland increased from 3.26 to 3.33 (incomplete statistics of the number of nurses, only found 15.73 in 2014 and 15.84 in 2015). In Norway and Iceland, the corresponding number of doctors grew from 4.77 to 5.51 and from 3.5 to 3.87 and the number of nurses increased from 19.48 to 20.78 and from

14.82 to 15.36 respectively. The data from Nordic Statistics also reflects (in spite of incomplete) that the number of nurses in Nordic countries is increasing. But at the same time, it can be noticed that the beds in Nordic countries have been reduced. Currently, the number of hospital beds per 1,000 inhabitants is not considerable in international comparisons.

On the other hand, aging and globalization pose new challenges to Nordic welfare countries. For example, under the conditions of economic globalization, the Nordic economy is influenced by the international market, thus the expansion of financial resources and the operation of redistribution mechanisms in its welfare system need to consider a more complex social policy decision-making background. Taking the challenge of aging as an example, the group of retirees in Nordic countries is constantly expanding, resulting in an increasing demand for pensions and elderly care services. Furthermore, the retirement population increasingly rises, with a growth rate of 28 percent (Denmark), 51 percent (Finland), 65 percent (Norway), 142 percent (Iceland), and 31 percent (Sweden) in the seven years from 2010 to 2017, which puts severe pressure on social security and services, and accounts for the relatively small number of hospital beds per 1,000 inhabitants.

5. Public Resources

In different countries and market relations, some welfare deliveries are mainly by the government, while others are mainly by the welfare market. In Nordic countries, the structure of their social service system is oriented towards public services, and the development of various welfare services for the public is mainly the responsibility of local governments. Meanwhile, a huge public sector has emerged as the welfare state system develops. Up to 70 percent of employees in the public sector of Nordic countries is engaged in work related to welfare public services, which indicates that with the development of the Nordic welfare system, the government's ability in welfare governance is also constantly strengthening, forming a "social service state" that involves in citizens' lives and assists with social services.

Actually, the delivery of social welfare should also be promoted through private institutions, volunteer organizations and commercial institutions. Since the 1990s, Nordic countries have promoted the privatization process of welfare reform, encouraging the privatization of public service institutions such as hospitals and schools. The reform has weakened the public service systems of Nordic countries (number of hospital beds per 1,000 inhabitants, as mentioned above), and has had a certain negative impact on vulnerable groups. The reform policies of Nordic countries aim to advocate for the involvement of private resources and promote diversified welfare policies, but these reforms have not achieved the expected results. After 10 years of reform, except for private hospitals, other public sectors are still served by the state. The legitimacy of welfare states has not fundamentally shaken, and the public welfare departments of Nordic countries still maintain the nature of public welfare (to the extent that some scholars discuss the return of welfare states).

In Nordic countries, social organizations and non-profit organizations play an active role in civil society. In the 1980s, under the influence of the neoliberal political system, governments attempted to introduce market mechanisms to encourage social participation and transform national welfare into a system where multiple parties participate and collaborate, including the government, enterprises, foundations, and non-profit organizations. Its purpose is not only to obtain more efficient public services, but also to reduce government expenditure budgets. However, although there are many volunteers in Nordic countries with high social participation, their active willingness to participate is based on their own interest in cultural and sports activities. Its role is mainly reflected in creating and cultivating a positive civil society, rather than in social welfare and poverty alleviation, which have been widely recognized by the public as the responsibility of the government.

On the other hand, Nordic countries generally believe in Protestantism, with up to 80 percent of Lutheran believers. The existence of religious values will guide volunteers to be willing to participate in public charitable causes. In fact, many volunteer groups participate in small-size charity activities to express goodwill and sympathy towards the victims and provide assistance within their capabilities. But these charitable activities cannot help people rely on charity to solve the livelihood problems of the poor. In the Nordic welfare system, people pay a higher proportion of taxes under an olive-shaped social structure. The middle class is developed, while the proportion of the wealthy and the poor is relatively small. Due to the scarcity of private welfare resources and private property, the main financial resources are transferred to the national treasury through tax payment, and the remaining financial resources of the public are very limited. Therefore, in Nordic society, the supply of social welfare is mainly achieved through public finance or redistribution by the state, while the power of folk charity is relatively weak.

In addition, the construction of a welfare state is inherently linked to the construction of an active civil society. The task of building a welfare state system is not only achieved through national policy formulation or through high welfare based on high taxation, but also requires a mass foundation with class unity and active support from civil society.

Therefore, the active involvement of non-governmental organizations provide a social foundation for social consensus. At the same time, the Nordic people actively advocate for life quality and democratic politics, believing that these democratic concepts should be reflected in daily life, and through social democratization and rule of law governance, a society with high transparency should be formed. In Northern Europe, clean politics is one of the fundamental elements for the public to support the state power. The Nordic countries have the highest ranking in Corruption Perceptions Index in the world, and their moral consciousness is also a derivative of consensus politics. Such social environment is precisely formed in the practice of daily life. The Corruption Perceptions Index of Nordic society ranks among the top in international rankings, providing conditions for an open civil society and a stable social order. It also lays a social foundation for winning social trust from the public, ensuring transparent and clean usage of tax, return to taxpayers and improve their life quality.

6. Analysis and Conclusion

Under the Nordic social democratic model, its economic system is based on the system of private property ownership. Through a series of factors such as class cooperation, social compromise, tripartite negotiations, social coordination, and consensus politics, it corrects market failure, achieves equal distribution of social wealth, avoiding excessive government intervention in economic system. On the basis of consensus politics, Nordic countries have established a model of inclusive social security systems. Certainly, this model has been widely criticized because of its burden on public finance. This prompted Nordic countries, especially Sweden, to actively promote privatization oriented reforms in the 1990s. However, the reform in the past decade has not achieved the expected positive results.

The development experience of Nordic countries also shows that common prosperity and social cohesion and solidarity within a country influence each other. The concept of "social solidarity" in Nordic countries is based on cross-class collaboration and cross-group social trust, and is formed due to the relatively equal distribution of income. In order to achieve class cooperation and consensus politics, it is necessary to fully consider the interests of each social class, respect the laws of the market economy, open up the source of social wealth, and ensure the legitimacy of social mechanisms through the operation of national social policies, maintaining the sustainable development and growth of the system.

However, the Nordic welfare state system also faces serious challenges. The challenges it faces mainly come from the issues of economic development and expansion of revenue and expenditure base, as well as the challenges of aging, rather than the legitimacy crisis and institutional defects of the welfare state system itself. To this end, Nordic countries adopt active social policies, encourage the orientation of work welfare, strengthen the cultivation of human resources, and reduce corporate taxes to stimulate entrepreneurial innovation vitality. At the same time, they are also keeping up with the times, encouraging the international development of their own enterprises, and assisting the development of export-oriented economies. In today's globalized world, only by enabling domestic economy to compete for resources from the international market is the long-term solution. In response to this demand, Nordic countries have strengthened their innovation orientation and enhanced the vitality of the Nordic welfare state system. Its basic policy direction includes increasing investment in education, expanding the international market, maintaining GDP growth rate and inflation rate at 1 percent, and ensuring institutional and fiscal sustainability. At present, these policies have achieved positive results, enabling Nordic countries to rank among the top in global competitiveness.

In conclusion, in the study of comparative welfare state systems, we can see that the Nordic welfare state model, as a unique economic and social system different from other European countries, has made significant contributions to promoting economic growth, social stability, and social justice, and will continue to maintain its sustainability for a long time to come. In these countries, social security provides everyone with a safe life, and individuals enjoy a safety net of public services, making the social welfare a fundamental social right of citizens. The establishment of the Nordic model also requires support from a certain class foundation and structure. The olive-shaped society dominated by the middle class formed in Nordic society provides the foundation for establishing a civilized and collaborative social atmosphere. Nordic society is a wealthy society, with 70 percent to 80 percent of the people in Nordic countries belonging to the middle-income group, basically achieving the goal of common prosperity. The achievement of above results is not only a product of the synergy between its economic and social system, but also an outcome of the development of social policies and service systems, as well as the result of ideological construction and social solidarity. The development experience gained by these societies is of great help for us to consider how to deal with the coexistence of public goods supported by public finance and the development vitality derived from market development, and how to achieve modernization goals such as prosperity, positive efficiency, and freedom of life. Therefore, the unique economic and social system of Northern Europe, as well as the experience of economic prosperity, social stability, and harmonious society, provide helpful reference and inspiration for us to think about the issue of common prosperity and explore the path of economic and social reform.

Spain*

1. Basic Information

After Brexit, Spain became one of the four major countries in the European Union. However, in terms of total GDP and per capita income, there is still a significant gap between Spain and Germany, France, and Italy. According to the Spanish National Institution of Statistics, Spain's GDP increased from EUR 1.03 trillion to EUR 1.24 trillion①, showing a slight growth trend year by year, ranking 14th in the world. From 2010 to 2019, the per capita net monetary income grew from EUR 10,858 to EUR 12,292 (see Table 6-1).

Table 6-1 Per Capita Income in Spain (2010-2019) Unit: EUR

Year	2010	2011	2012	2013	2014	2015	2016	2017	2018	2019
Per Capita Income	10858	10795	10531	10391	10419	10708	11074	11412	11680	12292

Source: The website of Spanish National Institution of Statistic: INE, Living Conditions Survey (LCS). Year 2019.

Final results, https://ine.es/en/prensa/ecv_2020_en.pdf.https://ine.es/en/prensa/ecv_2020_en.pdf.

---

* Author: ZHANG Min, Institute of European Studies of Chinese Academy of Social Sciences.

① INE, "The Spanish economy recorded a volume growth of 2.0% in 2019, Gross Domestic Product (GDP) at current prices stood at 1,244,772 million euros in 2019", Annual National Accounts of Spain: Main aggregates Years 2017-2019, https://ine.es/en/prensa/cna_pa_2019_en.pdf.

1.1 Significant Wealth Gap in Spain, Compared to Other EU Members

In 2014, 10 percent of the wealthy in Spain owned 52.8 percent of the national wealth①. From 2007 to 2017, the income of the top 1 percent of the wealthy in Spain increased by 24 percent, while the per capita income of the 90 percent at the bottom of society grew by less than 2 percent.② In terms of the income proportion of people with different income levels, from 2010 to 2017, the poorest 40 percent of the population in Spain accounted for 17.5 percent, with the richest 10 percent and 1 percent accounting for 26.2 percent and 9.8 percent③.

The population below the poverty line in 2020 increased from 20.7 percent to 21.0 percent. Among the population at risk of poverty, the poverty rate is relatively high among those under the age of 16, with an average annual rate of over 26% from 2010 to 2019. The situation was most severe in 2013, with 30.1 percent of this age group at the risk of poverty. The proportion of people at risk of poverty or social exclusion (AROPE ratio) rose from 25.3 percent in 2019 to 26.4 percent in 2020. Meanwhile, 7 percent of the total population in 2020 faced severe material scarcity, which was 4.7 percent in 2019.④ In 2019, 4.7 percent of Spanish cannot afford an automobile, the proportion of those who default on mortgage loans or rentals was 81 percent, and 33.5 percent

---

① El País, "Spain's richest 10% hold more than half the country's wealth", https://english.elpais.com/elpais/2017/01 /25/inenglish/1485333552_076842.html.

② CIARÁN GILES, "UN expert says Spain fails badly in tackling poverty", AP NEWS, February 7, 2020, https://apnews. com/article/ 44da80a35311586fd9f777246a70d6bf.

③ Eurostat: Income Quintile Share Ratio (S80/S20) of Disposable Income by Gender and Age-EU SILC survey, http://appsso. eurostat.ec.euro-pa.eu/nui/submitViewTableAction.do.

④ INE, "Living Conditions Survey (LCS), Year 2019", https://ine.es/en/prensa/ecv_2020_en.pdf.

of individuals or families were unable to afford a week of vacation expenses within a year.①

1.2 Significant Regional Differences in Spain②

In 2019, the autonomous regions with the highest per capita income were País Vasco (with an annual per capita income of EUR 15,813), Navarra (EUR 15,094) and Madrid (EUR 14,580), and the autonomous regions with the lowest per capita income were Extremadura (EUR 9,147), Murcia (EUR 9,850) and Canarias (EUR 9,935). From the perspective of At Risk of Poverty Or Social Exclusion ratio (AROPE ratio), autonomous regions with higher value were Extremadura (38.7 percent), Canarias (36.3 percent) and Andalucía (35.1 percent) and autonomous regions with the lowest AROPE rate were the Navarra (12.0 percent) and País Vasco (13.9 percent). Furthermore, the highest risk rate of poverty was found in Extremadura (31.4 percent), Canarias (29.9 percent) and Andalucía (28.5 percent), and the lowest in Navarra (9.9 percent) and País Vasco (10.0 percent)③.

1.3 Gap of Wealth

The S80/S20 ratio and Gini Coefficient can effectively measure the degree of inequality and in Spain. In 2019, the S80/S20 ratio in Spain was 5.8, a decrease of 0.1 from 2018, indicating the income gap between

① Eurostat: "Key Figures on Europe", https://ec.europa.eu/eurostat/cache/digpub/keyfigures/.

② INE, "The percentage of the population at risk of poverty or social exclusion (AROPE rate) increased to 26.4%, from 25.3% in 2019", https://ine.es/dyngs/INEbase/en/operacion.htm?=Estadistica_C&cid=1254736176807&menu=ultiDatos&idp=125473 5976608.

③ INE, "Living Conditions Survey (LCS), Year 2019", https://ine.es/en/prensa/ecv_2020_en.pdf.

the richest and poorest groups has slightly narrowed. From the changes of Gini Coefficient in Spain over the years, it can be seen that income inequality is mitigated, with a Gini Coefficient of 0.321 in 2019, a reduction of 0.009 compared to 2018 (see Table 6-2).

Table 6-2 S80/20 Ratio Gini Coefficient and in Spain (2010-2019)

Year	2010	2011	2012	2013	2014	2015	2016	2017	2018	2019
S80/20	6.3	6.5	6.3	6.8	6.9	6.6	6.6	6.0	5.9	5.8
Gini Coefficient	0.340	0.342	0.337	0.347	0.346	0.345	0.341	0.332	0.330	0.321

Source: The website of Spanish National Institution of Statistic: Living Conditions Survey. https://ine.es/en/prensa/ecv_2020_en.pdf.

Spain has a relatively sound healthcare system. In 2019, the public health expenditure was approximately EUR 74 billion, accounting for 6.4 percent of GDP, with the per capita value of EUR 1,594. There are a total of 468 hospitals nationwide, with 1,120,000 beds and 320,000 medical staffs. [①] Spain is one of the EU countries with the highest per capita life expectancy, with a female life expectancy of 86.1 years old, ranking first in the 27 EU countries and an average life expectancy of 84.3 for male, ranking third in EU countries. From 2006 to 2018, the life expectancy increased from 84.3 to 86.1 for female and from 77.7 to 80.4 for male[②] (See Chart 6-1).

① Ministry of Health of Spain, "KEY DATA FROM SPAIN'S NATIONAL HEALTH SYSTEM", https://www.mscbs.gob.es/en/estadEstudios/portada/docs/KEY_DATA_SNHS_ENG_A4_062020.pdf.

② Ministry of Health of Spain, "2019 ANNUAL REPORT. NATIONAL HEALTH SYSTEM EXECUTIVE SUMMARY", Https://www.mscbs.gob.es/estadEstudios/estadisticas/sisInfSanSNS/tablasEstadisticas/InfAnualSNS2019/ExecutiveSummary_2019.pdf.

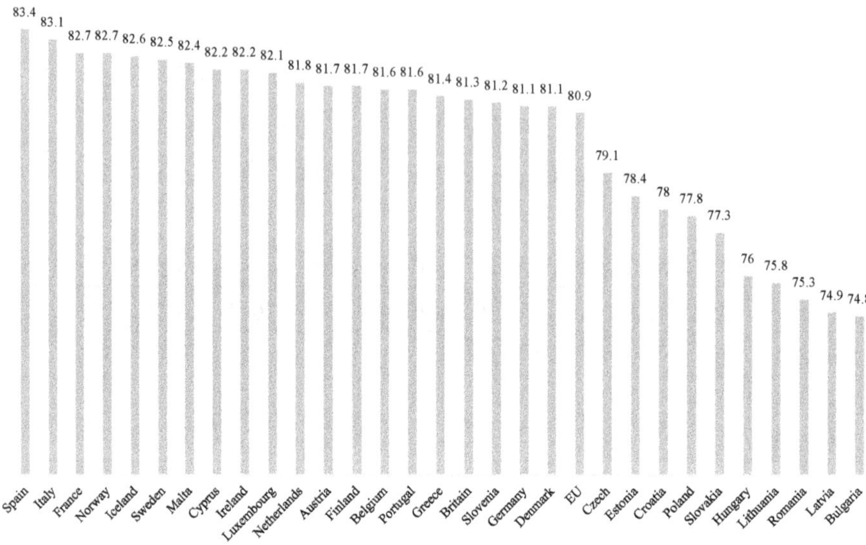

Chart 6-1 Spain, One of the EU Countries with the Highest Per Capita Life Expectancy

Source: OECD, "Life expectancy in Spain is the highest in the EU, State of Health in the EU", Spain Country Health Profile 2019, https://www.oecd.org/publications/spain-country-health-profile-2019-8f834636-en.htm.

2. Primary Distribution and Related Policies

2.1 Characteristics of Employment and Unemployment

Since Spain's accession to the EU, creating employment opportunities, improving the elasticity and flexibility of the labor market, and reducing unemployment rates for women and youth have always been important strategic objectives for its social development. Economic growth is closely related to the prosperity of the employment market. However, due to the late start of economic development and the existence of inherent deficiencies in the economic structure, it has led to insufficient cultivation of new industries, weak high-tech R&D capabilities, slow transformation and upgrading of traditional industries, and difficulties in creating a large number of employment in agricultural areas. Therefore, through various labor market reforms, establishing a flexible employment system that combines full-time and part-time employment to improve employment rates is one of the measures to ensure basic livelihood.

However, the high unemployment rate has long plagued Spanish society and has become one of the largest unstable factors in society. Compared to other European countries, Spain's high unemployment rate is widespread in terms of time and space, with unemployment problems particularly severe in the southern region and among young people. In the 1990s, the European economy experienced stagflation, and Spain's unemployment rate reached a record high of 24 percent in 1994, setting a record for a European country. Due to the severe impact of the European debt crisis, 6 million people in Spain were unemployed in 2014, with higher unemployment rates for young people and foreigners, about three times as much as before the European debt crisis and around one third of the foreigner was unemployed.① In 2019, the eligible age workforce in Spain was 230,271,000, with an actual employment of 1,977,930,000, while 3,247,800 people were unemployed with an unemployment rate of 14.1 percent. Among the employed population, services accounted for 75.5 percent, industry for 14.1 percent, construction for 6.0 percent, and agriculture for 4.0 percent.②

Compared to other EU countries, the COVID-19 has had a significant impact on the Spanish economy, leading to an increase in unemployment rates. The measures taken during the pandemic, such as quarantine, shutdown, and reduction of air transportation, have caused a huge

---

① The Center for Economic and Social Rights (CESR), "Spain: Visualizing Rights: A Snapshot of Relevant Statistics on Spain", January 2015, https: //www.cesr.org/sites/default/files/FACTSHEET_ Spain_2015_web.pdf.

② INE, "Anuario Estadístico de España 2020", https://ine.es/prodyser/pubweb/anuario20/anu20_completo.pdf, p.249.

influence on the tourism industry, hotel and catering industry, commercial trade, cultural industry, etc. In 2020, the total GDP decreased by as much as 11.1 percent.① As of the fourth quarter of 2020, the number of unemployed people in Spain reached 3,719,800 people.② Even after resuming work and production, the impact of the pandemic on vulnerable groups is still difficult to eliminate in the short term. It is estimated that GDP will decline by 14 percent in 2021, and the unemployment rate will grow to 25 percent. In 2022, the unemployment rate will still remain high at around 20 percent, and the youth unemployment rate will be about 40 percent.③ Above consequences will affect Spain's national income and wealth situation.

2.2 **Structure of Tax and Distribution**

Spain's tax system is managed by the central government, autonomous prefectures and local governments at the same time, with different focuses at three levels. Taxes are mainly used to support the construction of public services and facilities. In the process of decentralization, the central government continuously distributes taxes to the autonomous prefectures, dominated by national taxation. Usually, taxes are collected uniformly by the state, and the central government transfers tax funds to the autonomous prefecture governments and local governments through fiscal allocation.

---

① INE, "Quarterly National Accounts of Spain: main aggregates", Fourth quarter of 2020 Preview, https://www.ine. es/en/daco/daco42/daco4214/cntr0420a_ en.pdf.

② INE, Última Nota de prensa, "Encuesta de población activa. EPA. Cuarto trimester 2020", https://www.ine.es/dyngs/INEbase/es/operacion.htm?c=Estadistica_C&cid=1254736176918&menu=ultiDatos&idp=1254735976595.

③ William Chislett, "COVID-19 ups Spain's income inequality", https://blog.realinstitutoelcano.org/en/covid-19-ups-spains-income-inequality/.

An OECD report shows that Spain's tax revenue as a proportion of GDP is moderate, ranking 20th (see Chart 6-2). The Spain's tax system structure in 2019 featured following characteristics: individual income tax, corporate tax, and various value-added taxes were slightly lower than the OECD average, while social security contribution tax, property tax, etc. were higher than the OECD average (see Chart 6-3).

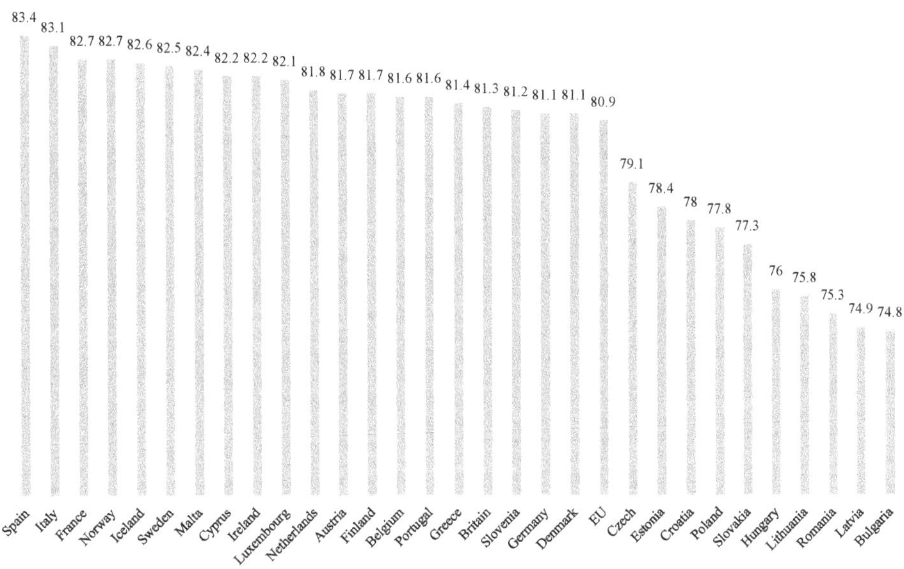

Chart 6-2 The Proportion of Tax to GDP in OECD Countries in 2019 (%)

Source: OECD, "Revenue Statistics 2020-Spain", https://www.oecd.org/tax/revenue-statistics-spain.pdf.

Taxes in Spain can be divided into direct taxes and indirect taxes. Direct taxes include income tax (corporate tax, individual income tax, non-resident income tax) and asset tax (property tax, inheritance and gift tax), while indirect taxes contain value-added tax, fiscal transfer and stamp tax, special tax, import tariff, and insurance premium tax. Autonomous prefecture taxes are generally the portion of national taxes that are distributed to each autonomous prefecture. In 2020, total

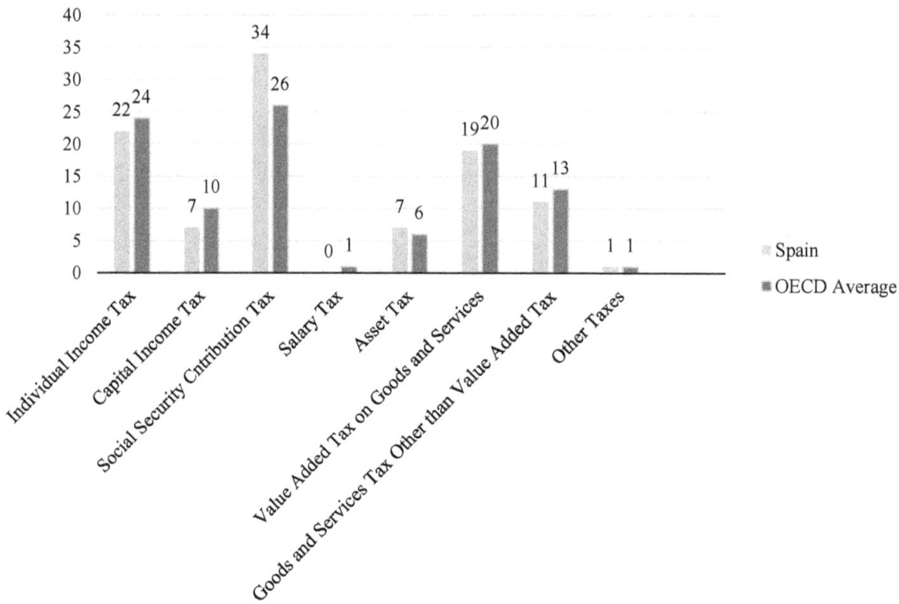

Chart 6-3 Comparison of Taxes in Spain with the OECD Average (2019)

tax revenue in Spain was EUR 194 billion, a year-on-year decrease of 8.8 percent.① Under the existing tax system, corporate tax is uniformly collected by the central government, individual income tax is levied by 50 percent respectively by the central government and autonomous prefecture governments, asset tax, inheritance tax, and other taxes are collected by local governments. Furthermore, País Vasco and Navarra enjoy historical privileges and have their own tax systems.

Corporate tax is a national tax that is uniformly collected by the central government. According to the *Corporate Tax Law* issued in March 2004 and the *Corporate Tax Regulations* issued in July 2004, the taxpayer of corporate tax is an entity established by Spanish law and located in Spain, with actual management premises. Currently, the corporate tax rate in

① Agencia Tributaria, "Tax Revenue in 2020", https://www.agenciatributaria.es/static_files/AEAT/Estudios/Estadisticas/Informes_Estadisticos/Informes_Anuales_de_Recaudacion_Tributaria/Ejercicio_2020/AnnualReport2020.pdf.

Spain is 25 percent. Some autonomous prefectures enjoy tax exemptions or preferential policies, such as Navarra, País Vasco, and Canarias. The tax rate for banks and petroleum companies is 30 percent. Companies in Spanish increase capital investment in research and development, scientific research, reinvestment of capital gains, export promotion, employee training, job creation, and social housing can enjoy tax deductions and other tax incentives.

Individual income tax is a vital tax lever for the central government to regulate the income gap between rich and poor. It has been jointly collected by the state and autonomous prefectures, with a progressive system since 2021. For high-income individuals, the maximum individual income tax rate can reach 52 percent (2012-2014) (see Table 6-3).

Table 6-3 Distribution of Individual Income Tax Rates in Spain (2021)

Starting Point (EUR)	Upper Limit Point (EUR)	National Tax Rate (%)	Tax Rate in Autonomous Regions (%)	Total Tax Rate (%)
0	12450	9.50	9.50	19.00
12451	20200	12.00	12.00	24.00
20201	35200	15.00	15.00	30.00
35201	60000	18.50	18.50	37.00
60001	300000	22.50	22.50	45.00
300001	+	23.50	23.50	47.00

Source: Spain Accountants, "Rates and Allowances", https://www.europeaccountants.com/spain/tax-rates.

Value added tax is divided into three types: standard tax rate of 21 percent, discount tax rate of 10 percent and super discount tax rate of 4 percent, applicable to different goods and services. Standard tax rate applies to all goods and services that do not belong to reduced rate, discount tax rate applies to non basic food, hotel services, passenger transportation, and new residential buildings and super discount tax rate applies to basic food, certain drugs, books and magazines. The goods and services exempt from value-added tax include education, training, sports services, cultural services, insurance, stamps, artists, writers, and composers provided by the state.

The social security contribution accounts for 28-31 percent of the total wage income, and the proportion paid by employees is 4.5-7.5 percent. There is no minimum regulation for contributions, and the maximum rate applies to individuals with an annual wage of EUR 48,850 or above. The statutory lowest annual wage in Spain is EUR 13,300, in the form of 14 months' payment. The minimum wage in Spain is EUR 7.3 per hour, determined by collective bargaining among various industries[①].

Asset tax is a newly added tax in the past decade, first proposed in the 2011 Spanish Fiscal Emergency Rescue Plan to alleviate the debt crisis. At present, this tax is collected by the autonomous prefecture governments and applies to residents and non residents possessing assets in Spain. The minimum amount of asset tax imposed by the state is EUR 0.7 million, but varies between different autonomous regions.

Each autonomous region collects its own inheritance and gift tax. As inheritors, beneficiaries, and recipients of domestic and foreign property, the Spanish is required to pay inheritance and gift tax. Spain's relevant laws also provide for corresponding exemptions and deductions for some inheritance and gifts of property, and there are differences in tax rates among autonomous regions, with the highest tax rate reaching 36.5 percent. The tax rate is calculated based on the following three aspects:

① Spence Clarke Tax Guides, "Tax Tables For Spain 2021", https://www.spenceclarke.com/wp-content/uploads/guides/Tax -tables-for Spain 2021.pdf.

net inheritance amount, the relationship between beneficiaries and donors and the beneficiaries' individual wealth before accepting the inheritance.① This regulation may help prevent the loss of family or individual wealth, as well as prevent criminal activities of money laundering.

Table 6-4 Distribution of National Asset Tax Rates

Tax Rate Scope(EUR)	Accumulated Asset(EUR)	Tax Rate %	Tax Bracket	Accumulated Tax
700000.00	700000.00	0.00%	0	0
167129.45	867129.45	0.20%	334.36	334.26
167123.43	1034252.88	0.30%	835.63	1169.89
334246.87	1368499.75	0.50%	2506.86	3676.75
668499.76	2036999.51	0.90%	8523.36	12200.11
1336999.50	3373999.01	1.30%	25904.35	38104.46
2673999.02	6047998.03	1.70%	71362.33	109466.79
5347998.03	11395996.06	2.10%	183670.27	293137.08
More Assets		3.50%		

Source: SPENCE CLARKE TAX GUIDES, TAX TABLES FOR SPAIN 2021, https://www. spenceclarke.com/wp-content/uploads/guides/Tax-tables-for-Spain-2021.pdf.

Spain also has tax reduction and exemption regulations for special groups. The basic individual exemption for the group under the age of 65 is EUR 5,550, EUR 6,700 for those aged 65 and above and EUR 8,100 for those aged 75 and above. Spanish living with children under the age of 25 can apply for the following additional allowances, EUR 2,400 for one child, EUR 2700 for two children, EUR 4,000 for three children, and EUR 4,500 for four children. The additional allowance for each child under 3 years old is EUR 2,800. If the offspring lives with parents or

① Spence Clarke Tax Guides, "Tax Tables For Spain 2021", https://www.spenceclarke.com/wp-content/uploads/guides/Tax -tables-for Spain 2021.pdf.

grandparents with the total income less than EUR 8000, the group aged 65 and above can apply for a subsidy of EUR 1150 per year, while those aged 75 and above can apply for a subsidy of EUR 2,550. In addition, charitable donations, payment of union dues, and expenses for renovating or renting houses can enjoy tax exemptions.

Capital income tax is the tax on the sale of assets or investment income. Spanish residents are required to pay taxes on assets sold globally. Non residents are required to pay capital gains tax when selling property belonging to Spain. The tax rate for capital gains is 19 percent for the amount above EUR 6,000, 21 percent for the amount between EUR 6,000 and EUR 50,000, 23 percent for the amount between EUR 50,000 and EUR 200,000, and 26 percent for the amount above EUR 200,000. The tax rate for foreign nationals is 19 percent.[①]

According to articles 138, 156, 157, and 158 of the Constitution, the financial funds of the autonomous regions in Spain mainly include six parts, i.e. taxes allocated by the State Administration, central taxes, taxes collected by autonomous regions, special donations from autonomous region, inter-regional compensation transfer funds, and other funds from the national general budget. Due to differences in natural endowments and uneven distribution of industrial structure, there are differences in the development of different regions in Spain. The contribution rate of each autonomous region to the national GDP varies, and there are also significant differences in income. Therefore, through fiscal transfer funds between regions, local governments can determine tax rates and make other institutional arrangements on their own to further narrow regional

---

① Spain Accountants, "Rates and Allowances", https://www.europeaccountants.com/spain/tax-rates.https://www. europeaccountants.com/spain/tax-rates.

differences.

According to the *Spanish Constitution of 1978*, the central government gradually delegated power, especially fiscal power, to various autonomous regions. In this way, the proportion of fiscal revenue controlled by local governments has been increasing yearly. Prior to the defeat of the People's Party in the 2004 general election, the approximate distribution ratio of fiscal revenue between the central government, autonomous regions, and local governments was 40:40:20.[①] In the process of financial decentralization, the social and economic differences between regions have still expanded. Therefore, the central government has established a regional compensation fund mechanism specifically for developed regions to assist underdeveloped areas.

3. Social Distribution and Related Policies

The social security system in Spain is mainly composed of pension, medical care, work-related injury, unemployment, and family insurance, basically achieving full coverage of the Spanish.

The pension security system in Spain has always been a pay-as-you-go system with public management as its core, covering 11 types of employment involving industry, commerce, and service. The insured population has been on the rise. The latest data shows that as of July 2021, the total number of people participating in social security is 19.591728 million people, a year-on-year increase of 4.29 percent, of which 9.073677 million are females with a rise of 4.78

① ZhANG Min: *Economy and Politics in Contemporary Spain*, Social Sciences Academic Press, 2016:89-90.

percent[①].

The pension system in Spain includes three pillars, namely public pension, employer pension, and individual account. Public pension consists of general plans, special plans, and non-contribution plans. The general plan is the core part of the pension system, fully covering employees aged 16 and above who are not covered by other special plans, and implementing a pay-as-you-go-system. Special plans include the special plan for self-employed persons, agricultural workers, domestic servants, fishery workers, coal mine workers and government employees (see Tables 6-5).

In addition, Spain has established a supplementary pension system, mainly including employer pension plans and individual account plans. The employer pension plans are actually composed of a pension plan and a collective insurance plan, accounting for approximately 20 percent of the Spanish workforce. These plans are usually provided by financial institutions and multinational corporations, specific standards of which need to be collectively negotiated by the senior management of the enterprises. Individual account plan is the third pillar of Spain's pension system, covering a population of approximately 8 million, with assets accounting for about 5 percent of GDP. These individual account products are mainly provided by banks and insurance companies, with relatively high management fees.[②]

---

① Ministerio Trabajo y Economía Social, "Interesting fact", https://www.mites.gob.es/en/index.htm.

② Ministerio Trabajo y Economía Social, "Anuario de Estadísticas 2018", https://www.mites.gob.es/es/estadisticas/anuarios/2018/index.htm.

Table 6-5 Categories of Social Security Expenses in 2017 (Unit: EUR million)

Category	Social Insurance Premium	National Finance	Others	In Total	Proportion
General Plan	90789.33	4865.24	990.63	96465.20	67.74%
Self-employed	11933.93	2296.50	136.75	14367.19	9.64%
Fishery	377.41	146.56	5.42	529.39	0.36%
Mine	128.48	11.61	1.40	141.49	0.09%
Work-related Injury and Occupational Diseases	7331.17	100.83	3574.65	11006.66	7.39%
Others			20606.95	20606.87	13.83%
In Total	110560.32	7240.74	25315.80	143116.87	96.05%
Non-contributory		5843.90	45.67	5889.56	3.95%
In Total	110560.32	13084.64	25361.47	149006.43	100.00%

Source: Ministerio Trabajo y Economía Social, "Anuario de Estadísticas 2018", https://www.mites.gob. es/es/estadisticas/anuarios/2018/index.htm.

The modern social security system in Spain was established relatively late, similar to the German model with a lower degree of generosity. Firstly, the social security funds such as retirement pension, unemployment compensation, pensions for orphans, widows and the disabled, etc. are raised from multiple sources, including national finance, social security premiums paid by insured enterprises, and other individual commercial insurance. Secondly, Spain implements a universal free medical insurance system, and Spanish citizens who pay social insurance premiums can enjoy free medical care in public hospitals. Thirdly, foreign citizens who participate in insurance can also enjoy pension and free medical insurance as long as they meet the statutory years of insurance payment and receiving, reflecting greater international inclusiveness. Fourthly, the degree of social security in Spain is linked to the industry, so there are differences in pensions between different industries. Retirement pensions from general pension plans, special pension plans, and supplementary pension plans (employer and individual accounts) vary, and over 65 percent of employees participate in general pension plans.

The medical security system is an important component of social security. The *Spanish Constitution of 1978* and the Article 1.2 of *Basic Law of 2000* stipulate that Spain's medical security rights shall cover all Spaniards residing in Spain, eligible nationals of EU member states that have signed bilateral treaties or agreements with the Spanish government in accordance with *European Union Law* and nationals of Non EU member states who meet the conditions under bilateral agreements. Spanish civil servants and dependents enjoy a special safeguard system (i.e., MUFACE, ISFAS, and MUGEJU) through civil military or judicial mutual assistance funds. Since 1999, medical expenses have no longer relied on social insurance contributions, but mainly come from general national taxes, which are collected and paid by the central government in a centralized manner, and are allocated to 17 autonomous regions based on the number of individuals, operated and managed by each autonomous region.

Other social security programs include unemployment insurance, work-related injury insurance and family allowance. Among them, the Unemployment insurance is jointly contributed by employers and employees. Meanwhile, the government provides irregular financial subsidies, covering 11 occupational categories including industrial, commercial, and service servants and employees from public sector. The work-related injury insurance covers all employees, including employees from public sector, self-employed individuals, and agricultural workers who voluntarily pay for it, exclusive of service servants. There are special plans for some types of work. The family allowance is a kind of mean test-based subsidy system that comprehensively covers all families with children legally living in Spain. Among them, families who give birth or adopt two or more children are exempted from the mean test.

4. The Third Distribution

The third distribution of social wealth is reflected in two aspects. Firstly, develop social welfare organizations and individual donations to gradually form a conscious concept of everyone's participation and willingness to contribute to society. Secondly, assist more countries in the form of development cooperation. The establishment of the concept of everyone participating in social public welfare voluntarily or voluntarily in an organized manner, assisting vulnerable and disadvantaged groups as well as the continuous growth of the the number of institutions and organizations voluntarily participating in social public welfare activities in various municipalities are the mass foundation and development concepts for common prosperity.

Table 6-6 Number of Non-profit Social Groups at All Levels in Spain (2007-2018)

Year	Number of Non-Governmental Organizations for Public Welfare	Year	Number of Non-Governmental Organizations for Public Welfare
2006	—	2013	16139
2007	3998	2014	16044
2008	7557	2015	15145
2009	10096	2016	16144
2010	10994	2017	16956
2011	10933	2018	15865
2012	10901		

Source: https://www.plataformaong.org/ARCHIVO/documentos/biblioteca/1594621854_lpec.2006.2018.pdf (Non-Governmental Organizations).

Table 6-7 Number of Volunteers in Voluntary Services of Public Welfare Organizations

Year	Number of Volunteers	Year	Number of Volunteers
2006	282574	2013	384023
2007	274426	2014	384265
2008	331204	2015	390772
2009	349393	2016	391038
2010	353008	2017	382178
2011	364326	2018	410994
2012	366844		

Spain's per capita annual income and average household income have not reached the highest level of wealth among EU countries, with an average household income of EUR 30,690 in 2019[①]. But Spanish are enthusiastic about public welfare, and the number of people participating in social donations and helping vulnerable or disadvantaged groups continues to grow every year. 95 percent of these public welfare social organizations are local, 3 percent of which are provincial, and only 2 percent of which carry out public welfare activities at the level of autonomous regions. The number of people attending volunteer services continued to increase from 2006 to 2018, with 282,574 in 2007 and 410,994 in 2018.

The Spanish are enthusiastic about public welfare and charitable activities, providing various types of helps and assistance services to the elderly, weak, sick, disabled, or groups facing difficulties in daily life and work through donations or voluntary social services. The total amount of various donations received by public welfare organizations in 2018 was EUR 363.4 billion (including revenue received by blind lottery

① INE, "Living Conditions Survey (LCS), Year 2019", https://ine.es/en/prensa/ecv_2020_en.pdf.

charity organizations), of which private donations accounted for 16 percent, totaling EUR 582 million. Services and selling goods provided by public welfare organizations accounted for 67 percent, while public donations from government departments account for 17 percent. In 2019, the total number of donations contributed by Spain to various charitable organizations was 21.8 million, involving cancer treatment, development assistance to the third world, child assistance, disaster relief, humanitarian assistance, education, medical care, etc.

Table 6-8 Annual Income (Including Donations) o fNon-profit Social Organizations (2006-2018)

Unit: EUR

Year	Donation Amount	Year	Donation Amount
2006	360826035.41	2013	3246264244.75
2007	3726429142.14	2014	3271042667.74
2008	3593507145.44	2015	2939393124.91
2009	3469164741.39	2016	3155426919.07
2010	3479420741.66	2017	3310082840.80
2011	3473528422.09	2018	3634987855.32
2012	3331786264.36		

Despite the severe impact of the COVID-19 in recent years, charitable donations from all walks of life in Spain have remained stable.① On January 13, 2021, the 2020 Annual Report of the Asociación Española de Fundraising (AEFr) showed that 37 percent of Spanish citizens had donated to charity organizations in 2020, of which 13 percent were related to the fight against the COVID-19. In 2020, 15 million people donated

① Asociación Española de Fundraising, "Donations remain steady in Spain despite coronavirus", January 13, 2021, https://efa-net.eu/news/donations-remain-steady-in-spain-despite-coronavirus.

to non-profit organizations, 24 percent of which made regular donations.

The participation of Spanish in voluntary services and social donations has become an essential component of citizens' involvement in social affairs. The income of various public welfare organizations is returned to society, helping those in urgent need, forming a social morality and public welfare concept of mutual assistance, which contributes to common prosperity and development of society. Spain's per capita GDP can only be considered moderate, but its wealth distribution is relatively average.

European Union*

1. Basic Information

The members of the European Union (EU) are mostly developed industrial countries. Due to the progress of European integration and the continuous development of the governance system at the EU level, the EU and member states share authority in the economic and social fields. However, the distribution of authority between the EU and member states varies in different fields. Overall, the policy-making authority in the economic field has been transferred to a considerable proportion at the EU level, while member states still retain the leading authority in social policy-making. This is determined by the gradual process of European integration. With the free flow of factors and the continuous establishment of a unified internal market, intensified competition and the improvement of market efficiency, the polarization between member countries and regions aggravates, leading to the Matthew effect, which requires relevant social policies to narrow the gap between member countries and regions. The European Community introduced regional or structural policies at the union level as early as its establishment to support underdeveloped regions in Italy and narrow regional disparities.

---

* Author: DING Chun&CHEN Tenghan, Fudan University.

Later, this policy was extended to countries in southern Europe as well as Central and Eastern Europe.

From the perspective of the European Union (European Community), social policies are mostly instructive. *The Treaty of Rome* only specified principles on health protection conditions in the workplace. Since then, although the EU has introduced a series of guiding principles in social fields such as employment and promoted voluntary convergence among member states through an "open coordination" mechanism, the EU has not obtained the transfer of power and authority of member states in the social field, and different from economic integration, social convergence was known as "harmony" with the main policy tool controlled by member states. However, the EU must make a difference in narrowing the gap between member states and regions and achieving common prosperity to maintain the attractiveness of integration to the public.

The overall economic and social development of EU member states is among the top in the world. Table 7-1 shows the Human Development Index (HDI), Inequality-adjusted Human Development Index (IHDI)[①], and Life Expectancy of 28 EU countries (including Britain) from UNDP Human Development Reports for Year 2011, 2016 and 2020.

---

① IHDI combines the average achievements of a country in health, education, and income with the distribution of these achievements among the country's population, and calculate the average value of each dimension based on its degree of inequality by discounting. Therefore, IHDI has distribution sensitivity to the average level of human development. Two countries with different achievement distributions can have the same average Human Development Index. In the case of complete equality, IHDI is equal to the HDI, but lower than the HDI when inequality intensifies. The difference between IHDI and HDI is the cost of unequal human development, also known as the overall loss of inequality to human development.

Table 7-1 HDI, IHDI and Life Expectancy of 28 EU countries (including Britain) from 2010-2019

	Human Development Index (HDI)			Inequality-adjusted Human Development Index (IHDI)			Life Expectancy
	2019	2015	2010	2019	2015	2010	2019
France	0.901	0.888	0.884	0.820	0.811	0.798	82.7
Germany	0.947	0.916	0.905	0.869	0.853	0.853	81.3
Italy	0.892	0.873	0.874	0.783	0.773	0.773	83.5
Netherlands	0.944	0.922	0.910	0.878	0.861	0.842	82.3
Belgium	0.931	0.922	0.886	0.859	0.845	0.833	81.6
Luxembourg	0.916	0.892	0.867	0.826	0.822	0.817	82.3
Denmark	0.940	0.923	0.895	0.883	0.856	0.858	80.9
Croatia	0.851	0.818	0.796	0.783	0.743	0.691	78.5
Greece	0.888	0.865	0.861	0.791	0.758	0.777	82.2
Spain	0.904	0.876	0.878	0.783	0.775	0.787	83.6
Portugal	0.864	0.830	0.809	0.761	0.744	0.730	82.1
Austria	0.922	0.890	0.885	0.857	0.820	0.836	81.5
Sweden	0.945	0.907	0.904	0.882	0.846	0.849	82.8
Finland	0.938	0.883	0.882	0.888	0.834	0.848	81.9
Cyprus	0.887	0.850	0.840	0.805	0.758	0.757	81.0
Ireland	0.955	0.916	0.908	0.885	0.836	0.819	82.3
Hungary	0.854	0.828	0.816	0.791	0.769	0.759	76.9
Czech	0.900	0.870	0.865	0.860	0.823	0.818	79.4
Estonia	0.892	0.861	0.835	0.829	0.782	0.768	82.3
Latvia	0.866	0.819	0.805	0.783	0.730	0.733	75.3
Lithuania	0.882	0.839	0.810	0.791	0.754	0.736	75.9
Poland	0.880	0.843	0.813	0.813	0.760	0.750	78.7
Slovakia	0.860	0.844	0.834	0.807	0.791	0.775	77.5
Slovenia	0.917	0.880	0.884	0.875	0.829	0.828	81.3
Bulgaria	0.816	0.794	0.771	0.721	0.722	0.699	75.0
Iceland	0.940	0.899	0.898	0.894	0.846	0.839	83.0
Britain	0.932	0.907	0.863	0.856	0.829	0.824	81.3
Malta	0.895	0.839	0.853	0.823	0.767	N/A	82.5
EU Average (Including Britain)	0.903	0.871	0.858	0.829	0.799	0.792	80.6
EU28 Standard Deviation	0.036	0.026	0.039	0.046	0.043	0.049	2.526

continued

	Human Development Index (HDI)			Inequality-adjusted Human Development Index (IHDI)			Life Expectancy
World Average	0.737	0.724	0.699	0.587	0.557	0.525	71.8

Source: Compiled and formulated based on the data of UNDP "Human Development Report" for three years of 2011, 2016 and 2020.

From Table 7-1, it can be seen that firstly, the overall HDI and IHDI of the EU have improved from 2010 to 2019, indicating that the EU has made continuous progress in human development from an overall perspective. Secondly, from the standard deviation of the two major indicators between 28 EU countries, it shows the degree of regional difference is decreasing from 2010 to 2015. However, from 2015 to 2019, the degree of regional difference within the EU did not improve or even intensified. Thirdly, the HDI and IHDI of 28 EU countries belong to high indicator countries globally, but within the EU, there is a clear advantage in Western Europe and Nordic member countries over other regions, with the disadvantage of Central and Southern Europe being particularly evident.

Table 7-2 indicates the per capita GNI of the European Union from 2015 to 2019, the Gini Coefficient of 2020, and the Proportion of Urban Population of 2019 from the World Bank.

Table 7-2 Basic Economic Development Index of 28 EU Countries (including Britain) (2015-2019)

	Gini Coefficient * 100	Proportion of Urban Population	Per Capita GNI, Calculated Based on 2020 PPP in USD				
	2020	2019	2015	2016	2017	2018	2019
France	32.55	74.7	41100	39070	38270	41080	42290
Germany	32.33	80.7	45750	44250	43650	47140	48550
Italy	35.92	77.4	32980	31950	31340	33810	34830

continued

	Gini Coefficient * 100	Proportion of Urban Population	Per Capita GNI, Calculated Based on 2020 PPP in USD				
Netherlands	28.31	70.7	49810	46900	47110	51250	53010
Belgium	27.57	91.9	45540	43360	42460	46060	47960
Denmark	28.50	91.2	60510	58040	56690	61340	64000
Croatia	29.80	88.0	12970	12380	12680	14080	14990
Greece	36.47	57.2	20140	18590	17940	19050	19690
Spain	36.69	79.4	28430	27530	27070	29320	30330
Portugal	34.9	80.6	20440	19930	20040	22030	23150
Austria	30.44	65.8	47450	46200	45030	49030	51390
Sweden	30.00	58.5	58420	54360	53030	55640	56090
Finland	26.89	87.7	47150	45500	47790	48230	49960
Cyprus	33.50	85.4	25980	24710	24710	26990	27930
Ireland	30.77	66.8	50390	51860	53750	60450	64740
Hungary	29.76	63.4	13250	13100	13190	15010	16530
Czech	25.43	73.9	18370	17670	18310	20520	21930
Estonia	32.18	69.1	18680	18410	18820	21320	23230
Latvia	33.71	68.2	15100	14780	14830	16520	17730
Lithuania	36.98	67.9	15180	14890	15270	17440	19000
Poland	30.19	60.0	13310	12720	12730	14150	15350
Slovakia	25.77	53.7	17670	16790	16600	18300	19200
Slovenia	24.84	54.8	22250	21770	22120	24580	25910
Bulgaria	37.15	75.3	7450	7430	7640	8560	9570
Iceland	28.41	93.9	49940	54910	60230	67760	72930
Britain	33.12	83.7	44340	42940	41280	41740	42130
Malta	29.74	94.7	25230	23590	24140	27090	28340
Luxembourg	35.11	98.0	72470	68670	66380	70840	N/A
EU Average (Including Britain)	31.18	74.61	33399.3	32170.7	31812.6	34495	34795.9

Source: Formulated based on data from the World Bank Databank.

Note: The missing GNI data for Luxembourg in 2019 is not included in the table.

Data in Table 7-2 shows firstly, except for Nordic countries, the Gini Coefficient of most EU countries exceeds the overall average, indicating that the wealth gap in Nordic countries is relatively small, and there is improvement potential in other countries (although the overall Gini Coefficient of the EU is far beyond the global average). Secondly, the per capita GNI in most member countries with a low proportion of urban population is also slightly lower than the EU average, excluding France, the Netherlands, Sweden, Austria, and Ireland, the correlation of which needs to be verified. Thirdly, the per capita GNI of Western Europe and Northern Europe is significantly higher than that of Southern Europe and Central and Eastern Europe.

Table 7-3 demonstrates the education expectancy for EU countries in 2020, the number of hospital beds per 1,000 inhabitants in 2017 and the proportion of health expenditure to government fiscal expenditure in 2018 from the World Bank.

Table 7-3 Key Public Service Data in the EU

	Education Expectancy (in 2020, Unit: Years)	Number of Hospital Beds Per 1,000 Inhabitants (in 2017, Unit: Beds)	Proportion of Health Expenditure to Government Fiscal Expenditure (in 2018, Unit: %)
France	15.6	6.0	14.8
Germany	17.0	8.0	20.0
Italy	16.1	3.2	13.2
Netherlands	18.5	3.3	15.4
Belgium	19.8	5.7	15.0
Luxembourg	14.3	4.7	10.7
Denmark	18.9	2.6	16.6
Croatia	15.2	5.5	12.3
Greece	17.9	4.2	8.5
Spain	17.6	3.0	15.2

continued

	Education Expectancy (in 2020, Unit: Years)	Number of Hospital Beds Per 1,000 Inhabitants (in 2017, Unit: Beds)	Proportion of Health Expenditure to Government Fiscal Expenditure (in 2018, Unit: %)
Portugal	16.5	3.4	13.4
Austria	16.1	7.4	15.5
Sweden	19.5	2.2	18.6
Finland	19.4	3.3	13.3
Cyprus	15.2	3.4	6.6
Ireland	18.7	3.0	20.2
Hungary	15.2	7.0	9.9
Czech	18.7	6.6	15.5
Estonia	15.2	4.7	12.5
Latvia	16.2	5.6	9.6
Lithuania	16.6	6.6	12.7
Poland	16.3	6.6	10.8
Slovakia	14.5	5.8	12.7
Slovenia	17.6	4.5	13.8
Bulgaria	15.5	7.5	11.6
Iceland	19.1	3.1	16.6
Britain	17.5	2.5	19.2
Malta	16.1	4.5	15.6
EU Average (Including Britain)	16.9	5.4	13.9
World Average	12.7	2.9	N/A

Source: Formulated based on data from the World Bank Databank.

Note: Missing data on the proportion of global average health data to government expenditure is not included in the table.

From Table 7-3, it is clarified that firstly, the education expectancy of 28 EU countries exceeds the global average, basically around 16 years. Secondly, except for a few countries (mainly Central and Eastern European countries), the difference in the number of hospital beds per 1,000 inhabitants in 28 EU countries is relatively small compared to the global average, while the difference in the number of hospital beds per 1,000 inhabitants within the EU is basically consistent with the performance of EU countries during COVID-19. Thirdly, among EU member states, Western European countries have a higher proportion of health expenditure to their government fiscal expenditure compared to other EU member states, and the proportion in the vast majority of member states (excluding Greece, Cyprus, Hungary, and Latvia) is over 10 percent.

2. Primary Distribution: Labor and Employment

To promote common prosperity, the EU has three main policy measures on primary distribution, i.e., Active Labor Market Policies (ALMPs), Public Employment Services (PES) and Employment Protection Legislation with the aim of balancing the primary distribution process through labor and employment policies. Among them, ALMPs and PES are policy framework requirement (Soft Laws) such as mandatory documents and resolutions promoting coordinated action among member states through the role of mechanism networks, rather than serving as tools for monitoring, evaluation, rewards and punishments. On the contrary, the Employment Protection Legislation refers to mandatory policy framework requirements (Hard Laws), requiring member states to meet the minimum requirements in relevant indicators.

2.1 Active Labor Market Policies

The main goal of ALMPs is to increase job opportunities for job seekers and improve the balance between labor supply and demand, thereby promoting employment and GDP growth, reducing unemployment and welfare dependence. The scope of ALMPs includes training provided by institutions and workplaces, indirect employment incentives (job retention, job sharing, recruitment incentives), establishing sheltered and supported employment and providing direct employment opportunities and entrepreneurial incentives. It has both advantages and disadvantages. From the existing evaluations of different ALMPs projects, it can be seen that the effectiveness of "recruitment incentives" is relatively complex as it's not easy to choose appropriate incentive methods, while the direct provision of employment by the public sector is considered the least efficient and ALMPs, aiming at retaining employment, such as short-term employment plans, should only be applied in the short term and during periods of severe recession. Generally speaking, there is a delay between the implementation of ALMPs and their impact on the labor market. Therefore, it is necessary to design ahead, but how to adopt activation methods in an economically declining society and accurately balance the priority between "training" and "employment" in a limited market are challenges. Finally, there is the issue of evaluation methods. Monitoring and evaluation are crucial for improving efficiency, but ALMPs are usually not regarded as a rule for monitoring and evaluation.

2.2 Public Employment Services

PES is the main labor market institution directly responsible to the government, aimed at promoting job seekers' involvement in the labor market and paying benefits to the unemployed in some cases. It integrates "positive" measures (training, employment incentives, employment and rehabilitation support, direct employment creation and start-up incentives) and "negative" measures (unemployment security, income maintenance, early retirement, etc.) to provide more reasonable and efficient employment services. On June 18, 2014, the *Decision on Strengthening PES Cooperation* came into effect, establishing a formal PES network covering the whole of Europe. By comparing the effectiveness of various services provided by countries, the network is committed to identifying effective measures and learning from each other to strengthen the capabilities, effectiveness, and efficiency of PES. At present, the representative measures of EU PES include implementing a PES registration system in labor supply, providing alternative support to improve the labor market from the perspective of balancing supply and demand.

2.3 Employment Protection Legislation

Employment Protection Legislation includes rules and procedures for hiring or dismissing employees, mainly involving the legality of probationary periods, statutory notice periods and severance payment (compensation for employees who terminate contracts in advance), sanctions for unfair dismissal, conditions for the use of temporary or fixed-term contracts. The policy levers of Employment Protection Legislation include solving the problem of labor market segmentation by narrowing the gap between employment protection legislation for permanent contracts and temporary contracts, increasing the flexibility of specific types of contracts without modifying permanent contracts or collective dismissal rules, so that employees have sufficient protection to face labor market risks, seeking support from other social partners to ensure the sustainability of legislative reform, choosing appropriate sequence and timing of reforms as weakening Employment Protection Legislation during economic downturns may result in severer employment destruction. The current legislative reforms in the EU on employment protection strengthen restrictions on fixed-term contracts, especially for temporary employees, increase the term of a fixed-term contract and the possibility of extending the term. For example, Belgium has passed the *Single Identity Law*, which basically coordinates the notice period between blue and white collar workers and redefines the definition of unfair dismissal. France has clarified the specific circumstances in which individuals can be dismissed for economic reasons, providing greater flexibility for companies to set working conditions. Italy has carried out comprehensive labor market reforms in the form of the *Employment Act*, revised the dismissal rules for open-ended contracts, simplified non-standard forms of contracts, and increased flexibility within the company. Lithuania has shortened the notice period and reduced severance payment through the amendment of its labor law, thereby reducing the cost of individual dismissal and introducing new types of contracts. The Netherlands has imposed restrictions on severance payment for unfair dismissals and provided clearer regulations on the means of termination, while shortening the maximum term of temporary contracts. Poland has imposed restrictions on the number and maximum duration of continuous fixed-term labor contracts.

3. Social Redistribution

3.1 Transfer, Renewing, and Convergence of Social Security Systems

The core of social redistribution is the transfer of fiscal payments represented by social security, while the initiative for most fiscal transfers still lies with the governments of member states. Except for a few public finance areas where have dominant policies authority, the EU mainly sets goals and non mandatory guidance frameworks for member states.

Although the EU has not obtained specific social authority, it has made efforts to promote the effectiveness of the social security system for the transfer and renewing of citizens within the EU through soft measures such as the "open coordination mechanism", allowing for free population movement, and providing national treatment for cross-border personnel of member states, which has promoted the universality and convergence of the social security within the EU. For example, the EU coordinates the transfer and renewing for the elderly care security system of citizens in cross-border member countries and launches domestic universal medical cards.

3.2 Family Policies

Unlike other countries, the EU's unique concept and focus on social redistribution in terms of common prosperity is the EU family policies, which typically aims to implement income redistribution, encourage childbirth, and promote gender equality. As for specific content, the EU family policies mainly include three following aspects. First is child care recommendation, which promotes member states to take effective measures to encourage males and females to coordinate their responsibilities of occupation, family, and education. Second is maternal protection directive, aiming to improve the safety and health status of pregnant workers. Third is family leave directive, which specifies the minimum mandatory implementation standards. The family leave directive is applicable to both male and female and emphasizes the individualized leave rights, which has progressive ideological significance and attaches the EU the authority to integrate the minimum degree of family leave in various countries.

From the perspective of policy intensity, family policies appear in the form of directives, belonging to the soft law at the EU level without a unified

EU standard. However, it also sets minimum requirements for member states and urges their implementation. For example, in February 1998, the European Commission issued a report on the implementation of child care recommendations. In March 1999, a report on the implementation of the maternal protection directive was issued. In addition, a report on the implementation of the family leave directive was released in June 2003.

The EU has also updated policies according to the needs of the situation. For example, in December 1997, a part-time work directive was issued, proposing the necessity of establishing measures conducive to the "coordination of family and employment". In January 1999, a fixed condition work directive was issued, proposing to "improve the quality of labors' life" and "promote equal opportunities for male and female". In July 2006, a directive was released to implement the principle of equal opportunities and equal treatment for males and females in employment and occupation, aiming to simplify, modernize, and integrate existing legislation on equal treatment for males and females. Meanwhile, the directive explicitly prohibited any gender discrimination, and proposed the implementation of paternity leave and adoption leave. In October 2008, a maternity leave recommendation was issued, extending the minimum duration of maternity leave and requiring mandatory maternity leave to ensure labors' right to return to work and request flexible working hours. In March 2010, a directive was released to implement the revised framework agreement for family leave, which stipulated the extension of family leave duration, recognized the right to return to work after family leave, and ensured greater protection for those on leave.

3.3 EU's Social Assistance Policies

In addition to social security and family policies, the EU's third largest policy driver for common prosperity in social redistribution is social assistance policies (see Table 7-4). The EU has implemented the National Action Plans on Social Inclusion to establish a more integrated society and has initiated to establish an indicator system for measuring poverty. A typical case is as follows.

Table 7-4 Social Assistance Policies in Some EU Member States

Belgium	mainly focused on recent policy measures: the approach of "proactive welfare state"; integrated key elements of the labor market
Denmark	developed an integrated labor market in the best possible way to achieve social integration; provided financial support; improves the living conditions of vulnerable groups
Germany	published the first poverty and health policy report in April 2001; implemented policies of "proactive welfare state"; avoided falling into the poverty trap
Greece	NAP/incl (National Action Plans on Social Inclusion) included a large number of policy measures; three responses; unemployment and transfer payments under the new economic conditions, transmission of social policies, and processing of information
Spain	reformed employment policies; the multidimensional nature of social exclusion made it difficult for the government to implement a consistent social integration policy
France	implemented the NAP/incl method since 1998; developed two strategies, namely the acquisition of employment and the application of social rights
Ireland	formulated the National Anti-Poverty Strategy, re-examined this Strategy after the implementation of NAP/incl
Italy	established the NAP/incl based on the National Social Plan implemented in 2001; planed a new budget for social protection expenditures; implemented a new plan for policy integration based on partnerships and multi departmental collaboration
Luxembourg	an active social state; provided sufficient income for everyone; developed social integration in work to prevent potential poverty
Netherlands	implemented policies based on employment and income security to ensure the minimum wage

continued

Austria	integrated economic, employment, and welfare policies; implemented NAP/incl based on existing policies
Portugal	NAP/incl reduced other quantitative targets to eliminate child poverty and general poverty
Finland	preserved the basic framework of the social security system while prioritizing employment
Sweden	gave full play to the role of flexible employment in poverty alleviation; In 2004, NAP/incl required an increase in employment rates and an end to dependence on social assistance
Britain	implemented long term strategy; promised to increase employment to eliminate poverty, and committed to eliminating child poverty within 20 years

Over the past 20 years, the minimum income protection in the social assistance systems of EU countries has shown a continuous downward trend. This trend has been partially affected by the economic crisis, and countries with higher public debt in GDP show a decrease in the adequacy of social assistance income. Some related services in social assistance are based on means test, while others are inclusive. Affected by the European economic crisis, welfare expenditure has been reduced, thus some countries have begun to re-examine the role of such social assistance. In 2014, EU countries accounted for 11 percent of the total social expenditure through means test. There are significant differences in welfare payments among member countries based on means test, with lower proportion countries represented by Estonia, Latvia, Sweden, and the Czech Republic accounting for less than 3 percent, and higher proportion countries such as Ireland and Denmark accounting for more than 30 percent. The proportion of welfare expenditure based on means test also varies among different service sectors, with a smaller proportion in health care and elderly dependant welfare, while a larger proportion in the fields of social exclusion and social housing, the expenditure of which is basically aimed at low-income and low asset groups.

4. The Third Distribution

4.1 Public Charitable Causes

Based on social donations, Charity collects public resources for public welfare. It is a special approach of benefits distribution and resources allocation, playing an indispensable role in promoting common prosperity. The EU is unable to develop mandatory measures for public charitable causes, and there's no explicit soft laws. Despite the European Parliament's repeated calls for "donations", no relevant policy directives have been issued. Still, several models of public charitable policies within the EU have been spontaneously formed with member states as the main body.

From Espin Anderson's classification of three worlds of welfare capitalism, the member states of the EU have representatives of liberal welfare systems, such as Britain. There are also representatives of conservative welfare systems, such as Germany and France and representatives of social democracy, such as Sweden. The representative countries of these three welfare systems also have distinct characteristics in the field of charity. These three different models of charitable regulatory systems are rooted in the cultural, economic, political, social, and legal environments of countries. Different institutional concepts result in different systems, which jointly form a normative network within the EU.

4.2 Corporate Social Responsibility

The European Commission first proposed corporate social responsibility in the 2001 EU Green Paper on Corporate Social Responsibility, titled

"Promoting a European Framework for Corporate Social Responsibility", which claimed that corporations integrate social and environmental issues into their operations and interactions with stakeholders voluntarily. In October 2011, the EU adopted the *EU Strategy 2011-2014 for Corporate Social Responsibility*. The definition of corporate social responsibility has changed, which is more defined as policies and regulatory measures. Europe has also decided to integrate corporate social responsibility into its foreign policy. In June 2012, a seminar on "Better Initiating Corporate Social Responsibility among Small and Medium Enterprises" was held in Berlin, Germany, in support of the "EU Strategy 2020" proposed in 2010, which regards social responsibility as a driving force for corporations to improve market competitiveness and develop innovative economies rather than the pressure on them. In December 2014, the EU's *Revised Directive on the Disclosure of Nonfinancial and Diversity Information by Certain Large Companies and Groups* officially came into effect, claiming qualified companies to disclose non-financial information on policies and effects taken in social, environmental, human rights, employee, anti-corruption, and other aspects annually, and requiring EU member states to convert this directive into domestic law by the end of 2016. Since its proposal in 2001, the concept of promoting social and economic development through corporate social responsibility has been continuously increasing in the EU's policy intensity, developing from simple policy recommendations to current soft laws, and there might even be a trend towards hard laws in the future.

5. EU's Regional Policies and Fiscal Transfers for Common Prosperity

The most direct measures at the EU level aimed at narrowing the wealth gap and alleviating poverty among regions and individuals are policy-based fiscal transfer payment measures such as Regional Policies, European Financial Stability Facility and European Union Solidarity Fund.

5.1 EU's Regional Policies

Before the regional policy reform in 1988, the European Community's regional policies roughly consisted of three main parts. First is to provide extensive financial assistance to underdeveloped areas, second is to ensure that the policies and measures of the Community take into account regional issues, and third is to assist member countries in implementing their respective regional policies. From an economic perspective, regional policies during this period were mainly reflected in the use of regional development funds, with actual effects being difficult to measure. The main reason was that the use of regional policy funds at the Community level was often integrated with the regional policies of member countries. In February 1988, member states unanimously decided to carry out fundamental reforms in regional policies. After this reform, the position of regional policies in the entire policy system of the EU has been increasingly strengthened. From the perspective of fiscal budget, regional policies have become the second largest policy after the Common Agricultural Policy. Subsequent revisions were made based on this foundation. After undergoing four regulatory reforms in 1993, 1999, 2003, and 2007, the EU ultimately formed a regional policy framework based on the 2007 Reform. The main starting point for formulating policy principles is to improve the efficiency of policy implementation, expand policy participation, and prevent the implementation of policy tools from bringing adverse effects such as moral hazard and investment crowding out effect. From the perspective of policy objectives, the current EU regional policies have set three major goals, i.e., convergence, competitiveness & employment, and regional cooperation. The two most important tools in the current public fiscal transfer implemented by the EU to balance regional development are European Financial Stability Facility (EFSF) and European Union Solidarity Fund (EUSF).

5.2 European Financial Stability Facility(EFSF)

The European Financial Stability Facility is a brand new industrial policy tool pioneered by the EU, consisting of the European Social Fund (ESF), the European Regional Development Fund (ERDF), the European Agricultural Guidance and Guarantee Fund (EAGGF), and the Financial Instrument for Fisheries Guidance (FIFG). ESF mainly provides vocational training and employment assistance to address the employment issues of youth and women. ERDF is the largest of the four funds, accounting for approximately half of the total EFSF. Its main purpose is to support the development of small and medium-sized enterprises in underdeveloped areas, promote investment, and improve infrastructure. EAGGF mainly provides financial support for the adoption of new agricultural technologies, improvement of agricultural industrial structure, and development of non-agricultural industries in rural areas. FIFG is established to assist fishermen in coastal areas with declining fishery production. The funds of EFSF are paid by EU member states according to a certain proportion of their GDP and included in the EU's fiscal budget, playing a significant role in the stability of the EU economy and society. After continuous improvement, it has successfully supported the development and structural adjustment of economically underdeveloped and industrial recession areas in the EU.

On July 17, 2003, the EU published a report summarizing EFSF's "Six Year Plan" from 1994 to 1999, claiming the EU has achieved significant results in utilizing EFSF, promoting economic growth, employment, and sustainable development in underdeveloped areas within the EU. According to statistics, from 1994 to 1999, the EU has invested EUR 1,140 in EFSF to the "Target One" region, accounting for two-thirds of the total amount of EFSF. From the actual effect of implementing EFSF, the regional imbalance of member countries has been improved to a certain extent, the infrastructure construction of recipient countries has been strengthened, the health and education industries of recipient countries have further developed, and there has been greater progress in protecting and improving the environment, the cultural and educational level and basic qualities of residents in recipient countries have been improved to a certain extent and the scope of employment has been expanded thus nurtured the labor market of recipient countries. Meanwhile, the most underdeveloped region in the EU has received approximately EUR 210 billion in public and private investment, creating 800,000 job opportunities, constructing 4,100 kilometers of highways and 320,000 kilometers of ordinary roads, with 21000 small and medium-sized enterprises and 8 million people being assisted. During this period, the per capita national income growth rates of Greece, Portugal, and Spain receiving regional development assistance were at least 1 percentage point higher than the EU average. The economic growth rates of Portugal and Germany's "First-Class Target Areas" reached 4.7 percent and 4 percent respectively. On average, for every EUR 1 of EFSF invested in this type of region, it increases the local GDP by EUR 1.33. In 1999, EFSF increased the per capita GDP of Greece, Ireland, and Portugal by nearly 10 percent, while 4 percent in Spain. Taking Ireland as an example, its per capita GDP was only 64 percent of the European Community average in 1983, and by 1995 it was close to 90 percent of the EU average. In 2000, its per capita income was USD 22,660, which was 115.2 percent of the EU average, already approaching Britain, is known as the "Celtic Tiger" and has successfully achieved economic boom, becoming a role model of rapid development benefiting from EFSF. The EFSF has indeed achieved significant results in narrowing regional disparities, promoting employment and economic growth in underdeveloped areas. More importantly, with the tangible help of EFSF, the people in the recipient regions and newly joined countries have greatly enhanced their sense of identification with European integration and "European identity", laying the ideological foundation for the further expansion and deepening reform of the EU in the future. Although the EFSF has achieved significant results in narrowing the gap between member states, it has minimal effect in narrowing the gap between internal regions within member states, as well as between central and peripheral regions of the EU.

5.3 European Union Solidarity Fund(EUSF)

In 1991, considering the impact of the operation of the European Economic and Monetary Union (EMU) on widening the wealth gap, the European Council established the EUSF at the request of the poorest four member countries, Spain, Portugal, Ireland, and Greece, aiming to compensate these four member countries for the negative polarization of EMU and provide financial support for environmental projects and cross European projects such as transportation, energy communication network to help them catch up with developed member states. The operation of the EUSF follows the regulations of the Council, which came into effect on May 26, 1994 and was revised in 1999. The allocation of indicators for the EUSF is based on precise and objective criteria, mainly including population, land area, and per capita GDP. The support provided by the EUSF is tied to conditions, such as requesting recipient countries to implement a plan to promote economic convergence. Member states choose and implement projects on their own, but the applied projects must relate to transportation infrastructure or environmental protection infrastructure under the supervision of the European Commission. The requirements for the EUSF to assist member countries include, in addition to the conditions for per capita GNP, that the recipient country should not have excessive national debt and budget deficits. If the recipient country has an excessive fiscal public deficit, the Council can terminate the fund and no new projects will be accepted until the excess deficit is eliminated. Union countries can choose feasible projects according to their needs, but the financing ratio for projects related to transportation infrastructure and environmental protection infrastructure should be maintained at 1:1. The assistance provided by the EUSF usually needs to be adapted to the EU's economic transition plan. If member states do not align with the transition plan, the European Commission will notify the Council.

The EUSF is a special fund provided by the EU to assist underdeveloped member states. An evaluation conducted by the London School of Economics and Political Science on the EUSF shows that it has played a positive role in the economic development and job creation of these countries. For example, during the Six Year Plan period from 1994 to 1999, the GDP growth in Spain, Greece, Portugal and Ireland was 5.1 percent, 4.8 percent, 4.4 percent and 3.8 percent respectively. In the Seven Year Plan period from 2000 to 2007, the assistance amount of the EUSF reached EUR 18 billion, accelerating the economic development of these four countries. The Fund has provided significant assistance for infrastructure construction in Greece, Spain, Portugal, and Ireland. Between 1994 and 1999, EUR 1.994 billion of the loan funds from EFSF, EUSF, and European Investment Bank on transportation infrastructure was invested in roads, railways, subways, aviation and other types of mixed transportation facilities in Ireland, Greece, Portugal, Spain and Italy, helping these countries achieve significant improvement in railway, road, and telecommunications networks. In 1991, the automobile and highway network density of these countries was still 20 percent lower than the average level of the 15 EU countries, and by 2001, it had exceeded that average level by 10 percent. From 1986 to 1996, the per capita GDP of Spain, Portugal, Greece, and Ireland increased from 65 percent of the EU average to 76.5 percent. Among them, Ireland climbed from 63.8 percent in 1988 to 111.7 percent in 1999, becoming one of the wealthiest countries in Europe. From 1996 to 2002, the employment rate of these four countries increased by 8 percent, reaching 60 percent in 2002, which is only 4 percent lower than the average employment rate (64 percent) of the 15 EU countries, and the gap has narrowed by twice as much as six years ago.

Britain*

Britain is a typical liberal welfare state that emphasizes welfare distribution based on market mechanisms, with the government's main role being to fill gaps. Overall, in addition to the universal free healthcare system, Britain's social security model is relatively conservative, with low levels of protection and a relatively high level of wealth inequality.

1. Primary Distribution and Related Policies

1.1 Gini Coefficient

The average Gini Coefficient of OECD member countries in 2018 before tax and transfer payments was 0.41, while it reduced to 0.31 after government interventions through public policies such as tax and transfer payments. Britain's Gini Coefficient (0.361) after government interventions ranked the third, with Chile(0.459) taking the first place and the United States(0.385) as the second. The three countries with the lowest Gini Coefficient were Slovenia (0.246), Czech (0.241) and Slovakia(0.232).

The Gini Coefficient in Britain remained relatively low before 1980, which has shown a significant growth since 1980 when the Conservative

* Author: ZHENG Chunrong, Shanghai University of Finance and Economics.

Government led by Margaret Thatcher vigorously promoted privatization and deregulation reforms and reached 0.34 in 1990s. Although experienced some fluctuations, it remained basically stable and arrived at 0.35 in 2019 (see Chart 8-1).

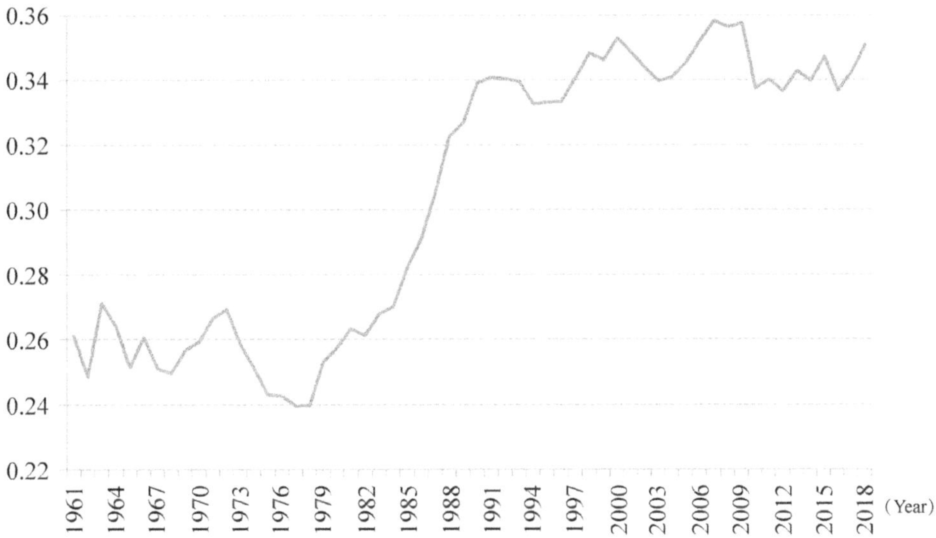

Chart 8-1 Historical Gini Coefficient in Britain

Source: Bourquin, P., Joyce, R. and Norris Keiller, A. (2020), Living Standards, Inequality, and Poverty: 2020, IFS Report 170.

1.2 Wealth Gap

The Resolution Foundation, an economic think tank focused on tracking and analyzing the living standards of British, has released a report claiming that the wealth gap in Britain has been widening over the past 10 years. From the report, one end of the wealth scale is 1 percent of the British population, which indicates approximately 4,880,000 people possessing nearly 14 percent of the country's assets, equivalent to £ 11 trillion. While, on the other end of the scale, 7.3 million British people (15 percent of the British population) are desperately poor or constantly struggling to repay debts.[1] From the perspective of development trends, the polarization in Britain will become increasingly severe in the future, with the income of the poor, who make up half of the population, decreasing while the living standards of the wealthy, who comprise about the other half, will continue to improve.

The efforts made by the British Government in the mid-1990s to alleviate the social wealth gap saw a reduction in the wealth gap at that time. From 1995 to 2005, the proportion of total assets owned by four out of five British in the lower class increased from 35 percent in 1995 to 45 percent in 2005. However, after reaching its peak in 2005, this situation changed again.

The reason for the widening wealth gap is that most of the newly added jobs are of high income type, with little involvement in middle-income and low-income groups. Research shows that by 2020, Britain is expected to add 2 million high-income professional and managerial jobs. Although jobs in low-skilled service industries will also increase by 700,000, such as retail, nursing, and leisure services, more traditional middle-income jobs in management and manufacturing requiring skills are gradually disappearing.

The disparity in income distribution has brought about social division. On June 23, 2016, in the "Brexit" referendum, the low-income group in Britain was firm "Brexiter" and to some extent dominated the voting results. Low and middle-income people oppose globalization and European integration and require a tight immigration policy. Since the EU's eastward expansion in 2004, an increasing number of poor people from less developed Eastern European countries have integrated

---

① Resolution Foundation (2017), "The generation of wealth: Asset accumulation across and within cohorts", https://www. resolutionfoundation.org/app/uploads/2017/06/Wealth.pdf.

into Britain. Over the past decade, Britain has accepted over 1 million Eastern European immigrants, who have to some extent occupied job opportunities for low-income individuals in Britain and shared the British social welfare.

2. Social Distribution

2.1 Britain's Financial and Tax Policies

2.1.1 Total Financial Revenue

From an international comparison perspective, the proportion of tax revenue in Britain is approximately in the middle of developed countries. In the fiscal year 2019/2020, the British tax revenue was £ 757 billion, with approximately £ 14,000 in tax revenue per person if evenly distributed. The proportion of tax revenue to British national income is 34.4 percent, which reached the highest value since the 1940s.

In addition to taxes, the British Government also has a small amount of other income, such as profits paid by state-owned enterprises and interest income from student loans. Adding in these revenues, the total government revenue is £ 811 billion, accounting for 36.9 percent of the national income, which is the highest value since the 1980s.

2.1.2 Structure of Financial Revenue

As shown in Chart 8-2, compared to other developed countries, Britain receives more financial revenue from property taxes, especially business real estate taxes and receives less financial revenue from social insurance taxes. This is related to the British social security system, which has characteristics of the Beveridge model with the focus on filling gaps, thus weakening the social insurance system.

If Britain follows the social insurance system of continental European countries, it needs to increase the income tax on the working class. In the fiscal years 2016-2017, the tax rate for the median income group of full-time employees in Britain was 28 percent, while the average in other developed countries was 44 percent.①

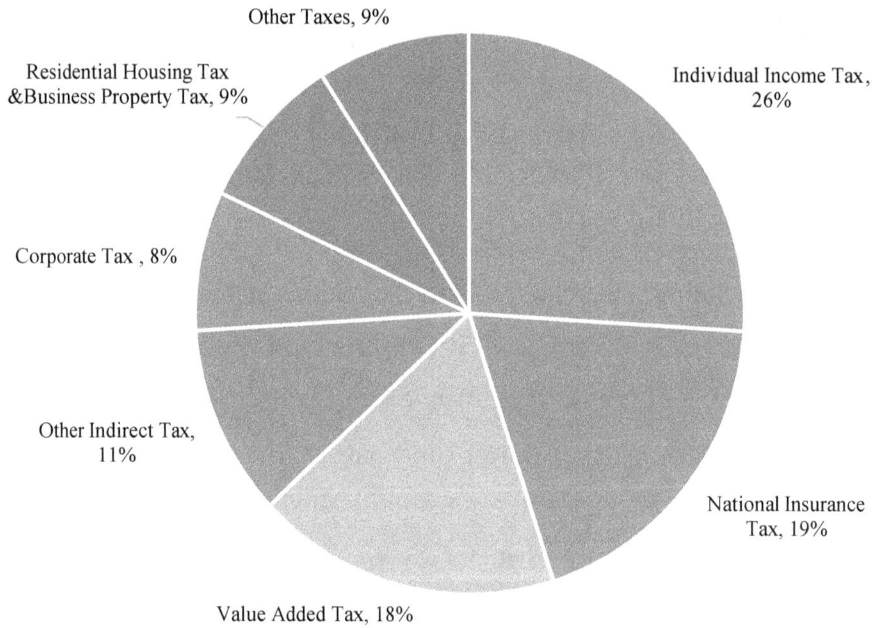

Chart 8-2　Structure of British Financial Revenue in 2019

Source: OBR, Economic and Fiscal Outlook: March 2019, https://obr.uk/efo/economic-fiscal-outlook-march-2019/.

2.2 The Total Expenditure and Structure of Britain's Social Security

2.2.1 Total Expenditure of Social Security

According to the British Government's statistical standards, the total annual expenditure on social security cash and tax credits in Britain is £ 225 billion, accounting for approximately 10 percent of GDP and

① Adam, S. (2019). How high are our taxes, and where does the money come from. IFS Briefing Note BN259.

1/4 of total financial expenditure. According to the Office for Budget Responsibility (OBR) in Britain, by the late 2060s, the proportion of social security expenditure to GDP in Britain will increase to 12 percent (see Chart 8-3).

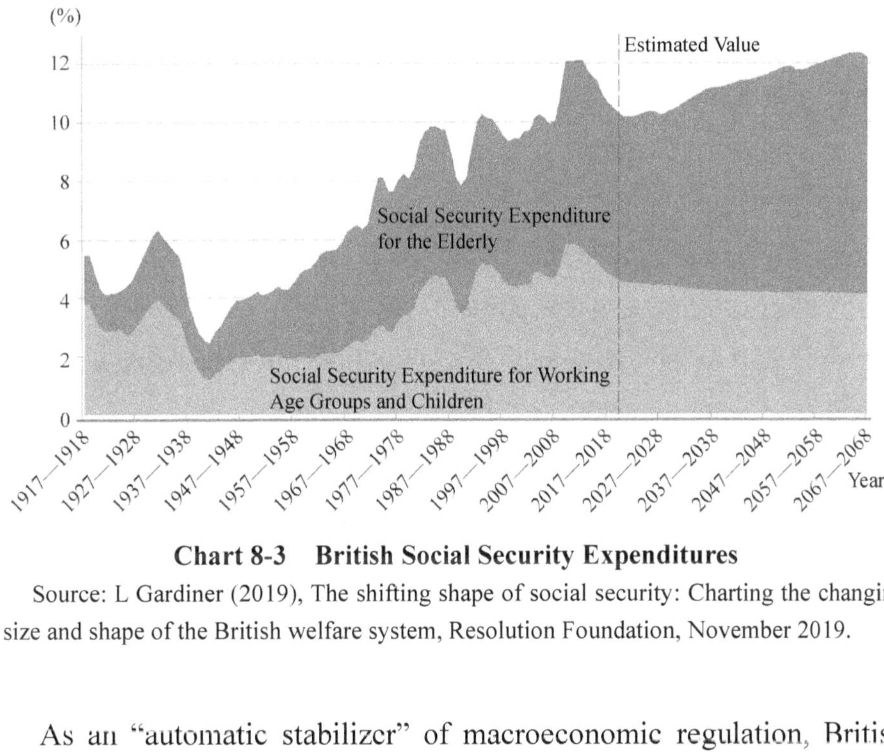

Chart 8-3 British Social Security Expenditures

Source: L Gardiner (2019), The shifting shape of social security: Charting the changing size and shape of the British welfare system, Resolution Foundation, November 2019.

As an "automatic stabilizer" of macroeconomic regulation, British social security expenditure has a certain degree of cyclical volatility. After removing the volatility, it can be seen that the proportion of social security expenditure to GDP is increasing year by year. The reasons for this are as follows:

(1) Economic factors. Firstly, during economic downturns, the government will introduce new social security policies to revive consumption or care for vulnerable groups, such as increasing subsidies for children's allowances or relaxing the conditions for their distribution. These new policies will be challenging to eliminate once the economy recovers. Secondly, due to

the strict conditions for receiving unemployment insurance benefits, some individuals who have lost their eligibility to receive unemployment benefits turn to applying for disability benefits, minimum income security benefits, etc. This has led to changes in the structure of social security expenditure and pushed up the level of expenditure.

(2) Aging factors. According to the analysis of the HM Treasury, the British Government needs to spend £ 2,800, £ 1,6000, £ 1,100 per person per year on social security for those aged 1-15, 16-64 and 65 and above respectively. Undoubtedly, the large-scale retirement of baby boomers will greatly increase social security expenditures.

2.2.2 Structure of Social Security

From Chart 8-4, it can be seen that since 2010, the proportion of social security expenditure (i.e., the proportion of social security expenditure to GDP) has decreased. Meanwhile, from a long-term perspective, both the proportion of social security expenditure for the elderly and the proportion

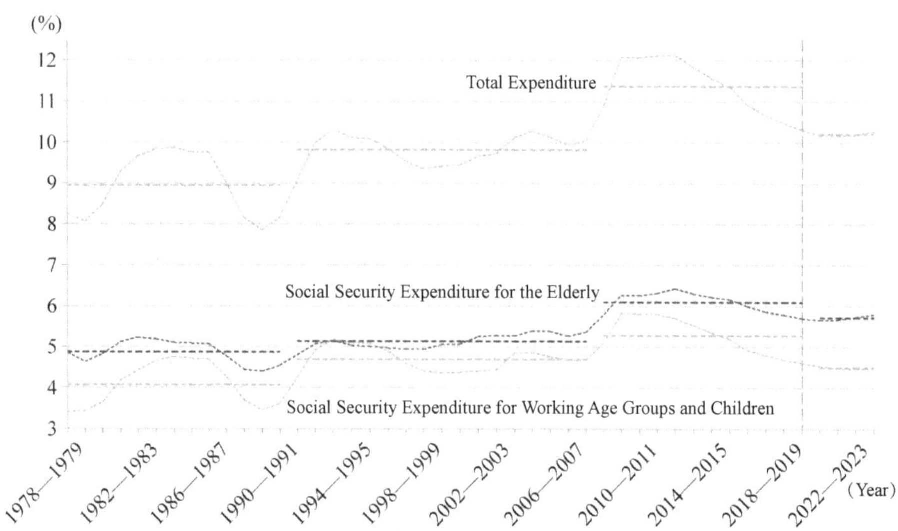

Chart 8-4 Structure of British Social Security Expenditures

Source: L Gardiner (2019), The shifting shape of social security: Charting the changing size and shape of the British welfare system, Resolution Foundation, November 2019.

of social security expenditure for working age groups and children have increased. Furthermore, the proportion of social security expenditures for the elderly is growing rapidly.

In addition to the increase in the proportion of elderly people in social security, the focus of social security expenditure in Britain has transformed from income related unemployment benefits (incapacity benefits, income support, and unemployment benefits) to tax credits, housing benefits, and disability benefits.

2.3 Britain's Pension Insurance System

The concept of basic pension payment in Britain is to ensure basic payment, wide coverage, and strong incentives. On the one hand, it emphasizes ensuring the basic living expenses of the elderly, maintaining a low replacement rate for basic pension, in order to reduce the burden on enterprises and individuals, and make room for occupational pension and private pension. As shown in Chart 8-5, the proportion of basic pensions to the average social wage in Britain has rebounded in recent years, but it is still less than 20 percent. On the other hand, the basic pension payment in Britain prioritizes equality, uniformly implements fixed basic pension funds which are not linked to the payment base, highlighting the social mutual assistance function of pension insurance.

It is predicted that for new employees entering the workforce in 2018, if their lifetime wage remains at the social average level, the net replacement rate of their pension will reach 28.4 percent, lower than the OECD average (58.6 percent) and the EU average (63.5 percent)[①]. Even with the addition of voluntary pension plans, the replacement

① OECD (2019), Pensions at a Glance 2019: OECD and G20 Indicators, OECD Publishing, Paris .

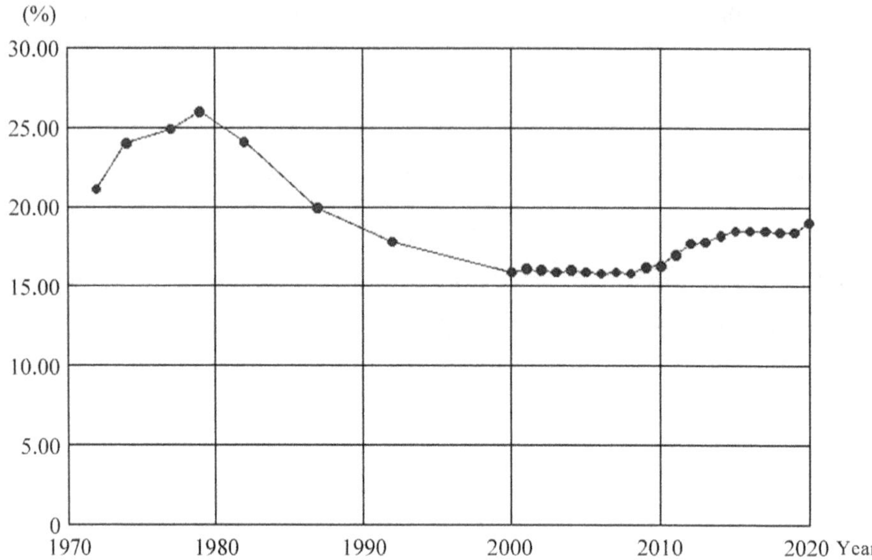

Chart 8-5 Proportion of Basic Pensions to the Average Social Wage (%)

Source: Pensions Policy Institute. (2021). The pensions primer: A guide to the UK pensions system, May 2021.

rate for large caliber pensions in Britain only reaches 61.0 percent, still lower than the OECD average (65.4 percent) and the EU average (67.0 percent).

Although there are many criticisms on the low level of pension benefits, some scholars believe that due to the implementation of the free healthcare system in Britain, it has dramatically reduced the medical expenses of elderly people, making the relatively low level of pension benefits acceptable to some extent.

In order to stimulate long-term retirement savings and alleviate the financial burden of aging population on the public pension system, Britain carried out the pension insurance system reform-the Auto-Enrollment Program (AE Program)-in 2012. Starting from October 2012, employees with an annual income of £ 7,475 or above, aged between 22 and the statutory retirement age, have not participated in any occupational pension program could automatically join the occupational pension program. When an employee joins a company, they automatically join the occupational pension program provided by the employer, unless the individual voluntarily and explicitly proposes that he or she doesn't want to join the employer pension program.

The contribution rates of employers and employees in the AE Program have gradually increased since 2012(see Table 8-1). Starting from April 6, 2019, the total contribution rate of the AE Program increased from 5 percent (employer and employee contribution rates were 2 percent and 3percent respectively) to 8 percent (employer and employee contribution rates were 3 percent and 5 percent, respectively). This growth is the last step in a series of increased contribution rates implemented since the launch of the AE Program in 2012.

Table 8-1 Adjustment of Contribution Rates for the AE Program

Duration	(Minimum) Contribution Rate for Employers	Contribution Rate for Employees	Total Contribution Rate
Octobcr 1, 2012~April 5, 2018	1%	1%	2%
April 6, 2018~April 5, 2019	2%	3%	5%
After April 6, 2010	3%	5%	8%

Note: Currently, the actual contribution rates for employees and employers are 5 percent and 4 percent respectively, and the contribution rate for the British Government is 1 percent through tax reduction.

The AE Program sets an automatic enrollment earning threshold, exemption, and payment ceiling. The threshold for the fiscal year 2019-2020 is annual wage of £ 10,000, with an exemption of £ 6,136 and a payment ceiling of £ 50,000 (see Table 8-2).

Table 8-2 The Exemption, Threshold and Payment Ceiling of the AE Program

Year	Exemption (£)	Threshold (£)	Payment Ceiling (£)
Fiscal Year 2012-2013	5,564	8,105	42,475
Fiscal Year 2013-2014	5,668	9,440	41,450
Fiscal Year 2014-2015	5,772	10,000	41,865
Fiscal Year 2015-2016	5,824	10,000	42,385
Fiscal Year 2017-2018	5,876	10,000	43,000
Fiscal Year 2018-2019	6,032	10,000	46,350
Fiscal Year 2019-2020	6,136	10,000	50,000

(1) When an employee's annual wage is lower than the automatic enrollment earning threshold but higher than the exemption amount, the employer may not initiate an AE Program for the employee. But if an employee requests to participate in the Program, the employer shall not refuse and shall be required to fulfill the supporting contribution obligation. When an employee's annual wage is lower than the exemption amount, there's no obligation for the employer to pay the supporting contributions.

(2) The portion of an employee's annual wage that exceeds the exemption amount and is lower than the contribution ceiling is used as the contribution base.

For example, an employee's annual wage is £ 22,000, and after deducting the contribution exemption of £ 6,136 in the 2019/2020 fiscal year, the amount of payable income is £ 15,864. As the contribution rates for employers, employees, and governments are 3 percent, 4 percent and 1 percent respectively, with contributions of £ 476, £ 635 and £ 159, the total amount of contributions entering into the employee's individual account is £ 1,269.

In 2012, matching the AE Program, the British Government established the National Employment Savings Trust (NEST), a low-cost pension fund investment platform funded by the government, to care for employees of small and medium-sized enterprises. NEST is a non-profit organization with the goal of providing employees and employers with low administrative fees, high transparency, and simple retirement security plans. The administrative fee charged by it every year is 0.3 percent of the total cumulative investment of the insured. The initial expenses of NEST were supported by government loans, and subsequent operations were maintained through administrative fees. NEST is a non-profit and non-departmental public body, with basic independence in daily operations. However, the government has a responsibility to ensure its effective operation. Currently, there are six types of funds on the NEST, i.e., Pre-retirement Fund, Lower Growth Fund, Higher Risk Fund, Ethical Fund, Sharia Fund and Retirement Date Fund.

Overall, the AE Program in Britain has created contribution incentives for employees and expanded the second-pillar pension. According to the *Automatic Enrollment Evaluation Report 2018* released in December 2018, since the operation of AE Program in 2012, over 9.9 million employees have joined the Program, and over 140 employers have fulfilled their matching contribution obligations. The coverage rate of the second-pillar pension in Britain has increased from 55 percent in 2012 to 84 percent in 2017.

However, critics argue that this Program sets a threshold, and actually, low-income individuals still cannot participate in Program and don't have the opportunity to enjoy government tax incentives. In addition, some employees with lower incomes may have participated, but the contribution exemption results in lower matching contributions from employers and the government, thus this group still faces the risk of elderly poverty in the future.

2.4 Britain's National Health Care Services

In 1948, the British Government announced the establishment of the National Health Service (NHS), providing free healthcare services to all citizens. With social changes and advances in health care as well as the change in British population composition, there's a trend towards aging. According to data from the Office for National Statistics, the population aged 65 and over has reached 18 percent, which is estimated to 24 percent by 2042. The expenditure on health care for the elderly is 2.5 times of that for young people. Meanwhile, the trend of sub-replacement fertility has led to a decrease in the workforce and an increase in pensioners, resulting in weak growth in financial revenue. On the other hand, a large elderly population has caused an increase in various chronic diseases, and the treatment of multiple comorbidities has aggravated the burden on the healthcare system.

As healthcare expenses become increasingly high, the NHS budget has not been increased accordingly, facing financial pressure. When the NHS was established in 1948, the plan required an annual budget increase of 3.7 percent. On the 70th anniversary of the NHS in 2018, its budget reached £ 156 billion with its carrying amount increasing nearly 12 times, but the actual growth rate was not as expected. Since the Conservative Party took office in 2019, the NHS budget has been reduced due to financial difficulties, with an average annual increase of only about 1 percent. Although it was later raised to 3.4 percent, but after excluding the impact of inflation, the NHS's budget grew by an average of only 1.4 percent from 2009-2010 to 2018-2019. According to estimation, there is a gap of at least £ 20 billion to £ 30 billion between this budget and the expected development goals of the NHS.

Due to the tight budget, NHS has improved efficiency through various means, among which outsourcing business to more efficient private enterprises is one of them. As early as the Labour Party's reign in 2000, non medical services in the NHS, such as accounting, IT, and other logistics offices, were largely outsourced to private enterprises. In recent years, medical services have gradually been outsourced to private medical institutions, as health officials believe that this can increase medical energy and shorten waiting times. As a result, during the 2019 election, the Conservative Government was criticized for "privatizing the NHS".

In addition, although rigorous tiered healthcare allows patients to be diverted, the problem it brings is long waiting times. The maximum waiting time set by NHS for referral under non emergency medical conditions is at 18 weeks, as patients need to be referred to a general practitioner before undergoing further examination or receiving the care of a specialist. However, in reality, it may take longer to see a doctor.

2.5 Britain's Universal Credit System

In history, there have been numerous welfare benefits in Britain, including low-income benefit, unemployment benefit, housing benefit, child benefit, etc. At the end of April 2013, Britain promoted a new Universal Credit to replaced the six categories of social benefits, including Income Support, Income based Jobseeker's Allowance, Income-related Employment Support Allowance, Housing Benefit, and Child Tax Credit and Working Tax Credit, etc.

If the applicant meets all the following conditions, it is possible to receive the Universal Credit. Firstly, the applicant is in a low-income or unemployed state. Secondly, the applicant is over 18 years old, and the applicant or the applicant's spouse is below the national statutory retirement age. Thirdly, the applicant and his or her spouse have a deposit of no more than £ 16,000. Lastly, the applicant resides in Britain. It should be noted that if the applicant and his or her spouse (including unmarried couples) live together, the income and savings of the applicant's spouse will also be included in the evaluation and consideration of the applicant. Meanwhile, if the applicant has children, it does not affect whether the applicant is eligible for the Universal Credit, but it may affect the applicant's payment treatment (see Table 8-3).

Table 8-3 The Standard Allowance Amount of Universal Credit

Applicant's Condition	Standard Allowance Amount Per Month (£)
Single and Under 25 Years Old	342.72
Single and Over 25 Years Old	409.89
Applies With Spouse, Both Under 25 Years Old	488.59 (in total)
Applies With Spouse, One of Them Over 25 Years Old	594.04 (in total)

On the basis of the standard allowance amount, the additional amount will be determined based on the applicants' child, health status, or whether they need to pay the rent.

The amount of Universal Credit received by the applicant every month=the amount of standard allowance+additional amount

Furthermore, if the applicants' health condition limits their working capacity, they will receive an additional allowance of £ 341.92 per month. If the applicants have started receiving health-related Universal Credit or income-related Employment and Support Allowance(ESA) before April

3, 2017, they are able to receive an additional £ 128.25 per month. The housing allowance is based on the applicants' age and actual situation, including rental fees, housing loans, and service fees (see Table 8-4).

Table 8-4 Additional Amount of Universal Credit Unit: £

First Child	281.25 (Born Before April 6, 2017)
	235.83 (Born After April 6, 2017)
Second Child or More than Two Children	235.83 (For One Child)
If the Applicant's Child is Disabled	128.25
If the Applicant's Child is Severely Handicapped	400.29
If the Applicant Pays Child Care Fees	A Maximum of 85 Percent will be Subsidized (Up to 646.35 for One Child; For Children of Two or More, the Maximum is 1108.04)

The British Universal Credit System has set a 5-week delay period for the first disbursement of allowance. For those who rely on relief funds for survival, the long-time wait left them penniless and unable to make ends meet. During the period of delayed disbursement, the British Government will provide a certain prepayment (similar to overdraft or loan, which should be repaid), but for those who have limited financial income. this kind of prepayment cannot help them get through difficulties.

In addition to the long-time delayed disbursement, the allowance sanction rule in Universal Credit System and the debt accumulation caused by the sanction are also the main reasons for the survival difficulties of applicants. The allowance sanction rule is a punitive mechanism. After reaching consensus with the employment guidance, the applicant signs an agreement and applies for the allowance according to regulations. If the applicant violates more than one regulation in the current month, a certain amount of relief fund will be sanctioned in next month.

Affected by the British fiscal reduction policy, since the first introduction of Universal Credit System in April 2013, it has only slightly increased by 1 percent in fiscal years 2014 and 2015 respectively. Since then, the payment amount has remained unchanged for five consecutive years (2015-2019).

3. The Third Distribution

3.1 Individual Charitable Donations

As one of the early birthplaces of charity in the world, Britain has a very long history and culture of charity. The social atmosphere of charitable donations and volunteer activities among the British public is relatively strong, establishing the cornerstone of the long-term and sustainable development of charity in Britain.

According to the British Government's statistical classification, charitable donations are divided into two categories: one is one-time donations, and the other is multiple sponsorships, which means donating funds in installments over a period of time, often with the equal amount of funds donated each time. For a long time, the funds donated by individuals in Britain have remained around £ 10 billion per year, with a total amount of £ 101 billion in 2018, £ 10.3 billion in 2017, and £ 9.7 billion in 2016.[①] From the perspective of funding, the amount of sponsorship is lower than that of direct donations.

The main recipient of charitable donations in Britain in 2018 was children or young people (accounting for 26 percent), animal welfare

---

① The Trustees of the Charities Aid Foundation, *CAF UK GIVING 2019: An overview of charitable giving in the UK*, May 2019.

(26percent), medical research (25 percent), hospitals and shelters (20 percent), as well as homeless people, lodgings and refuges(18%).

3.2 Charitable Organizations

In March 2019, there were over 186,000 registered charitable organizations in Britain.① However, the actual scale is much larger. In addition to registered charitable organizations, there are also a large number of charitable organizations that are exempt from registration or whose income falls below the registration threshold. It is estimated that there are about 600,000 to 90,0000 informal community organizations without clear legal forms (which may or may not have charitable goals) and an unknown number of non charitable organizations, including over 14,000 Community Interest Companies (CICs)②

From 2018 to 2019, the total revenue of registered charitable organizations in Britain exceeded £ 79 billion, of which £ 23 billion was reported as voluntary donations. However, there's a huge income gap between various charitable organizations.

Various charitable organizations and forms of charity, such as foundations, clubs, social service organizations, charitable trusts, etc., are generally similar to the operation mode in China. The most different type is charity companies (registered as both enterprises and charitable organizations), which will be further subdivided in Britain and have corresponding operational standards. This type of organization can maintain its operations and contribute to charity through various means such as daily commercial operations, investments, membership fees,

① Data here only includes England and Wales.

② Source: https://uk.practicallaw.thomsonreuters.com/8633-4989?transitionType=Default &contextData=(sc.Default)&first Page=true#co-anchor_a603657.

donations, stock returns, loans, etc.[①] The diversified implementation methods of charitable organizations in Britain have promoted various ways for charitable organizations to attract donations from the British public. According to statistics, the largest source of donations to charity in Britain is from the public, with the second largest source being the government. Other income includes investment income, national lottery, institutional donations, and income from paid services.

---

① CHEN Xiaode&ZHANG Zixuan: The Main Experience of British Development of Charity and Our Thoughts, *China Philanthropy Times*, 2020-1-24.

Russia*

1. Basic Information

As a transitional country, Russia's Constitution defines it as a socialist country, which determines its distribution system. The characteristics of Russia's distribution system are that in the primary distribution, the proportion of labors' wages to GDP is greater than 50 percent, and in the redistribution and third distribution, the government assumes the majority of social responsibilities to residents. The Russia's experience shows that reasonable distribution is the foundation of social stability, which has been an important condition for Russia's successful transformation and economic growth in the past 12 years, while unequal distribution policies can lead to social instability, which makes continuous economic growth impossible.

In the past 10 years, Russia's economic development has stagnated. In 2010, the total GDP of Russia was USD 1,520 billion, with a per capita GDP of USD 10,672, while in 2020, Russia's total GDP was USD 1490 billion, with a per capita GDP of USD 10,000.

In spite of economic stagnation, Russia's Gini Coefficient has remained at around 0.4. The first reason is that Russia spends a large portion of its

* Author: XU Yanli, China University of Labor Relations.

financial revenue on public expenditures such as education, healthcare, housing, and vulnerable groups. Secondly, for many years, the real wage growth rate after deducting inflation has been consistently higher than the GDP growth rate.

In terms of social development, the life expectancy of Russians is not high, which was only 73.42 years old in 2020. However, the number of doctors per 1,000 inhabitants in Russia was 4.01 and the number of hospital beds per 1,000 inhabitants in Russia was 8.2, ranking 18th and 10th respectively.

2. Primary Distribution and Related Policies

With the transition of the economic system, Russia's employment policy has transformed from "full employment guaranteed by the state" to "free choice of employment under market competition", and the labor market has basically been established. However, due to the slow progress of economic restructuring and limited efforts in enterprise reform, surplus personnel are rarely reduced. The Russian Government regards "prioritizing the retainment of current job positions" as its guiding concept.

Russia's labor market policy places equal emphasis on ensuring full employment and achieving free choice of employment. The *Russian Federal Employment Act* (passed on April 20, 1996 and amended for the 8th time on January 10, 2003) clearly stipulates that the state implements policies aimed at promoting residents' realization of complete, productive and freely chosen employment rights. The measures taken for this purpose are mainly as follows. First is to promote the rational allocation of productivity through financial credit, investment, and tax policies, improve labor mobility, develop temporary and independent employment, encourage flexible employment, take various measures to stabilize existing positions, and develop new job positions. Second is to implement legal regulation in employment under the premise of protecting the legitimate rights and interests of citizens and providing national security. Third is to formulate and carry out the employment promotion plan. Fourth is to establish an effective mechanism for implementing active employment policies and provide most effective employment assistance for the unemployed through categorizing the unemployed according to the characteristics of their occupational activities, education level, gender, age, etc., based on labor market conditions. Fifth is to provide social assistance to legally recognized unemployed individuals. Sixth is to establish a federal employment institution. The *Act* also specified if individual federal entities exist serious labor market issues, the federal government can allocate funds from the federal budget for mitigation.

Small enterprises are an important channel for expanding employment. The Russian Government has formulated preferential policies to support the development of small enterprises, including simplifying registration procedures, providing discounted loans and low-rent commercial housing, establishing small enterprise funds, reducing taxation, providing free legal consultation and market analysis, encouraging and promoting technological innovation activities, and organizing training and further education.

Strict control of illegal layoffs in enterprises is one of the key considerations of the Russian Government. It also pays special attention to solving the employment problem of college students.

In order to ensure the reasonable wage level and various rights and interests of labors, Russia has established a model based on social partnership and mediated labor relations through collective bargaining. The introduction of the Labor Code has put forward higher requirements for innovative collective bargaining mechanism.

The above measures ensure the proportion of wages in the primary distribution.

As of June 2019, the unemployment rate and employment rate in Russia were 4.4 percent and 59.4 percent respectively and the wage reached 49,840 Rubles per month.

The highest to lowest income ratio in Russia is 6.6:1. According to the Federal State Statistics Service (Russia), the average monthly wage of the Russian in 2017 was 28,345 Rubles, thus the group with monthly income from 221,000 Rubles to 567,000 Rubles can included in the middle class, accounting for approximately 38 percent of the total population of Russia. In the past 30 years, 80 percent of Russian people's income has decreased by about 21 percent and the income of the wealthiest group in Russia has almost halved. The shrinking middle class has aggravated the sense of social insecurity, while having a child or retiring contribute to the further reduction of this class.

3. Social Distribution

Russia's social insurance is the most essential part of the social security system, which includes mandatory social insurance, voluntary social insurance, and state-guaranteed social insurance. Among them, the dominant one is mandatory social insurance, including the Pension and Social Insurance Fund of the Russian Federation and the Federal Compulsory Medical Insurance Fund. Before 2002, there was an employment fund, and currently the Federal Service for Labour and Employment is an executive body responsible for ensuring employment and paying unemployment benefits.

The Pension Fund of the Russian Federation guarantees the payment of pensions for the elderly, the disabled, and those who have lost their dependents, and the Social Insurance Fund of the Russian Federation ensures and pays for temporary incapacity and maternity insurance, work-related injury and occupational diseases insurance. The Federal Compulsory Medical Insurance Fund allocates medical service funds for compulsory medical insurance programs in the healthcare sector.

Russia has achieved universal coverage of pension and medical insurance. However, the pension replacement rate is relatively low, only 3.5 percent. According to the Federal Service for State Statistics, if the current pension replacement rate should be maintained, Russia will increase the pension insurance rate by one percentage point every year from 2020 to 2050. However, the improvement of the rate will not only increase the tax burden, but also seriously reduce the investment attractiveness of the Russian economy. Alternatively, Russia can add the federal budget allocation to improve the proportion of the federal budget for pension security to GDP by one percentage point every five years. Namely, it is required to increase the proportion of pension security allocation to GDP by eight percentage points to 13 percent within 40 years.

4. Public Services

The Russian Government strives to achieve balanced development and social equity among regions through finance transfer payments between populations and regions.

4.1 Proportion of Public Finance Transfer Payments

From the expenditure structure of Russia's integrated budget and total extra-budgetary funds in 2019, social expenditure accounted for 61.2 percent of the total expenditure, ranking the first. Second is the expenditure on national defense, national security, and law enforcement activities, occupying 13.9 percent of the total expenditure, followed by the expenditure on national economic development accounting for 12 percent.

The fiscal revenue of various entities has increased, but the polarization trend of fiscal revenue in developed and undeveloped areas has intensified. In the future, the support of the Russian federal budget for local finance will be strengthened, and approximately 7.5 trillion Rubles will be transferred to local governments from 2020 to 2022, of which 2.2 trillion Rubles will be allocated for national projects and 2 trillion Rubles will be used to balance budget allocations. However, there is still an imbalance in the distribution of taxes between the central and local governments, and taxes shared by federal entities and the central government fail to cover fiscal expenditures.

In terms of federal fiscal expenditure in 2019, it is mainly targeted at education, health, culture, housing, etc., with a slight increase in education, health, social infrastructure and production infrastructure. According to *Federal Budget for 2020 and the Draft of Federal Budget for 2021 and 2022*, the budget allocation for population and health programs, education programs and housing construction programs from 2020 to 2022 is approximately 2.7 trillion Rubles, 380 billion Rubles and over 400 billion Rubles. The *Amendment* passed in March 2020 is expected to increase expenditure by 1.848 trillion Rubles (including an increase of 352.6 billion Rubles in 2020) within the next three years to implement the social security measures proposed by President Putin. Among them, the budget increased as subsidies for families with first child is 600 billion Rubles, and the budget for improving free meals for primary school students is 109 billion Rubles. Other funds are used to provide subsidies for low-income families with children aged 3-7 and increase teachers' salaries. In addition, salaries for staff in the fields of culture, education, health, and social services will be increased and the allowances for soldiers, military dependents and retired soldiers as well as undergraduate and doctoral students in federal educational institutions will also be improved.

4.2 Supporting Policies for Sustainable Social Development

Since March 2020, the Russian Government has taken a series of measures to assist enterprises, increase financial revenue and reduce the impact of the COVID-19, including temporarily reducing the social insurance premium paid by SMEs from 30 percent to 15 percent, delaying the collection of taxes from SMEs for six months, and providing preferential loans to SMEs. Since the outbreak of the pandemic, Russia has introduced multiple supportive policies, including tax reductions, refunds, improving unemployment benefits, and subsidies for families with children.

Russia has always focused on supporting measures, which account for approximately 4 percent of its GDP. The measures taken by Russia to support economic development and people's lives during the pandemic can help prevent the exacerbation of poverty. If the Russian Government has not taken measures to respond to the pandemic crisis since January 2020, the impoverished population in Russia might experience significant growth. Russia has better addressed this crisis than many countries with similar economic conditions and the COVID-19 has provided an opportunity for the reform of Russia's social welfare system. Russia's increased in support for families with children is a step toward the right direction.

5. Other Transfers: Charity and Tax Preference

Domestic large-sized enterprises in Russia naturally become the main group of charitable donations. Unlike Western European countries that rely on civil society to promote corporate philanthropy, Russia's unique institutional transformation background and national conditions determine that corporate charitable donations are primarily driven and influenced by the government.

The Russian Government focuses on guiding, promoting, and motivating charitable activities of domestic large enterprises. First, in terms of guiding, the government does not particularly advocate for "spot or sporty" charity in areas such as poverty alleviation and disaster relief, but focuses on supporting social infrastructure in sports, culture, healthcare, and education. Second is the government's promotion. The "public-private partnership model" promoted by President Putin in 2006 included corporate social responsibility into the national socio-economic development strategy. For example, local governments in Russia have introduced commercial resources by signing formal cooperation agreements, focusing on developing traditional fields such as sports, art, healthcare, and education that were left over during Soviet times as "social infrastructure", making them the fields where Russian corporations fulfill their charitable social responsibilities best and develop fastest. Last is the government's motivations. The Russian Government controls critical and scarce resources for enterprise production and development, and enterprises tend to seek government protection to ensure their stability in policy formulation and implementation in order to achieve development.

Japan*

1. Basic Information

Japan is a highly developed capitalist country with unique characteristics in social development. With the longest life expectancy per capita in nearly 86 years, Japan is currently the most affluent Asian country in terms of national wealth. Despite experiencing the so-called "Lost Two Decades", its per capita GDP in the past five years has exceeded USD 40,000 and reached a historic high of USD 42,589 in 2019and its per capita GNI in 2012 approached USD 50,000. Although there was a decline in per capita GNI due to the adjustment of Japan's global industrial layout, it had already broken through USD 40,000 again in 2018 and increased to USD 41580 in 2019. Meanwhile, Japan's employment rate remains stable at around 75 percent year-round, with a long-term unemployment rate of less than 1.4 percent, and its employment instability index is only 1.4, far below the average index of around 7 in OECD countries. The vibrant economy brought about by the continuous improvement of the per capita economic situation as well as stable and high employment rates and the formation of a long-lived society based on sound public health conditions have become Japan's first impression on the world (see Chart 10-1).

---

* Author: HUANG Guan, Xiamen University Tan Kah Kee College.

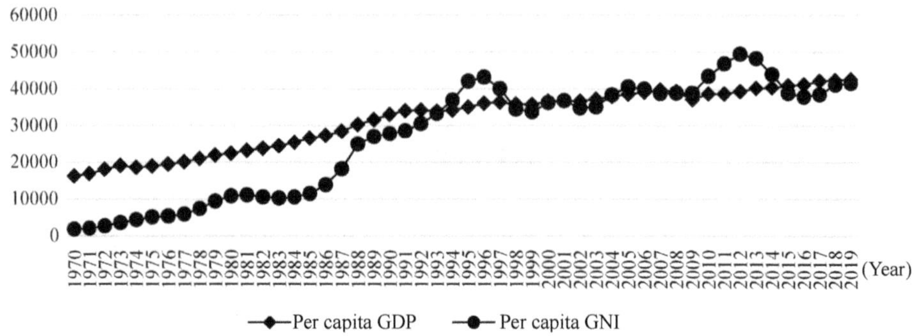

Chart 10-1 Japan's per capita GDP and GNI, 1970-2019 (USD)

Source: OECD and World Bank Open Data.

From a long-term historical perspective, Japan performed fundamentally different in terms of wealth distribution before and after World War II. After "Lost Two Decades", the "Abenomics" launched in 2012 has brought a new era to Japan's income distribution. Although there are differences in social wealth distribution methods, policy tools, and even institutional involvement in different historical periods, when it comes to the results, what persists is the low Gini Coefficient in Postwar Japan, which was near 30 in terms of disposable income (see Chart 10-2). Although there have been significant changes in the ways of achieving social equality, Japan's approach to achieving a relatively balanced distribution of social wealth, as well as the policy tools and governance experience adopted for this purpose, have great reference value for China, which is shifting towards "common prosperity".

During the Golden Age of Capitalism in Postwar Japan, the average annual economic growth rate was as high as 10 percent, and industrial upgrading continued to accelerate. In the process of export-oriented industrialization, small and medium-sized enterprises obtained advantaged development opportunities, created a large number of job opportunities, and thus triggered continuous labor flow towards high value-added

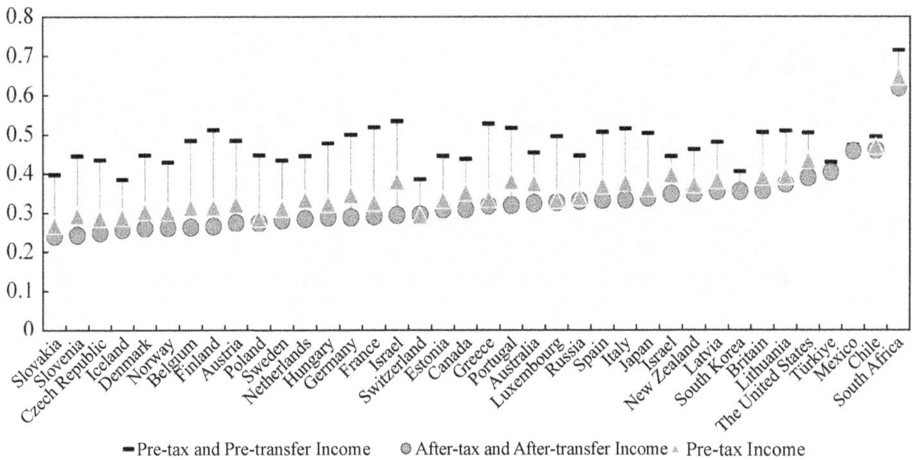

Chart 10-2 Changes in Gini Coefficient Before and After the Third Distribution in OECD Countries (2019)

Source: the OECD Social Expenditure Database.

industries. At the same time, as the egalitarian social solidarism formed in Japan after the war, the Japanese Government, in collaboration with industry associations and trade unions, jointly established and promoted a wealth redistribution system based on industry and social identity (Ito, and Wong, 2010). In the past, Japan relied on functional programs represented by public employment, agricultural subsidies, market competition restrictions, and job security, which not only achieved balanced distribution of social wealth among different industries, but also ensured "common prosperity" with low public expenditure and low wealth redistribution (Margarita, 2008). However, facing the widening gap of primary income distribution caused by "Abenomics", the rapid growth of public expenditure and the expansion of wealth redistribution have become new guarantees for Japan to maintain social equality.

After the "Abenomics" reform began in 2022, the Gini Coefficient of Japan's primary income distribution soared to over 0.5, but reduced to below 0.4 through tax adjustment. After the redistribution, Japan's Gini

Coefficient further dropped to under 0.35, regaining the equalization of social income distribution (See Chart 10-3). It is not hard to see from this that during the "Lost Two Decades" of stagnant economic growth in Japan, the iconic highly equal primary income distribution system in Japanese social income distribution has gradually collapsed, the coverage of the once proud lifelong employment and seniority wage system has gradually narrowed, and the marketization level of labor income has significantly increased. However, at the same time, the size and function of Japan's redistribution have also been expanded and strengthened, consolidating the function of tax revenue to regulate income disparities through targeted and significant increases in tax. Furthermore, the expanded public finance has also provided a stable expenditure source for the development of social security and welfare, thus bringing Japan's income redistribution to an unprecedented level. Among them, the expenditure of public finance on social security and welfare has continued to proliferate since the 1980s,

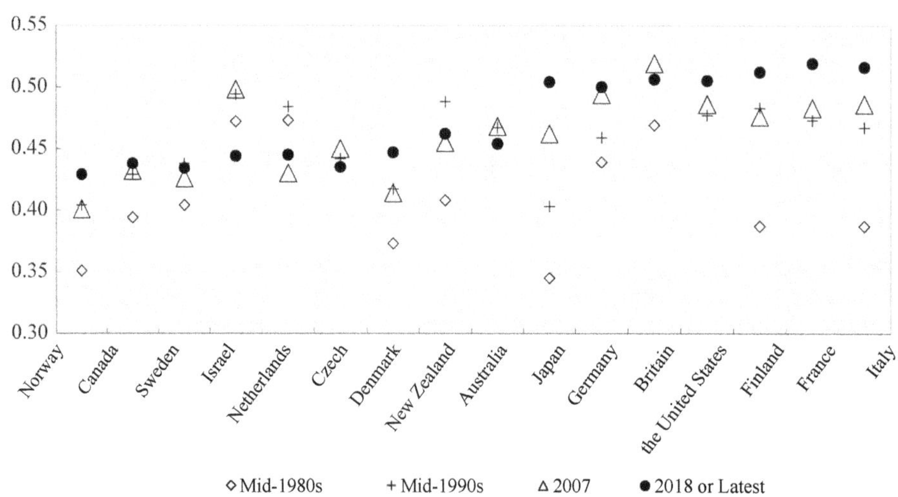

Chart 10-3 Changes of Gini Coefficient After Primary Distribution in OECD Countries During Different Historical Periods (Since the mid-1980s)

Source: the OECD Social Expenditure Database.

and the proportion of Japanese public's expenditure on voluntary social security and welfare projects to GDP has also significantly increased since 2000s. Obviously, in today's Japan, there is an increasing emphasis on social equality at both national and individual level.

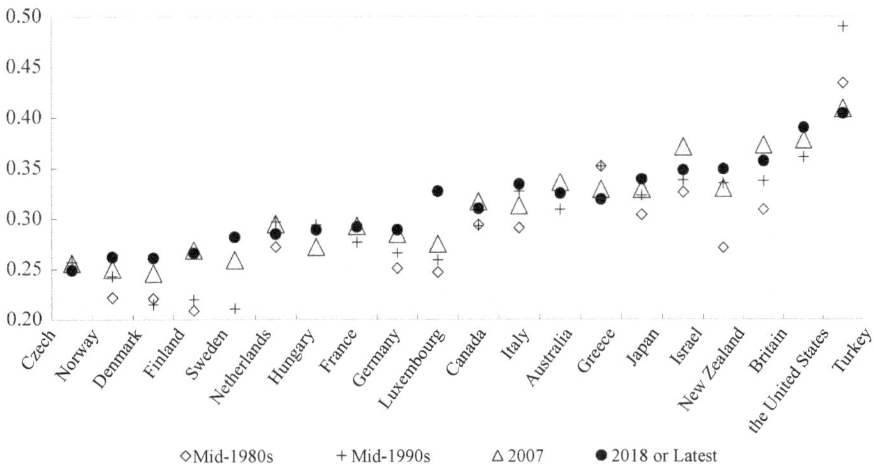

Chart 10-4 Changes of Gini Coefficient After Re-distribution in OECD Countries During Different Historical Periods (Since the mid-1980s)

Source: the OECD Social Expenditure Database.

2. Primary Distribution

The Japanese employment system, which consists of three core components, i.e., lifelong employment, seniority wage, and enterprise based trade unions, is considered the core support for its significant economic achievements in the second half of the 20th century. Subsequently, studies in 2000s summarized a fourth key core for Japan's employment system-community perception within the corporation-which refers to the reciprocal relationships and consensus based decision-making processes between personnel at different levels, vertically from high to low. The first three institutional employment designs contributed to the birth of the fourth social employment consensus, and the Japanese employment system jointly constructed and led by these four core element promoted the high degree of equalization in Japan's primary income distribution before the "Abenomics" reform. During the 1980s of the rapid growth of the entire Japanese economy, the Gini Coefficient of residents' pre tax income remained stable at below 0.35, the degree of equalization in Japan's primary income distribution ranked the second highest in the world and the income equalization after such redistribution as taxation and transfer payments was also close to top five in the world (Moriguchi, and Saez. 2006). This means that during the period of rapid economic growth, Japan mainly relies on market-oriented means to regulate the distribution of social wealth and achieves the common share of economic prosperity through relatively equal primary income distribution. But the impact of redistribution on income and welfare is minimal.

In terms of primary income distribution, Japan still continues and mainly relies on the "three core components" mentioned above to carry out its social wealth distribution function. However, in response to the changes in domestic and international economic forms since 2000s, more market-oriented competition has been introduced in human resource allocation, improving the horizontal labor mobility. Even so, the main body of Japan's employment system is still based on lifelong employment and seniority wage system. Currently, over 90 percent of graduates (with high school and university degrees or above) who enter the workforce each year still sign traditional lifelong employment contracts with corporations as the entire employment system in Japan is essentially based on lifelong employment. On the one hand, lifelong employment effectively reduces personnel mobility between different corporations, improves employees' career expectations and stability. On the other hand, it also allows corporations to provide comprehensive training at will for new employees who lack professional knowledge and experience to support their career development and make a promise to offer a one-time large subsidy of "buyout service" when employees reach the statutory retirement age, thus forming a stable and mutually beneficial cooperative relationship between employers and employees. The enhancement of the horizontal labor mobility actually reduces the bargaining power between trade unions and corporations, leading to a widening gap of the primary income between employees and employers.

3. Social Distribution

Before Abe's reform, due to the stable employment in Japan and the high equalization of income in the primary distribution, Japan also attached great importance to functional projects represented by public employment, agricultural subsidies, market competition restrictions, and job security in the construction of its social support system while invested less in typical social security and welfare projects that would expand the scale of redistribution. In the early 1990s, as the Bubble Economy burst, Japan left a contradictory impression on the world that Japan's national welfare was very "stingy", but the degree of social equality was very high in OECD countries with a tax level slightly higher than that of the United States and a social security and welfare expenditure less than 15 percent of GDP. Even in recent years, in the OECD's statistics on public expenditure in its member countries, Japan's public expenditure still accounts for less than a quarter of its GDP, ranking at the bottom of the OECD countries disproportionately to its economic size.

In the 1990s, impacted by the burst of Bubble Economy and the subsequent long-term economic stagnation, as well as the aging population and low fertility, the Japanese Government had to make adjustments and reforms to the above social equality achieved by primary distribution. Faced with emerging economic and social issues, the Japanese Government had to balance limited financial resources with the continuously growing welfare needs of the people. After nearly half a century of development, in 1995, the promulgation of *Reconstructing the Social Security System: Building a Harmonious Society in 21st Century* marked Japan's successful construction of a welfare state system that can meet the minimum living needs of all members of society, and national welfare became an indispensable component of people's daily lives.

Before World War II, the income distribution in Japan was extremely imbalanced, with the highest 1 percent of the population accounting for over 20 percent of its national income at its worst. By the end of World War II, as a defeated country, Japan had undergone comprehensive reforms under the supervision of the occupation forces, and its income distribution had reached an unprecedented equality. In 1947, when Japan had the most equal distribution of income, the value of the highest 1 percent of the population accounting for the national income had dropped to less than 10 percent while the top 10 percent of the population had occupied less than 30 percent of the national income. Since then, although the top earners were taking a rising share of national income, this group witnessed the largest decline in their income share due to severe economic turbulence such as oil crisis and the burst of Bubble Economy. On the contrary, although the proportion of national income accounted for by 40 percent of the middle-income group and 50 percent of the low-income group gradually decreased, there has been a significant increase in the past economic turmoil. This means that Japan's wealth distribution system not only allows the expansion of the wealth of a few high-income groups during the economic growth period, but also reduces the loss of wealth of middle-low income groups in the economic recession and requires a small number of high-income groups to bear the income losses caused by the economic recession, thus achieving a long-term balance in the distribution of wealth in Japan (see Chart10-5).

In terms of the design and evolution of the social security and welfare system to fulfill the redistribution, Japan as a welfare state basically adopts insurance projects with significant fund accumulation characteristics that are popular in various countries around the world today. Originating from the comprehensive and universal free national welfare supply system established by the Supreme Commander of the Allied Powers (SCAP) to solve postwar chaos and restore order, the Japanese Government began to restructure its social security and welfare system with public funded insurance projects as the core after regaining national sovereignty and reviving the economy. Due to the extremely limited resources available to the Japanese Government during the occupation period to fund its social security benefits, although the welfare programs established at that time for work-related injuries, unemployment, and relief were universal, they all used qualification review methods to define the beneficiaries, with relatively low degree of funding. Even so, these welfare programs still laid the foundation for Japan's social security and welfare system, and Japan's social security and welfare system also inherited and continued its previous tradition of relatively low revenue at the end of occupation.

The development process of Japan's postwar social security and welfare system can be divided into four stages, i.e., the foundation period from 1951 to 1960, the expansion period from 1961 to 1975, the adjustment

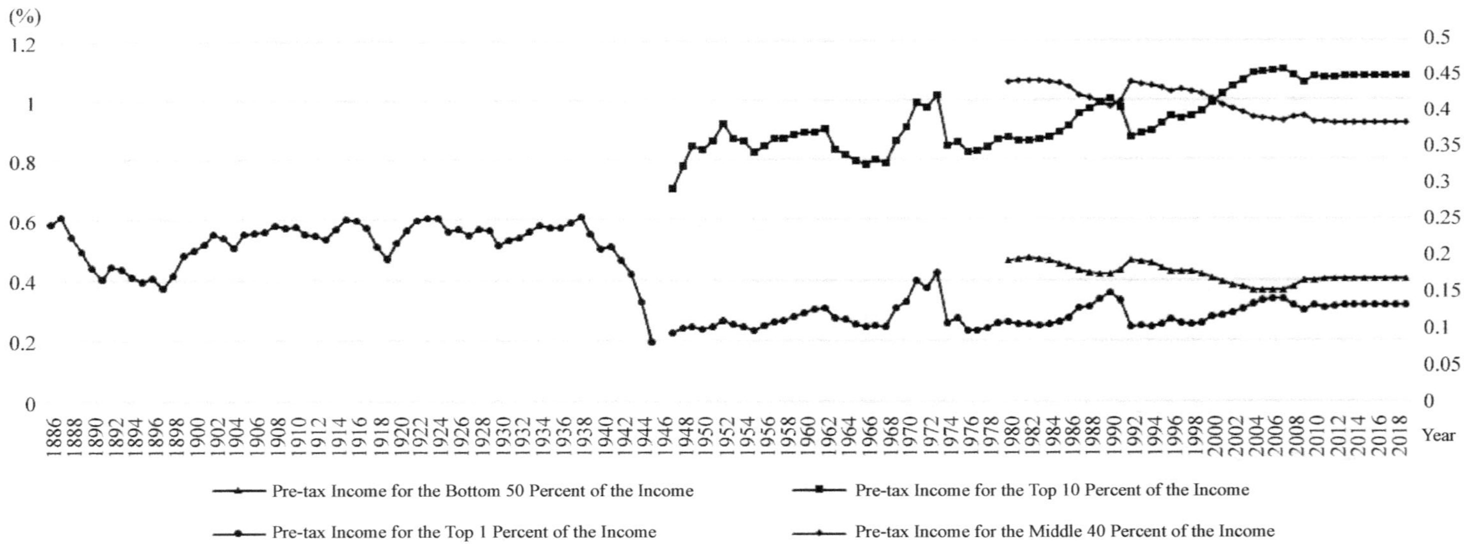

Chart 10-5 Changes of Japan's Income Inequality Degree (1886-2019)

Source: Japan's National Survey & www.wid.world.

period from 1976 to 1989, and the reconstruction period after 1990. In the first and second periods, with the background of rapid economic growth and government financial assistance, the coverage and scale of Japan's social security and welfare system rapidly expanded. Most Japanese scholars ignored the national welfare programs that existed before the Japanese Government regained its sovereignty and advocated that the Social Security Review Conference held in October 1950 was the beginning of Japan's social security and welfare system (National Federation of Health Insurance Societies, 2008). With the introduction of a pension and related insurance system that covered all citizens in 1961, the so-called comprehensive and universal welfare state system was established. Since then, a series of welfare programs such as child welfare, employment welfare, and even environmental welfare policies have been introduced into Japan's social security and welfare system.

1973 was known as "the first year of Japan's welfare", however, Japan was plunged into an "oil crisis" later that year when this announcement was made. Afterwards, the public finance became increasingly feeble in supporting expenditures on welfare state. In fact, the welfare state defined by Japan in 1973 essentially refers to the Japanese Government covering 70 percent of all residents' medical expenses and all medical expenses for the elderly, as well as the coverage of certain pension insurance programs for all social members. In other words, although this definition of the welfare state clarifies the universal coverage attribute of the main welfare projects, it only limits the general basic revenue of specific projects without a unified reference standard. To this day, the social security benefits enjoyed by people from different industries in different administrative regions of Japan still vary greatly.

Since 1973, the Japanese economy has ended its astonishing explosive growth and entered a stable development stage. Without the support of high economic growth expectations, the Japanese Government has begun to plan schemes to cope with the financial burden caused by the welfare state. The interim administrative investigation held in 1980 recommended that the government limits the growth of welfare state expenditures and explore ways to reduce the scale of welfare provided by the government as much as possible. Therefore, in response to the new economic, social, and financial environment, the Japanese Government canceled free medical care for the elderly in 1983 and instead established a new medical security system for the elderly with the main expenditure of this system coming from the funds of other medical insurance programs. In 1984, a medical fixed charge standard for patients to pay a rated fee for their medical consumption as well as medical assistance funded by the health insurance fund for retirees were implemented. In addition, in 1986, Japan began implementing the *National Pension Law*, which was a milestone event in Japan's pension system reform and established the current three-layers pension system. The newly revised *National Pension Law* expands the applicable scope of national pension to include all citizens over 20 and under 60 years old, becoming the basic public pension system for all Japanese citizens.

After nearly half a century of development, the promulgation of *Reconstructing the Social Security System: Building a Harmonious Society in 21st Century* in 1995 marked Japan's successful construction of a welfare state system that can meet the minimum living needs of all members of society, and national welfare became an indispensable component of people's daily lives. Impacted by the burst of Bubble Economy and the subsequent long-term economic stagnation, as well as the aging population and low fertility, the Japanese Government had to make adjustments and reforms to the above social equality achieved by primary distribution. Faced with emerging economic and social issues, the Japanese Government had to balance limited financial resources with the continuously growing welfare needs of the people.

In response to the expected increase in social security and welfare expenditures triggered by maintaining and expanding the basic state welfare supply in the upcoming 21st century, the Japanese Government adjusted and further coordinated the security functions of various departments of the welfare state to improve the overall effectiveness of the welfare state. Since 1989, the so-called "Golden Plan" - the "Ten Year Plan Strategy for Promoting the Health and Welfare of the Elderly", as well as a series of other social security and welfare projects, have been introduced successively. Since the 1990s, the Japanese Government has invested more effort in its emphasis on elderly care. It revised the Eight Laws for the Welfare of the Elderly in 1990 and integrated the relevant pension fund systems operated by different administrative levels. The implementation of long-term insurance, known as the "Fifth Insurance System", introduced in April, 2000 marked the formation of an elderly friendly welfare system. At the same time, the "Angel Plan" aimed at addressing the low fertility was also adopted during this period. Through such rapidly expanding social security and welfare programs, Japan's income redistribution function has been strengthened, and the level of income redistribution has also significantly improved. As a result, Japan's Gini Coefficient of primary income distribution, which had already reached 40 in the mid-1990s, has returned to around 30 after redistribution, ensuring income equality in Japanese society.

Unlike the weakened function of primary distribution to suppress income inequality, Japan is now a typical comprehensive welfare state, encompassing all nine major social security and welfare departments and covering all Japanese residents. Nevertheless, the Japanese welfare state still features significant fragmentation in different administrative divisions and industry, with a low degree of uniformity, and the absolute core of its entire welfare system has always been composed of public social security benefits and mandatory private social security projects. Among them, public social security benefits account for the absolute majority, but it should also be noted that the proportion of voluntary participation in social security projects in Japan's redistribution system has a significant upward trend (see Chart 10-6). However, in Japan and even all OECD countries, the scale of privately funded charitable projects is almost negligible, and their funding intensity is even lower than the "tax burden reduction". Among major social security and welfare departments, elderly care and public healthcare receive the most resource support. Since 1973, known as the "first year of welfare", medical insurance has reimbursed all medical expenses for the elderly and 70 percent of expenses for general patients. In terms of elderly care, the growth of elderly care benefits has also kept pace with the rise in prices and rents. In addition to retirement benefits and some special welfare programs for victims of World War II, pension, medical and employment benefits, as well as disaster insurance and nursing care insurance that came into effect in April 2000, account for the vast majority of Japan's welfare state budget. In other words, these programs collectively constitute the main body of Japan's welfare state. More strictly speaking, some scholars represented by Shogo Takegawa argue that the development of Japan's welfare state in the two most important welfare categories of elderly care and healthcare is comparable to that of developed Western countries (Takegawa. 2005).

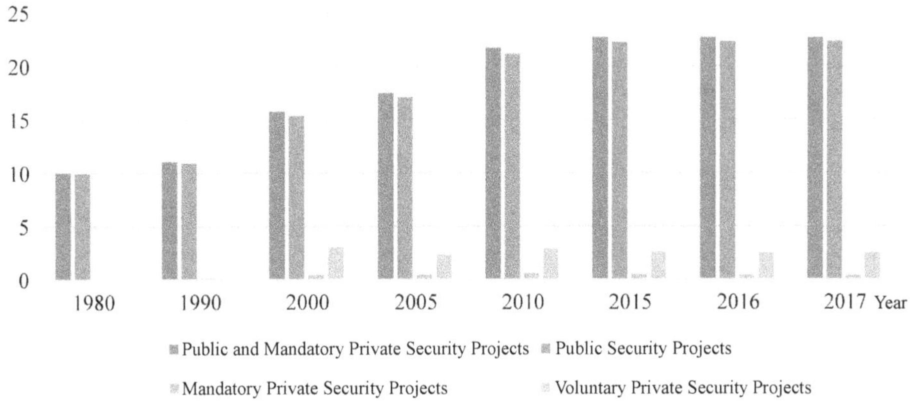

Chart 10-6 Composition of Japanese Social Security System During Different Historical Periods

Source: the OECD Social Expenditure Database.

4. The Third Distribution: Roles and Functions of Charitable Activities in Japanese Wealth Distribution

In the 2021 World Giving Index① released by the Charities Aid Foundation (CAF), Japan ranked 107, making it ineligible as a country with developed philanthropy. Among these Japanese respondents, only about 23 percent expressed their willingness to donate, about 24 percent of respondents were willing to help strangers, and only about 22 percent of them were willing to spend time on voluntary activities. The investigation conducted by Statista in 2019 on the "happiness through donations" among Japanese are consistent with the conclusions of the CAF. From Statista, only about 4 percent of Japanese respondents believe that donation can bring great joy, over 65 percent of respondents argue that donation does not bring any delight, with 39 percent of them

① According to a survey conducted by the Charities Aid Foundation (CAF), covering 125 countries and regions worldwide, with over 1.3 million respondents.

considering that donation is none of their business, and only about 30 percent of respondents believe that donation to a certain extent can bring some happiness.

In fact, as shown in the aforementioned statistical data, charitable activities were marginalized in Japan's past and present social wealth distribution system. As the cradle of charitable activities in Japan, the "Four Institutions" (a Hiden-in (welfare Institution), a Seiyaku-in (pharmacy), a Ryōbyō-in (hospital), Kyōden-in (Institution of Religion and Education)) were actually established by the first official temple in Japanese history, the Four Heavenly Kings Temple in Buddhism. Even in the 16th century, Buddhism and newly introduced Christian organizations played a crucial role in charitable activities in Japan, endowing traditional charitable activities with a profound religious color.

Even in Joint Labor, Neighborhood Assistance and Autonomy Organization with Japanese characteristics based on mutual agreements to carry out activities, there have emerged charitable organizations with economic functions centered around specific religious doctrines or beliefs, represented by "Mujin-ko" (financing through item guarantees) and "Tanomoshi-ko" (collective funding organizations). The main beneficiaries of these traditional charitable organizations are vulnerable groups such as farmers, the poor, and orphans, with generally limited assistance force.

During the Edo period, religious organizations such as Buddhism were suppressed, and the Meiji Government nationalized the authority of "public welfare" activities through the system of Public-Benefit Corporations, further resulting in the decline of Japan's folk charitable and public welfare activities. It was not until the end of World War II that social welfare organizations and private non-profit organizations gradually emerged, especially stimulated by student movements and public marches in the 1960s, private non-profit organizations began to become a means for the public to express themselves and engage in social activities, and thus increasingly appeared in charitable activities in Japan. During the Bubble Economy of the 1980s and 1990s, the enthusiasm of Japanese people to participate in charity activities was unprecedentedly high, and private non-profit organizations have gradually grown into the main operator of Japanese charity activities. However, the existing Public-Benefit Corporations system, which relies on the supervision of government agencies and implements top-down management, has severely restricted the free development of private non-profit organizations.

Under the circumstances, Great Hanshin Earthquake occurred in 1995 directly provided a large number of opportunities for the Japanese to engage in voluntary charitable activities at that time. Taking this opportunity, the Japanese Government promulgated a special law of civil law, the *Law to Promote Specified Nonprofit Activities* (commonly known as the *NPO Law*) in 1998, aimed at promoting the development of public welfare activities among citizens. Meanwhile, the outdated Public-Benefit Corporations system rooted in Article 34 of the Japanese Civil Code was completely abolished in 2006. At this point, Japan's management of non-profit organizations engaged in charitable activities has shifted to a General Corporations system based on the principle of registration and filing, and a new Public-Benefit Corporations system system based on Determinism, thus creating the current Japanese charitable system with non-profit organizations as the core. Nowadays, there are over 20,000 social welfare institutions and nearly 10,000 non-profit organizations for public welfare in Japan. Nevertheless, the improvement brought by charitable activities as the main body of the third distribution to Japanese living standard is still minimal.

5. Lessons Learned from Japanese Social Wealth Distribution

Through the above review and analysis, it can be found that Japan's "developmental nationalism" not only attaches great importance to economic growth, but also strengthens the residents' consumption ability power from the institutional level, thereby creating a necessary domestic market and a sustainable economic "internal circulation" system for its industrial upgrading. The performance of this system in terms of income distribution is to achieve and maintain a relatively equal distribution of income among Japanese residents through the mutual coordination of primary distribution and redistribution. The experiences of the design and evolution of Japan's income distribution system can be summarized as follows.

Firstly, the design and adjustment of income distribution system need to be in line with macroeconomic conditions. During periods of rapid economic growth with smooth vertical labor mobility, the primary distribution should play a major role in suppressing income disparities. While during periods of sluggish economic growth, it is necessary to moderately liberalize the horizontal flow of labor while enhancing the role of redistribution in suppressing income disparities.

Secondly, in the design of the primary income distribution system, it is necessary to pay attention to the distribution of social wealth between different industries, as well as its distribution among different production factors, strengthen the protection of employment and wage treatment for labors, enhance their collective bargaining power, and make those having got prosperous first in society bear more obligations to suppress economic fluctuations.

Thirdly, in the design of the redistribution system, it is necessary to not only avoid distorting market functions and disrupting competition mechanisms, but also fully leverage the role of taxation in regulating income distribution, and improve the overall social welfare through expanding public expenditure.

Finally, through the analysis of income and related economic data from Japan and other countries, it can be found that no matter how the social security and welfare system is designed, an increase in public expenditure does play a positive role in suppressing income inequality. Therefore, in the process of "common prosperity", it is essential to not only attach importance to the role of tax tools in raising public funds, but also gradually expand the scale of public expenditure.

Republic of Korea*

1. Basic Information

After World War II, the Republic of Korea (ROK) was generally in poverty. After 20 years of development, it has made remarkable achievements and created the Miracle on the Han River. The implementation of social welfare policies under the administration of Military Manpower before 1993 was targeted to achieve economic development and social stability. In this historical stage, the social welfare in ROK experienced a cycle of development and stagnation. During the period of rapid economic development, social welfare shrank, while when the economy stagnated, there was a boom in social welfare. Under the reign of Kim Young-sam from 1993 to 1998, the Government ended decades of military rule in ROK and gained political legitimacy, witnessing the social stability and decline in trade union activities and labor disputes year by year. The Kim Young-sam Government believed in the diversification of welfare providers, shifted the responsibility for national welfare to the people, and emphasized the neo-liberalism of market principles, ending the "Spring of Welfare", and even overturning the social welfare system. The Kim Dae-Jung Government, famous for welfare affinity and a tendency towards social progress, has encountered the worst condition since the founding of ROK. After Kim Dae-Jung took office in February 1998, a significant

* Author: GAO Chunlan, Changchun University of Technology.

reform of the welfare system was carried out, and ROK's social welfare policy entered a new development stage. Although successive leaders after Kim Dae-Jung attached different emphasis on social welfare policies, the ROK Government did not deviate from the productive welfare concept of "synchronous development of welfare and economy", stressing that individuals obtain necessary living security through working.

After rapid development in the 1970s and 1980s, the economy development in ROK has slowed down in the 21st century. In the 1970s, the per capita GDP of ROK was less than USD 1,000, and it had increased by nearly 20 times by the 1990s. Although it did not reach the average level of developed countries in OECD, the growth rate was astonishing. Impacted by the pandemic, both per capita GDP and GNI showed a decline from 2019 to 2020(see Table 11-1).

Table 11-1 GDP&GNI, Per Capita GDP&GNI in ROK Unit: USD, %

Year	GDP, USD Billion		GNI, USD Billion		Per Capita GDP, USD		Per Capita GNI, USD	
	Gross Value	Deflator	Gross Value	Deflator	Per Capita	Growth Rate	Per Capita	Growth Rate
2011	1253.43	93.9	1261.19	1.3	25100.4	8.74	25255.8	9.25
2012	1277.96	95.1	1291.33	1.3	25457.5	1.42	25723.7	1.85
2013	1370.56	96.0	1379.30	1.0	27178.1	6.76	27351.3	6.32
2014	1483.95	96.9	1491.14	0.9	29242.4	9.44	29383.9	7.43
2015	1465.34	100.0	1469.93	3.2	28723.8	-1.77	28813.6	-1.94
2016	1500.03	102.0	1505.51	2.0	29287.2	1.96	29394.3	2.02
2017	1623.31	104.3	1629.92	2.2	31605.2	7.91	31734.1	7.96
2018	1725.16	104.8	1732.11	0.5	33429.0	5.77	33563.7	5.77
2019	1646.33	103.8	1660.63	-0.9	31838.2	-4.76	32114.9	-4.32
2020 (Estimated)	1630.82	105.1	1644.29	1.3	31494.9	-1.08	31755.0	-1.12

Source: 2020 Social Indicators from Korea National Statistical Office, p234.

Note: Per Capita GDP=GDP/total population based on 2017.

The rapid economic growth contributed to the "Miracle on the Han River", but the financial crisis of the 1990s broke the belief that "economic growth is the only choice for a happy life for the people". ROK changed its development philosophy of "growth prior to distribution" and formulated various innovative social policies. In terms of the Gini Coefficient, government social policies have played an important role in promoting social equity and common prosperity. Although the Gini Coefficient of market revenue① exceeds 0.4 in most years However, the Gini Coefficient of household disposable income has significantly decreased due to the public transfer of income such as national annuity, basic annuity and child allowances, reaching its lowest point in 2019. The income quintile ratio reflects the gap between high-income and low-income groups. The income gap obtained by different groups in the market is as much as ten times that of each year, while the effectiveness of narrowing the income gap through public fund transfer is significant (see Table 11-2). However, from a global perspective, among the 36 OECD countries, ROK's Gini Coefficient and its income quintile multiplier ranked 28th and 29th respectively. Therefore, it is necessary to continuously improve the income distribution system.

Table 11-2 Gini Coefficient and Income Quintile Ratio Unit: times

Year	Gini Coefficient		Income Quintile Ratio	
	Market Income	Disposable Income	Market Income	Disposable Income
2011	0.418	0.388	11.21	8.32
2012	0.411	0.385	10.65	8.10
2013	0.401	0.372	10.29	7.68
2014	0.397	0.363	10.32	7.37

① The ROK Government has been calculating the Gini Coefficient and income distribution ratio through the "Domestic Means Test" since 2011. Starting from 2017, it adopted the "Household Financial Welfare Investigation" supplemented with administrative data and calculated according to OECD standards.

continued

Year	Gini Coefficient		Income Quintile Ratio	
	Market Income	Disposable Income	Market Income	Disposable Income
2015	0.396	0.352	10.41	6.91
2016	0.402	0.345	11.15	6.54
2017	0.406	0.354	11.27	6.96
2018	0.402	0.345	11.15	6.54
2019	0.404	0.339	11.56	6.25

Source: 2020 Household Financial Welfare Investigation from Korea National Statistical Office.

Note: The income quintile ratio is the average income of the upper 20 percent group divided by the average income of the lower 20 percent group

The disposable income is equal to the income that equalizes disposable income (market income+public transfer income - public transfer expenditure)

The public transfer income: public annuity (including national annuity), basic annuity, child allowances, disability allowances, etc

The public transfer expenditure: taxes, annuity payments, social insurance premiums, etc

In 2019, the life expectancy of ROK citizens reached 83.3, with 80.3 for males and 86.3 for females, which was far above the world average. The medical and social services in ROK are also close to or even higher than the OECD average. For example, the number of hospital beds per 1,000 inhabitants in ROK was 7.08 in 2018, exceeding the average level of OECD member countries (4.5).①

2. Primary Distribution and Related Policies

2.1 Primary Distribution in Republic of Korea

The main source of household income in ROK is recurrent income, including labor income, business income, asset income, public sector transfer

① Source: "Annual Report for Health and Welfare in 2020", from Ministry of Health and Welfare, ROK.

income, and private sector transfer income. In terms of its composition, labor income accounts for over 60 percent and business income accounts for around 20 percent with market income being the majority and primary distribution occupying a relatively high proportion (see Table 11-3).

Table 11-3 Composition of Income Source Unit:%

Year	Labor Income	Business Income	Asset Income	Public Transfer	Private Transfer	In Total
2011	62.5	26.8	4.5	4.3	2.0	100.0
2012	64.5	25.1	4.5	4.2	1.7	100.0
2013	64.9	24.9	4.1	4.5	1.6	100.0
2014	65.6	23.9	4.0	5.0	1.4	100.0
2015	65.6	22.9	4.5	5.6	1.4	100.0
2016	63.9	22.2	6.5	6.0	1.5	100.0
2017	63.8	21.8	6.7	6.2	1.6	100.0
2018	64.9	20.2	6.5	6.6	1.8	100.0
2019	64.0	19.4	7.0	7.7	1.8	100.0

Source: 2020 Household Financial Welfare Investigation from Korea National Statistical Office.

The Korea National Statistical Office uses multiple indicators to measure income inequality. From 2019, in addition to median income, quintile income, relative poverty rate, there was an additional indicator of the Parma ratio. The primary distribution of income in ROK varies greatly, with quintile income multiplier of up to 11 times in the market income. The ROK Government has introduced various policies to narrow the income gap through the transfer of the public sector. In 2019, the relative poverty rate[①] calculated based on market income in ROK was 20.8

① The proportion of the group with incomes below 50 percent of the median income to the total population.

percent, while the relative poverty rate calculated based on disposable income including social transfer payments is reduced to 16.3 percent. Nevertheless, the poverty problem in ROK remains prominent, especially among the elderly.

2.2 Policies and Measures Related to Primary Distribution

ROK's employment policy mainly focuses on expanding employment, lacking collective bargaining or other institutional arrangements to ensure labors' wage and social rights. The direction of employment promotion in ROK is 1) to actively create employment opportunities that are coordinated and promoted by labors, capital, citizen groups, and the government, in order to respond to the employment crisis in advance; 2) to cope with the Fourth Industrial Revolution and vigorously cultivate new industry and technological talents; 3) to develop adaptive policies for different objects; 4) to strengthen the construction of employment safety nets; 5) to shorten labor hours and raise labor efficiency through the improvement of working environment.

The ROK Government has introduced different policy measures targeting groups such as youth, women, and the elderly to increase their participation in the labor market. For the youth, subsidies have been provided to employers to reward the employment of young people, and employment centers have been established to provide employment consultations and assistance to young people. For women, employment support policies for women during childbirth and childcare period have been implemented. For the elderly, subsidies have been provided conditionally to enterprises that hire elderly people over 60 years old.

Compared with OECD countries, ROK's employment rate is in the middle of the list, with an employment rate of 60.9 percent in 2019, with 70.7 percent for male and 51.6 percent for female. Furthermore, the employment rate for the elderly aged 60 and above reaches to 41.5 percent, which is also a demonstration of severe poverty among the elderly in ROK.

Taxation in ROK includes corporate tax and individual income tax and legal persons pay corporate tax annually based on their income. The starting point for individual income tax is 12 million Korean Won per year (approximately RMB 66,000), and a progressive tax system is implemented. As wages increase, the tax standards and actual payments continue to rise. In addition to individual income tax, individuals bear a variety of taxes, including real estate tax, church tax, inheritance tax, gift tax, etc.

In order to prevent people with jobs from falling into poverty, the ROK implements the Earned Income Tax Credit (EITC) system and provides funds on a household basis based on family, income, and asset conditions. It divides families into one person household, one-earner household, and employed-couple household based on whether they have a spouse, children, and parents aged 70 and above. One person household with an annual income of less than 20 million Korean Won, one-earner household having a spouse, children, and parents aged 70 and above with an annual income of less than 30 million Korean Won, employed-couple household with an annual income of less than 36 million Korean Won and households possessing less than 200 million Korean Won of family assets are qualified for EITC and household with children under 18 years old can receive children's subsidy.

From 2008 to 2010, due to an increase in the minimum wage but no changes in the application conditions for EITC, the number of households receiving EITC decreased. From 2011, the conditions for applying for EITC began to liberalize, thus the number of qualified households increased. By 2019, the number had increased by 1.9 times compared to the previous year and the expenditure had risen by 2.9 times.

3. Social Redistribution

3.1 ROK's Social Insurance System

The social insurance system in ROK includes national annuity, health insurance, unemployment insurance, industrial accident compensation insurance, and long-term care insurance for the elderly. The long-term care insurance implemented in 2008 has become the ROK's fifth largest social insurance.

3.1.1 National Annuity

The national annuity officially come into effect on January 1, 1988. Initially applicable to corporations with more than 10 employees, it was expanded to corporations with more than 5 employees in 1992, extended to residents of agricultural and fishing villages in July 1995, expanded to urban self operated individuals in 1999, and finally covered enterprises with less than 5 employees in 2003.

Public annuity in ROK covers employees in special occupational fields such as civil servants, soldiers, teachers in private school, and postal clerks and other residents participate in the national annuity. Although the law stipulates that nationals over 18 years old and under 60 years old, as well as foreigners residing in the ROK should participate in the national annuity, the participation rate in the national annuity has not reached a very high level, especially for informal labors (see Table 11-4).

Table 11-4 Employees' Participation Rate in Public Annuity Unit:%

Year	Employees	Formal Employees	Informal Employees
2011	65.2	79.2	38.3
2012	66.8	80.4	39.2
2013	67.7	81.3	39.4
2014	68.1	82.2	38.5
2015	67.5	82.1	37.0
2016	67.7	83.0	36.4
2017	69.1	85.0	36.6
2018	69.8	87.5	37.9
2019	69.5	87.5	37.9
2020	69.8	88.0	37.8

Source: 2020 Social Indicators from Korea National Statistical Office, p221.
Note: The public annuity does not include community participants and dependents.

The payments of national annuity include elderly annuity, invalidity annuity, dependant annuity, etc. However, there's still a severe elderly poverty in ROK due to the low receiving rate(see Table 11-5).

Table 11-5 Proportion of the Elderly Aged 65 and Above Receiving Public Annuity Unit: person, %

Year	Receiving Rate of Public Annuity	Receiving Number of Public Annuity	National Annuity	Annuity of Civil Servants	Annuity of Private School Teachers	Annuity of Soldiers
2013	39.1	2353035	87.8	8.8	1.4	2.0
2014	41.1	2580260	88.1	8.6	1.4	1.9
2015	42.8	2802065	88.3	8.6	1.3	1.8
2016	44.6	3015710	88.3	8.5	1.4	1.8
2017	46.9	3313618	88.6	8.4	1.3	1.7
2018	48.6	3584900	88.7	8.4	1.3	1.6
2019	50.9	3914457	88.9	8.3	1.3	1.5

Source: Korea National Statistical Office: 2020 Data on the Elderly, p70.

Note: Public annuity receiving rate=receiving number of public annuity (aged 65 and above)/elderly population aged 65 and above*100 percent, based on the number of the elderly in 2017.

National annuity include elderly annuity, invalidity annuity and dependant annuity.

The replacement rate of national annuity is relatively low as well and has been decreasing year by year. In order to ensure the financial safety of annuities, increase the receiving age and reduce the replacement rate, the national pension payments include an equal portion calculated based on average income and the proportion of income calculated based on a constant ratio (see Table 11-6).

Table 11-6 Changes of Replacement Rate of National Annuity

Insured Time	1988-1998	1999-2007	2008	2009	2010	2011	2012	2013	……	2028
Replacement Rate	70%	60%	50%	49.5%	49%	48.5%	48%	47.5%	……	40%
Constant Ratio	2.4	1.8	1.5	1.485	1.470	1.455	1.440	1.425	……	1.200

Source: National Pension Service: Report on 2020 National Annuity, p305.

ROK has implemented the national annuity system since 1998. Due to the short duration, it has not covered many people and the participants can only receive the annuity in one go. For this reason, ROK has carried out a basic annuity system where individuals are not required to pay fees and are fully funded by the government. Elderly individuals or couples aged 65 and above can apply for a basic annuity if their income is less than the prescribed limit. Currently, approximately 66 percent of elderly people aged 65 and above receive basic annuities (see Table 11-7).

Table 11-7 Recipient of Basic Annuity

Year	All Elderly People (person)	Recipient (person)	Proportion (%)
2012	598060	3933095	65.8
2013	6250986	4065672	65.0
2014	6520607	4353482	66.8

continued

Year	All Elderly People (person)	Recipient (person)	Proportion (%)
2015	6771214	4495183	66.4
2016	6987489	4581406	65.6
2017	7345820	4868576	66.3
2018	7,638574	5125731	67.1
2019	8013661	5345728	66.7

Source: "Annual Report for Health and Welfare in 2020", p428, from Ministry of Health and Welfare, ROK.

Before July 2014, it was referred to as a basic elderly annuity, and later as a basic annuity.

3.1.2 Health Insurance

Health insurance is contributed 50 percent by both employers and employees, and is fully covered by individual community participants. As the mobility of informal professionals is relatively high, the participation rate is correspondingly low (see Table 11-8).

Table 11-8 Employees' Participation Rate in Health Insurance

Unit:%

Year	Employees	Formal Employees	Informal Employees
2011	68.4	80.9	44.1
2012	70.1	80.3	45.5
2013	71.4	83.6	46.3
2014	71.5	84.2	44.8
2015	71.6	84.8	43.9
2016	72.6	86.2	44.9
2017	74.2	88.4	45.3
2018	75.5	90.1	45.9
2019	75.7	91.5	48.0
2020	76.7	92.6	49.0

Source: 2020 Social Indicators from Korea National Statistical Office, p221.

Note: The participants in health insurance does not include community participants and dependents.

After the unification of the health insurance management agency in 2000, the coverage rate of health insurance continued to increase. However, due to the increase in expenses borne by non medical insurance individuals, the improvement in the coverage rate was not significant. Since 2005, the coverage rate for cancer, cerebrovascular disease, heart disease, and complex diseases has been increased in health insurance expenditures, reducing the burden on individuals and families. When the total amount of legal individual expenses borne by patients exceeds the upper limit of individual expenses according to individual income regulations, the excess shall be paid by the health insurance community, with the main purpose of reducing the medical burden on low-income patients through direct deduction and refund. Since the implementation of this system in 2007, the average annual increase in refund amount is 28 percent.

3.1.3 Unemployment Insurance

Unemployment insurance in ROK is aimed at promoting employment, improving labors' employment ability, and preventing unemployment, rather than providing basic income security for the unemployed. It mainly includes policies such as stable employment, vocational ability development, and employment subsidies. Currently, unemployment insurance in ROK has not achieved full coverage, and only 76.2 percent of the employed are insured in 2020, with formal labors accounting for 87.2 percent and informal labors accounting for 43.6 percent.[①]

3.1.4 Long-term Care Insurance for the Elderly

ROK has implemented the *Long-Term Care Insurance Act* since 2008. At that time, only 3 percent of the disabled at 65 or above received

① 2020 Social Indicators from Korea National Statistical Office, p221.

services, and after more than 10 years of development, this proportion increased to 10 percent. The long-term care insurance system for the elderly has played an important role in improving the life quality of disabled elders and reducing the burden on their families. Currently, the national awareness of care insurance is over 70 percent, and satisfaction is above 90 percent.

3.2 Social Assistance

Basic living security includes livelihood, medical care, housing, education, self-reliance, and other aspects of security. In addition to providing corresponding security for basic living support, ROK also reduces or exempts residents' taxes, television subscription fees, electricity fees, communication fees, and annual car inspection fees.

Livelihood security: Based on the family members, income, and caregivers, provides income security to eligible families and individuals according to household income and assets investigation.

Medical security: Provides basic medical security for low-income groups with financial difficulties.

Housing security: Provides housing security for those income below 45 percent of the median income and the total asset income below the prescribed limit.

Education security: Provides educational activity support fees for primary, secondary, and high school students from low-income families.

Self-reliance security: Provides suitable employment opportunities for low-income individuals and extends financial support to enterprises founded by two or more individuals who provide basic living support.

Youth Hope 1: Youth saving 50,000 to 100,000 Korean Won (approximately RMB 280 to 560) per month, getting out of insurance within three years can apply for labor rewards.

Youth Hope 2: Youth saving 100,000 Korean Won per month, working for three consecutive years and participating in relevant skill education can apply for labor rewards of 3.6 million Korean Won (approximately RMB 20,000).

Youth Savings: Youth saving 100,000 Korean Won per month, working for three consecutive years with national qualification certificate for further education can apply for rewards of 10.8 million Korean Won (approximately RMB 60,000).

3.3 Social Welfare

ROK provides welfare services for special groups such as the elderly, children, the disabled, and pregnant and postpartum women. For example, all pregnant women can receive free folic acid for 3 months and iron powder for 16 months. Children under 7 years old can receive a monthly subsidy of 100,000 Korean Won (RMB 560) and children aged from 3 to 5 who attend kindergarten can receive childcare fees. Meanwhile, kindergartens must be established in public residential areas with over 500 households. Furthermore, ROK provides Alzheimer's disease screening services for the elderly over 60 years old with an income below 120 percent of the median income and the senior who have been diagnosed with dementia and received treatment can apply for partial assistance for the individual -charged health insurance.

4. Expenditure on Public Services

In ROK, the concept of social services is more commonly used. In a broad sense, social services are welfare, healthcare, education, culture, housing, employment, environment, and other services provided to improve the well-being of individuals or society. In a narrow sense, social services refer to services provided to the elderly, children, and the disabled.

Overall, ROK's social welfare expenditure has increased as a proportion of GDP, reaching 12.2 percent in 2019, while it has not yet reached the average level of 20 percent among OEC D member countries.①

Frequent medical expenses refer to the total amount of healthcare services and medical products consumed by citizens within a year. Government expenditure refers to medical expenses incurred in accordance with government (central and local) requirements for compulsory participation in health insurance, industrial accident compensation insurance, long-term care insurance, and automobile liability insurance. Private medical expenses are medical expenses that are paid based on voluntary participation in commercial insurance, non-profit organizations and corporate insurance, covered by family and individual (including legal individual burdens, non-payment individual burdens). In 2019, the proportion of frequent healthcare expenses in ROK's GDP was 8 percent, below the OECD average. Among the frequent healthcare expenses, government expenditure accounted for 60.8 percent, with private expenditure accounting for 39.2 percent.②

Public education expenses refer to the deduction of expenses invested by parents outside of the school from the total education expenses. It contains all education and related administrative expenses invested by the government and private sectors, including government departments, private sectors, and overseas investment. 30 percent of the investment in

---

① 2020 Social Indicators from Korea National Statistical Office, 256.

② 2020 Social Indicators from Korea National Statistical Office, 166.

public education in ROK relies on the private sector, with government investment accounting for 70 percent. In 2017, the investment in the education sector is 5.0 percent, higher than OECD member states with an average of 4.9 percent.[①]

5. Carrier of Social Services

The majority of social welfare services in ROK are provided by non-governmental organizations, with the social welfare legal entity playing a critical role in these organizations. Social welfare legal entities are established in accordance with the *Social Welfare Law*, mainly divided into institution-oriented legal entities and capital-oriented legal entities. Those established for the purpose of establishing and operating social welfare institutions are institution-oriented legal entities, and those using their investment and income to support social welfare are capital-oriented legal entities. Generally, large corporations allocate a portion of their annual profits to establish independent social welfare legal entity and invest funds into social organizations through bidding, such as Samsung Welfare Syndicate, Pacific Welfare Syndicate, and Ehsan Welfare Syndicate. As of June 2019, there are a total of 2,985 social welfare legal entities in ROK, including 2,711 institution-oriented legal entities and 274 capital-oriented legal entities.

ROK also established the "Social Welfare Joint Fundraising Association" in 1998, which belongs to social welfare legal entities. Its main activities are to raise funds from the public, distribute, operate, and manage funds, and carry out investigations, publicity, research, and

---

① Korea National Statistical Office: E-National Indicator-Education Sector.

international exchange activities in the field of social welfare, including livelihood, diet and nutrition, mental health, education, environment, employment, information technology popularization, and gender equality. Currently, there is a central federation and a total of 17 local branches.

This book is the result of a co-publication agreement between China Social Sciences Press (China) and Paths Publishing Group LTD. (UK)

Title: Comparative Study on the Promotion of Common Prosperity
Author: Zhou Hong et al.
Translated by Jiang Mengyuan
Translation Review: Du Nan
ISBN: 978-1-80589-035-5
Ebook ISBN: 978-1-80589-036-2

Paths Publishing Group LTD.
www.pathspublishinggroup.com
Published in the United Kingdom